Conversations in Postcolonial Thought

Edited by Katy P. Sian

palgrave
macmillan

First published in 2014 by PALGRAVE MACMILLAN® in the United States—a division of St. Martin's Press LLC, 175 Fifth Avenue, New York, NY 10010.

Where this book is distributed in the UK, Europe and the rest of the world, this is by Palgrave Macmillan, a division of Macmillan Publishers Limited, registered in England, company number 785998, of Houndmills, Basingstoke, Hampshire RG21 6XS.

Palgrave Macmillan is the global academic imprint of the above companies and has companies and representatives throughout the world.

Palgrave® and Macmillan® are registered trademarks in the United States, the United Kingdom, Europe and other countries.

ISBN: 978-1-137-46565-8

Library of Congress Cataloging-in-Publication Data

Sian, Katy

    Conversations in postcolonial thought / edited by Katy P. Sian.
      pages cm
    Includes bibliographical references and index.
    ISBN 978-1-137-46565-8 (hardback)
    1. Postcolonialism. 2. Multiculturalism. 3. Postcolonialism.
4. Interdisciplinary research. 5. Race relations. 6. Marginality, Social.
I. Sian, Katy P., 1984–editor.

    JV51.C753 2014
    306—dc23   2014021686

A catalog record of the book is available from the British Library.

Design by Scribe Inc.

First edition: November 2014

Contents

Acknowledgments

First and foremost, I would like to sincerely thank all the thinkers that make up this collection. I appreciate all the time they have given and value their commitment to this project. I would also like to thank Ian Law, David Tyrer, Silvia Rodríguez Maseo, Marta Araújo, Barnor Hesse, and colleagues from the School of Social Sciences at the University of Manchester, particularly Brian Heaphy, Wendy Bottero, Paul Simpson, Claire Alexander, and Sivamohan Valluvan, for their ongoing encouragement throughout the course of this project. I must also thank my family and friends for their constant love, faith, and kindness, and especially my mother for her prayers and guidance. Lastly, I would like to thank the editorial team at Palgrave for their support with both the development and production of this book.

INTRODUCTION

The Quest for the Postcolonial

Postcolonial Snapshots: Biographies and Life Stories

Being embodied in the world is a condition of my philosophical voice. It is a voice that is located in, and a voice that is shaped by, a thick web of political sedimentations and other value-laden commitments. These introductory reflections, then, are grounded within my standpoint, my perspective, and my personal biographical location. I make no effort to do the impossible: to become invisible, apolitical, decontextual, to speak from nowhere.

—Yancy 2002, ix

This book offers a series of conversational interviews with a diverse range of thinkers in the social sciences and humanities engaging with debates around race, ethnicity, and postcolonial questions. Taking seriously Yancy's reflections from the opening epigraph, this text has been written with a self-aware yet unassuming voice that is mindful of personal standpoint, perspective, and biographical location and, at the same time, makes no attempt for claims of objectivity or neutrality. Uniquely, this book not only examines the key ideas of the thinkers interviewed but, through its compilation of conversations, also invites readers to share their biographical journeys to help one understand the experiences that led to the thinkers' work within the field.

The selection of thinkers included within this text may on the surface appear perplexing; however, the aim of this book is not to offer an encyclopedic index of thinkers (Sayyid 2006). It is rather to show how postcolonial thinking can been found across a range of disciplines, from sociology to history, gender studies to political science, geography to cultural studies, and literature to education. Fundamentally, one should see that what ties together this collection is that, although the various thinkers may differ to some degree in their approaches, they all see the postcolonial as offering a new way of thinking about the world—and the possibility of transformation that comes with that.

George Yancy (1998), in his book *African-American Philosophers: 17 Conversations*, offers a collection of engaging interviews with significant African-American intellectuals. He argues that the structuring of his collection is done so "according to a set of questions relating to early biography, formative influences, and significant contributions provided by the interviewee's areas of philosophical concern." Yancy goes onto comment that "each interviewee represents an embodied *Coginto* and a dynamically relational mode of existence," concluding that what then emerges from his volume is "a complex set of philosophical positionalities and thoughts exhibiting areas of commonality and diversity broadly informed by, though not simply reduced to, African-American culture" (Yancy 1998, 10). Taking Yancy's approach into account, the conversations that make up the chapters to follow are to be understood as various complex sites of enunciation of postcolonial discourse. Though there is a biographical element to the conversations, the biographies are not simply the reporting of highly individualized accounts; rather, they partake in the broader conversation of a general culture. In other words, the language that is deployed to express diverse concepts and concerns shares a common sensibility.

The insights farmed from these conversations can therefore be seen as the product of a set of dialectical exchanges between a series of key questions that orientated the major themes of the conversation as well as the interventions and responses of the interviewees as a means to open up various avenues when thinking about the postcolonial. An image that comes to mind is perhaps that of jazz, in which the art of improvisation is based on a carefully crafted riff.

Yancy's approach is one that has influenced the formation of this book; however, the object of this collection does not have the same clarity of definition as *African-American Philosophers*. This is perhaps because postcolonial studies are far more diffuse institutionally compared to conventional philosophy. The Heideggerian and Wittgensteinian distaste of the philosophical for its separation from life, its essentialism, and its rejection of lived culture found an eerie echo among the interviewees whose academic evolution involved struggle, often institutionally as well as personally, against the reification of the production of knowledge. This distaste for such a separation is also found in Yancy's interviews of 17 African-American philosophers.

The pioneering of interdisciplinarity by postcolonial thought has been necessary to rescue the object of postcolonial investigations from both receding out of their analytical gaze and fragmenting into discrete bounded ensembles of teaching and research. Metropole and empire denoted two planets, organized around different logics and different orders; for example, John Stuart Mill, a theoretician of liberty in Britain and servant of empire in India—two distinct beings unified in the same body but studied separately. The postcolonial appears as the precarious bridge between a Western planet and a planet without its own name—to travel from one to the other necessitates the crossing of intellectual and institutional boundaries. Thus the thinkers that make up this volume have different disciplinary affiliations, and often the postcolonial exists as a direct confrontation with the world that can no longer be mastered under the rubric of the colonial hierarchy of the "West over the rest" (Hall 1992).

This book emerges, then, not simply as a collection of interviews but, rather, as an attempt to map out the discursive configurations of the postcolonial as it appears through the medium of conversation that the selected thinkers are prompted to have about themselves and their influences. Its eclecticism is a product that is not purely pragmatic but also programmatic in that its reflections of the diverse nature of the field denoted by the postcolonial demonstrate its existence outside formal disciplinary framings. Postcolonial thought is thus not the sum of the outputs of postcolonial thinkers; rather, it produces postcolonial thinkers in their myriad ways by reflecting the idiosyncrasies of schooling and working, of place and context, and of biography and history. In the process, a textured series of overlapping questions and responses are brought to the fore.

The story to follow is based on biographies as a way to document the life histories and journeys of postcolonial thinking, which has been achieved through a series of semi-structured, in-depth interviews with contemporary postcolonial scholars. The biographical narrative represents the surface of inscription where cultural hopes, anxieties, and insertions present themselves through the writing of the self and of the other (Roberts 2001). This collection is not a quest to uncover the "real lives" of the thinkers that make up this text, nor is it a search to find the "truest" or most "authentic" postcolonial thinker. There has inevitably been an element of selectivity so that the figures, including myself as the narrator, represent the construction of oneself in a particular context (Rosenthal 1993)—that is, "individual lives are not understood merely in terms of their uniqueness—recognizing individuality—but also within a social context" (Roberts 2001, 34), and as Rosenthal suggests, "A life story does not consist of an atomistic chain of experiences, whose meaning is created at the moment of their articulation, but is rather a process taking place simultaneously against the backdrop of a biographical structure of meaning" (1993, 4). In other words, the central concern is the mapping out of the complex relationships between the individual and society, time and space, and context and circumstance. In short, the biographical approach is actually an attempt to understand *being* in a world without structures (Roberts 2001; Rosenthal 1993; Sayyid and Zac 1998).

This collection traces the biographies of postcolonial thinkers and attempts to recenter the continued influence of postcolonial thought in the social and political landscape, which is often currently described as being "post-racial"—that is, it examines the apparent paradox of how postcolonial thought seems to have retained its influence at a point in history when racism itself is frequently felt to have disappeared. The collection thus illustrates how the postcolonial condition shapes thinking in the social sciences, and the use of a biographical methodology facilitates the narration of the stories and journeys of those involved in struggles against racism and colonialism in different times and in different spaces.

In addition, it also explores the forms of subjectivity expressed and constituted through postcolonial thought and activism in specific historical settings. As such, the text observes the interplay among postcoloniality, knowledge production, and post/decolonial performances in the contemporary world. In doing so, it shifts away from the privileging of the postcolonial *qua* theory that continues to mark Western social sciences engagements and, instead, explores the ways in which postcolonial thought is drawn on in response to contemporary political questions and problems. The collection therefore engages with the relationship between postcolonial theory and the formation of subjectivities.

This book marks the development of a comprehensive biographical archive of postcolonial thinking and draws on a range of questions around personal experience to present a broad set of narratives and their relationship to contests over memory. The collection is not, however, concerned with memory in a historical sense but, rather, with the ways in which biographies problematize Eurocentric notions of memory. In doing so, it reflects the various struggles over the postcolonial itself. Colonial encounters involved ruptures, which problematized the histories and memories of colonized peoples. On the one hand, colonization denied the colonized history by instituting particular histories and temporalities (beginning with backwardness and ending with Westernization). On the other hand, history and memory have been used to problematize the agency of the racialized by representing them as being bounded by tradition, backwardness, and authenticity (Sayyid and Hesse 2006). The biographical narratives in this collection thus attempt to introduce an alternative framing that opens out memory and history as contested sites that shape narrations of radically different futures.

The collection engages with the political challenges presented by the thinkers that make up this volume and poses questions about the constitution of political subjectivities in relation to contested discursive visions of past, present, and future. This book, as such, aims to embed alternative memories and alternative visions of what the world can be like—that is, putting to the center the role of memory in postcolonial thought as something that is not just peripherally interesting or easily commodifiable ("the other's traditions") but centrally political. As such, this collection breaks with some of the important moves in current work on memory; for example, in recent times, there has often been an emphasis on memory as a response by victims to ruptures and traumas.[1] This is not to deny the significance of such works; however, this text goes beyond these narratives by focusing not on victims but on agency, and not on responses to ruptures but on introducing new ruptures. In this sense, the biographical approach underpinning the collection is bound up with attempts to institute different sets of social relations.

In other words, it is about the opening out of wider fields to contest. As such, it is not about a dead past but, rather, a living present and future to shed light on how postcolonial thinking contributes to instituting radically different types of social horizons and histories. This is perhaps even more so a crucial endeavor in a context in which racism is no longer deemed relevant (Sian, Law, and Sayyid 2013). This book fundamentally brings to the center the ways in which postcolonial thought is in fact part of a wider struggle over memory and history and, therefore, the future.

The postcolonial journeys that have led to the cultivation and craft of each of the contributing thinkers' works and ideas have been fascinating, moving, joyous, and at times painful, and through their personal biographies, readers are able to see how their experiences led to the formulation of their thinking. As such, the thinkers that make up this collection are nothing short of inspiring. From Bob Marley to the Black Panthers, Fanon to feminism, apartheid to the academy, Checkpoint Charlie to climate change, and Wittgenstein to the War on Terror, this book uncovers a set of thought-provoking adventures about intellect, resistance, and empowerment.

The etiquette of racism has undoubtedly changed;[2] many of the thinkers in this collection describe a turbulent backdrop of overt and oppressive racism as they fought on the frontlines for social, cultural, and political transformation. Today, the religion for the unfaithful that comes in the form of neoliberalism has replaced the "gollywogs" with glossy Benetton ads, and from Beyoncé to Obama, we are led to believe that racism has come to an end (Goldberg 2008). This is the world in which I was born.

In Pursuit of Happiness: The Neoliberal Junkie

> The best of postcolonialism is autocritical.
>
> —Spivak 2000, xv

Following Spivak's advice, the journey to follow is based on an autocritical engagement with the aim to bring about the "best of postcolonialism." My quest for the postcolonial stems from my PhD experience; by this point, despite obtaining a degree in the social sciences, I hadn't ever encountered the poetics of Fanon, Said, Lorde, or Du Bois—our "founding parents." My journey is set against the backdrop of 2006 Britain, where I came to a crossroads. Prior to my PhD, I was the good assimilated Brit—well integrated, different but not too different; I'd mastered the art of passing, and I did it well.

The world I came to inhabit was one of hedonism, self-indulgence, and a glittering hyper-reality in which I immersed myself, driven by the belief that anything was possible because everything was available—me, myself, and I; ego; and the devil walking by my side. Everything around me was dispensable: fleeting relationships, a dilettante searching for the next temporary high, blinded by the bright billboards lighting up the night sky. A healthy neoliberal, I bought into that lifestyle and was willing to keep paying to be part of that enchanting world full of wonderful distractions. The cost, I would later learn, was the giving up of my soul, the silencing of my voice, and a profound depoliticization.[3]

The embeddedness of racism is the legacy of Western colonialism.[4] The idea that the world has somehow overcome race—"the post-racial generation"—is a lazy fabrication fueling the strength of the neoliberal monster that attempts to reduce racism to an individual phenomena rather than a structural one. Racism is entrenched—people of color are still failed by education systems in the West; people of color are still overrepresented in prisons in the West; people of color still have the highest unemployment rates in the West; people of color still have the worst health in the West; people of color still disproportionately live in poverty; and the list goes on.[5] If, as we are more than often led to believe, Western society is meritocratic, why is it that, out of the UK's 18,510 university professors, only 85 are black (Gabriel 2013),[6] yet young black men in the UK account for around 40 percent of the population of youth jails in England and Wales (Travis 2011)?[7] This is not coincidence, this is not chance, and this is not a cruel twist of fate. It cannot be that people of color are all educationally inept, or criminals, or simply work-shy. The trick of the neoliberal masquerade is that it makes the individual responsible for his or her own destiny, and if he or she fails, it is the individual's fault and not the failure of the modern state (Goldberg 2008). This is the face of the 2000s, and beneath the gloss, it's ugly.

People of my generation, and those following, never experienced a sense of the Soviet Union. We are also too young to remember the cruelty of Thatcher: we lived at the height of the Blair brigade where the neoliberal consensus was cemented with his election. We were born at the end of history—no memory, no counterculture, no side to choose—in short, no politics (Mouffe 2005). And this is precisely the point: neoliberalism destroys the ability to imagine structures and, with that, destroys the possibility of alternative stories of the world to be told.

There are three main events that the current generation has been a witness to: first, the spectacle of the War on Terror.[8] We are living in a world where the United States and their allies are able to send drones to the Middle East, torture prisoners in detention camps in breach of human rights conventions, and break thousands of privacy rules through a strict regime of surveillance.[9] Second is the election of Obama. This hailed the "post-racial" and the subsequent belief that a black president led to the end of racism. Third is the economic crisis—the boom generation no more—and the West as the center of the global economy seriously undermined. These are significant events, and we continue to live in precarious times. But the "X-factor" generation appears more concerned with celebrification and consumerism, living for the moment, detachment, and narcissism, as the "I" is the center of the universe.

Neoliberalism has become what religion was to Marx: the opium of the people; as we inject this new opium, we turn our heads away from neo-imperial war crimes, racism, and inequalities that continue to plague our societies. Where is the voice of our generation shouting and forcing society to look at itself? That voice has been replaced by apathy—an apathy that enables the far right to gain power, an apathy that allows troops to enter Iraq and Afghanistan, and an apathy that allows us to deny that we have blood on our hands. We are disengaged, disillusioned, and "withdrawn from withdrawal" as we await our next fix of the neoliberal concoction that makes us forget (Heidegger 1962).

A life of racism didn't affect me, and I honestly believed that. I was born "here" (in the UK), so my parents' and grandparents' journeys in East Africa and India didn't impact me. No one verbally or physically racially assaulted me; I blended in quite well, so what did it matter? In short, questions of race were irrelevant to me. It was only when I awoke from my slumber that I came to realize that, beneath the manufactured elaborate production staged by a conveyer belt of clowns and puppets, was a hazy, zombie-like existence, and the deeper I delved, the more I knew that there was always a sense of disconnect and discomfort lurking below. Race often crept into the background of my thinking, so it wasn't like I had abandoned such questions completely, but I had repressed them in every way possible because I didn't want to face up to the reality of racism—it was easier to close my eyes or turn my head because I wasn't a victim; I was the parvenu, racially mobile (Arendt 1968).

The Art of Passing Post-racially

> The problem of the twentieth century is the problem of the color-line—the relation of the darker to the lighter races of men in Asia and Africa, in America and the islands of the sea.
>
> —W. E. B. Du Bois 1996, 13

Du Bois's critique of the color-line remains significantly relevant to understand the current racial configurations and hierarchies that haunt our contemporary "post-racial" times. Passing (across the color-line) is a phenomenon that has been analyzed mainly through the lens of the African-American experience. Other ethnically marked populations also have tales of extraordinary lives in which they manage to erase or domesticate ethnic difference, allowing themselves to be presented as ethnically unmarked; for example, stories of Jews pretending to be gentiles, "half-castes" who are able to step over racial boundaries and hierarchies even if problematically.[10]

Passing is part of the world of strict racial boundaries. The question that haunts us today is, how does one pass post-racially? In the post-racial, racial categorizations come (paradoxically enough) to be dominated by an emphasis on the phenotype (e.g., Modood 1994). As a consequence, where a phenotype is ambiguous, it makes available a space where questions can be asked rather than categorization assumed, so in my case, I didn't "look Indian"—whatever looking Indian meant at the time. Because I didn't look Indian, etiquette meant that there was always a certain amount of hesitancy in asking me to explain my failure to "look Indian."

Second comes the performance (Butler 1997).[11] As the repertoire of performing increases and as the general population becomes slightly more knowledgeable about the varieties and variations and the nuances of performing the part of "playing the ethnic," it paradoxically makes it easier to conceal ethnic marking. In my case, I didn't "act like an Indian," whatever acting like an Indian meant; from musical tastes to fashion choice, I was not easily part of the Indian crowd nor did I engage with a cultural schizophrenia (beloved of anthropologists and ethnographers of a certain hue),[12] wearing salwar kameez and eating samosas at home, and wearing miniskirts and devouring fish and chips outside my home. I was a method actress living the part but not playing it. At home, we were generally at ease with ourselves, expanding the range of what it meant to be a Sikh without reflection or engagement—just doing what came naturally.

Third, the horizon of the post-racial was no longer presented as exclusionary. Britain had become a meritocracy—or so it seemed. Where hard work, the right connections, and enterprise would allow you to achieve success, there was no color-line, let alone a glass ceiling. My family seemed to demonstrate that with successful family businesses—and not a corner shop in sight. Living in leafy suburbia we were whiter than white.

An Awakening

> It is more rewarding—and perhaps more difficult—to think concretely and sympathetically, contrapuntally, about others than only about "us."
>
> —Edward Said 1994, 408

The contrapuntal thinking Edward Said proposes is one based on respect for "other" components that also have their part to play in the performance of the melody. Syncopated rhythms allow for the weak beats to be heard as the splendor of a collective tune is recognized. Said is correct in suggesting that it is more difficult, but at the same time, he is equally correct in stating that it is more rewarding, as we will go on to see; subscribing to this type of thinking is the opening of oneself to a new synthesis of different sounds.

In the neoliberal world one comes to embrace, one finds that the will, the strength, and the courage to escape dissipates, and that's its very triumph; it paralyzes you physically, mentally, and spiritually as it throws you bread while you enjoy the circus show. I hadn't had the tools or the consciousness yet to formulate my ideas; it was almost like such questions were hidden in a chest waiting to be unlocked to reveal a treasure of knowledge that my soul yearned for. This unlocking came with my PhD journey, where I was introduced to the jewels *Black Skin, White Masks*; *Souls of Black Folk*; and *Orientalism*. I absorbed their words like a sponge to water. I had been thirsty, and I continued to drink the antidote that I had been searching for; I wept, I smiled, and finally, I spoke.

I soon learned how duped I'd been as a devotee to the cult of neoliberalism; the rabbit it pulled from out of the hat was no longer magic; it was just a trick. I saw the mechanisms, the strings; I learned how it all worked—and suddenly, I was brought back to life. The power of Fanon, Du Bois, Spivak, and Said was through the way in which they told me that a different story was possible to the one I had always been too scared to question, and that the possibility of new narratives was empowering, freeing, and politicizing. This wasn't a mere temporary or passing feeling of elation; it's permanent, not superficial or vacuous but meaningful—no longer an individual but part of a collective involved in a struggle to change the world.

What I've shared may sound like a clichéd story that the revisionist historians and neocon commentators warn us about (e.g., Riley 2012). A happy-go-lucky girl does sociology and ends up spouting Malcolm X. Sociology turned this hedonist's head; a PhD with a postcolonial vibe makes for a militant. Alas, if only that were true. The trouble is that the social sciences, like the academy, remain resolutely Eurocentric, so the question then becomes, how do I explain my turn? Just as revisionist historians forget, the colonizers didn't need European ideas to resist European empires, because resistance was in the blood.[13]

Looking back, the effects of racism and the knowledge of its cruelty and injustices were never entirely absent; they were simply well hidden. If anyone could connect the dots, they could see the whole picture, and all my degrees helped me draw blurred lines from dot to dot, seeing racism not as random interruptions of the normal, but something systemic and sustained. Racism didn't just happen to those poorer than me or to those darker than me; it happened to us all—black, brown, yellow, white. It just happened in different ways; racism wasn't just an attitude or a system of beliefs, and racism wasn't inside our heads but in our bodies, as a network of practices regulating and disciplining society (Sayyid 2010; Foucault 1995).

My mind became curious, my vision became clearer, and a new spirit entered my soul. The new direction I took proved more challenging with losses along the way as I found myself excluded from the space I once thought I belonged to. The truth is, I never did belong, and when I questioned the way things were, I didn't make sense to many of my peers anymore; I was the troublemaker, the nuisance, or the angry person of color. Although harder the path may well have been, I never looked back. I wanted more, and as I continued along my journey, I encountered all the thinkers included within this collection, excited by the way in which the contributors had used, interpreted, and developed the thinking of our founding texts. This collection is thus based on those who transformed me personally by helping me understand what it is to *be* as a person of color.

The challenge for the new generation of scholars interested in questions around race and ethnicity and postcolonial thinking is to look beneath the glittering veneer of neoliberalism and not to be fooled by the mesmerizing spell that it has cast on us, because beneath the mask, one is able to see the hunger strikers in Guantanamo awaiting fair trial, the constant and sustained monitoring of beards and veils, and the white supremacists who have replaced their shaved heads and tattoos with shirts and ties. Neoliberalism has made us lazy; we are distracted by the mass churning of vacuous messages as "the self" reigns prominent and the collective voice dismantled. It is easy to fall into this trap, and in terms of my own personal biography, I too was fooled; it's the safe option to pretend that things are OK. Such a view is perhaps more so than ever in vogue as anti-racism and anti-colonialism are increasingly branded unnecessary and such voices reduced to mere whispers.

This collection then tells the tale about how ideas can transform *being* and shows us how to survive in a world that has already told us a story about ourselves. Following in the chapters is the mapping out of this complex journey as it reflects on a series of 12 one-to-one conversational interviews with friends, who along the way have helped me unlearn and relearn a conceptual vocabulary and arm me with the necessary tools to make new connections and leave my footprint in the postcolonial sand. This book calls to the new generation of scholars entering these debates to take up the baton and continue to keep the flame alive that the thinkers in this collection have worked so hard to light.

Postcolonial Kaleidoscopes

We still need to work on understanding that such relations are not a matter of "high" and "low" cultures, of "thought" versus "action" but rather different ways of striving for social and cultural transformations.

—Mignolo 2000b, 199

Rather than clinching to conventional distinctions that immobilize collective action, Mignolo points to the promise of emancipation through the embracing of alternative routes for struggles for change. This is key for understanding the varied yet unified approaches to postcolonial thought. People talk about the postcolonial in many different ways; with one twist of the kaleidoscope the subaltern speaks, with another appears the souls of black folk. As we twist again, we see before our eyes those black skins, white masks, and in the final turn, we see the murky shadows from the Orient flickering in the horizon. The postcolonial takes many different guises; some call it subaltern studies, some call it *Orientalism*, and others call it liberation.

All the thinkers that make up this volume have been shaped by the anticolonial struggles and mobilizations of their time in unique ways. Anticolonialism refers to not only the national liberation struggles against the European empires but also the struggle for the autonomy and emancipation of black people (Larsen 2000). These thinkers, separated as they are in the theater of their activities, share a degree of commonality arising from the logic of resistance to systems of white privilege in its various manifestations. The thoughts of these diverse thinkers also point to their contributions to the weakening of Eurocentrism by challenging the centrality of the West. Their critique of Western colonialism is fundamental to postcolonial thinking and enables us to understand the way in which specifically Western systems of colonialism have enabled the West to articulate a global hegemony through the maintenance of the racialized Western/non-Western hierarchy that has come to shape the current world order (Said 1978; Hall 1992; Sayyid 2003; Alessandrini 2000).

Through their diverse set of critiques, these thinkers have been significant to the advancement of postcolonial debates and have contributed to the opening of new spaces to think about, question, and unsettle the privileged positioning of the West in political, academic, and cultural spheres. The thinkers in this collection also bring to light the nexus between postcoloniality and diaspora as a means of exploring the formation of complex deterritorialized collective identities by weaving together the different ways the relationship between culture and politics impacts questions of postcolonial identities in the contemporary landscape (Gilroy 1993; Brah 2003; Behdad 2000).

The female voices that make up this collection add to our understanding of the postcolonial as a site to destabilize both gendered and racialized global structures of oppression. Their work has contributed to the transformation of the very nature of feminism as a "universal" discourse. Bringing to the center their "lived" experiences, their compelling body of analytical work demonstrates the various ways in which non-Western women have been essentialized and reduced within conventional Western feminist discourses—and by extension, political and popular accounts (e.g., *Mail Online* 2006).[14] Their critique of Western feminism is underpinned by a close engagement with the category of intersectionality (Rajan and Park 2000). Many of the women interviewed in this collection were at the very beginnings of the feminist movement, and readers will be able to see how, through their activism, they have been pioneers in shifting the debate to a more critically reflexive arena.

Whichever way one chooses to turn the kaleidoscope, one should see that with the changing colors and developing patterns also comes the possibility of different stories to be told—however, not necessarily trapped within one lens. In our quest to find the postcolonial, readers will see that, in the conversations to follow, "another solution is possible. It implies a restructuring of the world" (Fanon 2008, 60).

Notes

1. For example, see literature on the Holocaust (Levy, Sznaider, and Oksiloff 2006) and on India's Partition (Butalia 2000).

2. For further details of the changing etiquette of racism in the UK context, see Sian, Law, and Sayyid 2013, 1–20.

3. For further analysis of neoliberalism and its consequences, see Žižek 2011, Bauman 1991, and Goldberg 2008.

4. For the argument that racism appears in multiple sites over many different periods, see Law 2009.

5. It is often pointed out that the effects of racism have been abated because various ethnically marked populations are demonstrating higher rates of upward mobility—for example, East Asians in America and Sikhs in Britain. The argument to move appears to be that, by demonstrating the heterogeneity of ethnically marked populations, one can assert the irrelevance of racism in contemporary society. The difficulty is that such ploys only work because what is maintained is an essentialist characterization of race and racism. Racism is not about the regulation of "races" as much as it is about the process of racialization. Thus group populations that are deemed "model-minority" often reflect the dialectics between racialization and de-racialization; this is a key feature of the operation of racism,

not evidence for its abandonment. For elaboration of this argument, see my conversation with Paul Gilroy in Chapter 12 of this volume.

6. For this discussion, see Gabriel (2013).
7. For this discussion, see Travis (2011).
8. For a critical discussion of postcolonial studies post-9/11, see Ray 2000, 574–84.
9. For example, the 2013 leaked reports exposing mass surveillance of foreign nationals and US citizens by the US National Security Agency (NSA).
10. For examples of cultural representations, see Tarantino's film (2009) *Inglourious Basterds* and Edna Ferber's 1926 novel *Showboat.*
11. This is in reference to Judith Butler's notion of performativity.
12. For such anthropological accounts, see Anwar 1998 as well as Ballard and Ballard 1977, 21–56.
13. "Blood" is used as a metaphor to refer to the corporality beyond power (Foucault 1995; Foucault 1998; Dreyfus and Rabinow 1983).
14. This is seen in various media and political debates around Muslim women and the veil.

CHAPTER 1

Sara Ahmed

Sara Ahmed is a professor of race and cultural studies at Goldsmith's College, University of London.

How did you first get into the field of race, ethnicity, feminism, and postcolonialism?

I guess it would help to go quite far back to my first experiences as a student. As an undergraduate, it was feminist theory that caught my attention. When I read works that reflected on questions of gender and sexual difference, they captured my imagination, as I could relate what I was reading to my own experiences growing up as a girl. I can't remember a time when I did not feel like a feminist. I had so many experiences of being a feminist killjoy at the family table, getting into trouble over gender; questioning ideas about what was appropriate for girls to be and to do. So feminism had always been quite a felt part of my life and my experience. When I encountered feminist theoretical texts, it was just amazing. My PhD was on feminist theory and postmodernism (later published as *Differences That Matter: Feminist Theory and Postmodernism*).

It took much longer for me to engage with questions of race and ethnicity, but the shift did occur when I was writing my thesis. It was quite ironic how it happened, because it felt like something that happened to me, which came *to* me rather than *from* me. I was writing this chapter on subjectivity for my thesis, and I was thinking that I needed an example to hang my argument on. I can even remember looking around the room for inspiration! And that's when I remembered this event that had happened when I was growing up in Adelaide, where I was stopped by two policemen. One had asked, "Are you aboriginal?" And the other one then said, "Or is it just a suntan?" It had been a disturbing event at the time, and it made me very angry. So this event came to mind, and I began to reflect on questions of "strangeness" and different differences that matter.

I began to realize that many of my childhood experiences, or experiences of growing up, were about the sense of not quite being at home, always being seen as "other" and different; for example, the constant references to my surname, jokey comments, and references to my complexion—that sense of not quite being from where I was. These things were very much part of how I had experienced growing up, but I had not been ready to think about them. However, once I let those memories in, once the thoughts came to me, it was very reorienting. Everything changed!

At that time, Chris Weedon was teaching at Cardiff, and she introduced me to Audre Lorde. I read *Sister Outsider* and was blown away. I was blown away by her capacity to describe everyday experiences of being the object of hate: how racism positions the body, how it makes you feel, how it feels to be the one who is presumed to be the cause of the problem, of your own problems. And it helped me make sense of my own experiences of being a stranger, which, of course, were different to her in terms of the context and histories. I began to think about those uneasy feelings of being in the wrong or being wrong and how they can accumulate. She also helped me think about how you can do conceptual and intellectual work differently. I was fascinated by how she was able to use personal experience and embed her conceptual innovations in description. And I think that she's probably inspired me more than anyone to think about these experiences that I have had of not being at home, whether that is within the neighborhood in Australia, whether it is at school, whether it is at home, whether it is in the institution or the university; these experiences are my pedagogy. They are the means by which I can think critically about who comes to be understood as a rightful occupant of time and space.

So encountering Audre Lorde, and re-encountering my own memories through her, was pivotal. Sometimes I think it takes a while to be able to work through these forms of estrangement. Initially, I wasn't ready. These experiences are so difficult when you're growing up, feeling different and excluded; it is so painful. You have to be at a certain place, I think, to be ready to work through that. But once I was ready, that was it. You know, everything was reinterpreted through that lens, and it allowed me to understand so much, not only about my own experiences, but also about the theoretical materials that I was reading. It was like reinhabiting the world.

I was never taught by anyone who was not white in my whole university experience, and not one person in primary or secondary school. I didn't realize that until quite recently! And when I thought about that—what it means to live and to work in proximity to whiteness—it just helped me understand how racial categories and social categories are so embedded in the institutions that we learn to not notice them. We need to unlearn that embeddedness, and that was and is a real challenge.

Postcolonialism was not a word I ever really strongly identified with, I think partly because I first encountered that word as a literature student in Australia. It was taught within the context of Australian literature, and *postcolonial* was used to index the relation between Australia as a nation and "the mother country." The way it was taught to me gave me the impression that the postcolonial was about white Australia (I have learned since that, if this whiteness was not remarked on, then *that* is the mark of whiteness). Postcolonial theory in this rendering did not have much to do with indigenous people or Asian Australians. And given that the colonizers did not leave in the Australian case, the "post" always seemed wrong.

But then coming to the UK, I became aware that the postcolonial was also a space in which those who experienced colonialism could challenge that legacy. I began to appreciate that *post* doesn't necessarily mean "after"; it can also mean an ambivalent relationship to the colonial as an unfinished history—colonialism as a structuring of the present. And I've been very influenced by reading Spivak, Bhabha, and Said, so I do think of this body of work as a ground on which I tread, though some of the decolonial literatures are probably more where I would locate myself politically.

Can you talk a bit about your biracial heritage?
Did this influence your intellectual trajectory?
To what extent do your early experiences relate to
the topics discussed throughout your work?

I think much of my awareness of the significance of biraciality was retrospective. When I was growing up, I did not consciously think of how important it was to have parents who came from such different worlds. Often, what does not reach conscious recognition is what is most important. My retrospective word for my experience would be "biworld" as much "biracial." If you have two parents that come from two different countries and cultures, however porous those cultures may be, they bring with them worlds that might otherwise have been kept apart or stopped from meeting, at least in certain kinds of intimate spaces. But in your own family and your own home, these worlds meet. You are a meeting point! I think there is a lot of pressure and anxiety in being a meeting point, but there are also good things: worlds open up when there is more than one world available to you.

I grew up in the 1970s and 1980s. My father was one of a generation of immigrants who assimilated because he thought it was the right thing to do. I even learned to mispronounce my own surname "Ahmed" because he wanted to make it more "sayable" to his English and Australian friends. He did not speak Urdu or Punjabi to us at home, so I don't speak those languages. We can inherit our parent's decisions. He thought with these decisions we would have more chances, but it meant we were cut off from being able to be from that "other" world. And there is a degree of sadness in that. I still have a close relationship with some of my Pakistani family, but I think that those decisions have had an impact on how I've connected with them.

I later really began to think through the kind of world-making aspects of being biracial or being mixed. For me, it is not a question about how you identify. I've never been interested in that; that's never been one of my questions. It is more about what is around you. I was interested in thinking about objects, for instance, the objects at home. Some of these objects pointed to my Pakistani heritage; they were things my father had brought to Australia with him from Pakistan. One of the objects I talked about in *Queer Phenomenology* was, funnily enough, an old volume of Shakespeare plays that he'd found in the house in Lahore that they came to during Partition. And these books captured my imagination. They were a kind of signifier of Englishness and its own imperial travels, but they mattered to me because they pointed to Pakistan. There would be other objects that arrived and mattered because of how they arrived; things brought by my aunties, such as rugs and spices, as well as what bodies brought with them, smells and sounds. Bringing things home makes home, and my home was shaped by these worlds.

So biraciality matters to me through matter—what is around you, the material that surrounds you. It is also, of course, a question of how you are addressed. Where are you from? Where are you *really* from? These are not simply questions addressed to biracial or mixed raced kids, but I think you are often asked these questions when you have a mixed background; I think we are familiar with these kinds of questions. They create the impression that you need to explain yourself! When you are constantly being asked where you are from, it does not allow where you are to become part of the background. This "where" occupies the foreground; you are aware of where. This can lead to a certain kind of consciousness, just as you can become more conscious of what home is when you are not at home. Even when you are asked these sorts of questions, it doesn't necessarily mean that you register what is going on at the time.

A lot of my consciousness of the significance of being mixed has come after, through reflecting back on what it does to be asked those questions. And I have always loved the work of other writers who reflect on these ways of becoming estranged wherever you are or of how you are not quite at home in any place (such as the work of Ien Ang). These are the sorts of questions that allow you then to ask questions about what it means to be at home, to have an identity, and so on.

How did you develop your sense of political consciousness?

I had always felt or thought of myself as quite a political person in the sense of being aware of questions of injustice, estranged from the kind of politics of what was around me. I had quite a conservative family. My father—who is a middle-class Pakistani doctor—would say things that I was uncomfortable with, often about gender but sometimes also about race. He would speak of those "unwelcome" immigrants who were not like him and those other good citizens who were doing the right thing. It was having that position articulated through his mouth that taught me how when you have to fight to be taken seriously, when you have to fight to be a legitimate person, it can make you identify with the norms that are excluding you.

I'm somebody who has found education politicizing as both a teacher and a student. I think of the excitement of doing women's studies and the excitement of reading someone like Frantz Fanon or Audre Lorde for the first time. It is just mind-blowing. It is partly, to use an old-fashioned word that I still quite like, about "consciousness raising." There is that sense you can acquire that you are not on your own, that there are others for whom the world is a place that is not safe and familiar. Trying to develop a language and a vocabulary to describe what is going on in what might seem like quite small instances (like the police stopping you and asking you questions) is for me political labor. Understanding the mechanisms can be politicizing.

In terms of events, I first got involved in student politics around the time of the first Gulf War. I became enraged by the use of certain kinds of scripts about the "others" who were "brutal," who were not human, and who "we" have a moral mission to exterminate or to civilize. When you begin to read the work of academic activists like Gayatri Spivak, you begin to realize that the contemporary discourse of empire is written in the language of "civilizing," "love," "care," "empathy," "freedom," and "democracy." Some of these words are words you might have been attached to, as words that seem to indicate something that you are for, but you learn these words can be used as tools to support what you are not for. Imperial language is often written in the language of love and saving, specifically the "saving" of women. It was politicizing to come up against contemporary imperialism through the lens of postcolonial theory because it allows you to hear the continuity; it gives you the history to that present.

In the Australian context, the struggles around indigenous sovereignty were politicizing. When I was growing up, and in my early days as a student, there was an absolute failure to create a space in which we could talk about the native title, the stolen generation, or reconciliation; it was absent from our classroom discussions, and it was absent from my own life. Since I left Australia, reconciliation has become a much more public and debated theme, but it still feels that reconciliation can be used as a kind of desire to be "over" race and to put it behind us. I have often felt alienated from some of the trends in academic Australian literature (particularly feminist ones) because they are often premised on love, sympathy, and goodwill, and I'm like, "No, I'm not going to do that—most definitely not!" I am much more interested in angry women of color! I've been glad in the Australian context to see the development of the Australian Critical Race and Whiteness Studies Association, which was originally led by Aileen Moreton-Robinson, one of the most important indigenous feminist voices in Australia. Working with her and others in Australia has been very important to me.

In the British context, where I have been based all my academic life, being part of black British feminism has been sustaining. I met Heidi Mirza just after getting my job at Lancaster in 2005, and she has been a real mentor. I felt that I was able to be not only part of the collection—the actual written collection that Heidi edited, *Black British Feminism*—but also part of a collective that identified as black British feminists. Heidi Mirza and Avtar Brah have been incredibly supportive to my generation of scholars. They have given me a sense that the work we do to get "here" is a relationship to "being here" and that *that* is a relationship that is worth conserving.

Which thinkers have most influenced you in your work?

Audre Lorde would be, without a doubt, the writer who has most influenced me. What I really like about her work is how she generates concepts through her description of experiences and situations. And that's why I always teach with her, because I think that there is a tendency to reify concepts, to think of theory as this abstract thing or as this tool that you use to dismantle or refashion the world in some way. Audre Lorde taught me that the point of description is to get to the point of description. Description is hard work, and I think of her as somebody who has shaped not just how I think but also my own writing practice. I want to write from experience and to bring concepts to life through experience.

I'd also say Frantz Fanon has been hugely influential. When I read *Black Skin, White Masks*, and also later *Wretched of the Earth* and *A Dying Colonialism*, it really was one of those mind-blowing experiences. Again, I think the way in which he is able to use dramatic instances of being in Paris, being hailed by the white boy, to describe what it means to become the object is important. And I learned again from how the description of a situation of being objects and "other" can be a way of speaking back, in this case, to a certain kind of existential landscape that was all about bodies and the "I can" (the classic formulation of existential phenomenology is the "I can" of the body that can). It is those who are made "nots" who might show the "I cannot." And we can think about, and from, what happens when we become objects of the gaze and cannot extend our bodies into the world; there is no capacity of ease or familiarity, and you are stopped. And I've been trying to develop what I call "a phenomenology of being stopped."

I have also been influenced by Spivak, and I still think her *Can the Subaltern Speak?* has been foundational for me, especially her ability to describe the colonial project and condense it into the "white men saving brown women from brown men." Spivak has this incredible capacity to describe complex world systems in a sentence! And Said, without a doubt, has been massively influential. I always teach *Orientalism*, and every year when I teach it, I think how easy it is to forget just how significant that book was. *Orientalism* allowed me to go back and look at the kinds of knowledge I take for granted as "academic knowledge"—that is, to think about how the construction of the "other" as a category is institutional. I also think that he has helped me think more about domestication. This term is not usually attributed to Said, but he shows us how Orientalism is not just about the creation of what we are not but also about bringing that "not" home and making it familiar.

I also would say Sander Gilman's work has been really helpful to me, as with other theorists who have shown how sexuality and gender are at stake in the colonial relation, including Anne McClintock's work (especially her book *Imperial Leather*). I have also found Homi Bhabha's article on mimicry useful; I returned to it when writing my book on happiness, as it helped me think through how empire becomes a "happiness mission." Bhabha's readings of education in the colonial context were powerful (e.g., his reading of Macaulay). I learned especially about whiteness as a form of imperial travel from his exploration of how the demand for the "other" to be Anglicized (a way of not being English through proximity) generates a subject that is "almost the same but not quite white." Whiteness becomes all the more powerful in the requirement to approximate its form, a requirement that is registered in the failure to approximate that form.

Do you see yourself as a postcolonial thinker? How far would you locate your work within the genre?

I'm not really sure about this. Only one of my books "signs" itself under postcolonialism, and that is *Strange Encounters,* which was published in 2000. I was interested that, when I published that book with Routledge, one of the readers said it was not postcolonial theory. They were very clear: "This is not postcolonial theory." I was interested in this not because I was attached to postcolonialism (I mentioned earlier how in the Australian context, the postcolonial had signified white) but because, as a judgment, it seemed very sure of what made something postcolonial (and what did not). I remember Spivak saying that, when she was at Lancaster University for a conference there, she wanted her book *A Critique of Postcolonial Reason* to be called "Don't Call Me Postcolonial." Even academics associated with postcolonial studies have a degree of hesitation about that name. Maybe it is because of the ease with which postcolonialism became a genre or even a canon.

I think there is hesitation because, even though most people who are using the term *postcolonial* know that the "post" does not mean after or that colonialism has ended in our current world, "post" can easily signify the "after" because "posting" is such a desire—a desire to register moving beyond this or that. So, even if we are not using "post" in that way, I think it can imply or create an impression, rather like post-feminism or post-racial. I think I am becoming again more uncomfortable with the term itself and more interested in other terms such as *decolonial*. I think the "de" registers a project, one that requires active, purposeful action and thought. So I would say yes and no, short answer.

Can you elaborate on what you regard as the main significance of postcolonial thinking in the social sciences?

My background is not in the social sciences, which I think does make a difference. I did my first degree in English and the history of ideas, and my PhD was in critical theory. Following that, I was based in women's studies for ten years, which is sort of between the humanities and the social sciences. So I am answering your question from the position of not being located in the social sciences.

I think what was significant, for me, about postcolonial studies was how, although it tends to be read as relating to other places and other people, it shows that this otherness takes us back home. When you think of Spivak's reading of *Jane Eyre*, she showed how a classic example of Victorian literature was predicated on a racialized discourse, in both the referencing of missionaries around the edges of the novel but also its center, in the representation of Bertha Mason. She showed how empire was at home.

The point of postcolonial critique was to create a disturbance in how literature was taught, how culture was taught. I think it is still too easy to think of postcolonialism as being about the study of the "other," what we do when we "go there." But colonialism is right here in how we constitute the very object of our disciplines (including sociology), and it has been here right from the beginning (just think of how some of the early work in British sociology was informed by eugenics). This, for me, is what postcolonialism should mean in the teaching of disciplines. Coloniality is the "darker side" of modernity, as Walter Mignolo (2011) has described. But I don't know if it has meant that—and I suspect it hasn't—so disciplines such as sociology have resisted being transformed by the critiques of coloniality.

I teach one session on race on a social theory course; all the other sessions include set readings by white men on topics that are taught as if they have nothing to do with race, including modernity. One of the things I try to do when I teach race is to not make race something that is particular. A struggle for postcolonial studies and critical race studies has been coming up against this constant desire to find race in this thing over *here* as a way of finding it *there*. So when you look at other courses that are not explicitly on race, they tend to be centered on an entirely white European male intellectual tradition that assumes Europe as their referent, an assumption that is not made explicit.

Doing the work of critiquing disciplines requires exploring the genealogy of the discipline. This is why working on race is also about working on institutions (and their reproductive technologies), and this is what *Orientalism* as a book asks us to do. It is not about offering new readings of old texts. It is about intervening in how institutions reproduce themselves around certain bodies—bodies of knowledge as well as physical living bodies. I think that a lot of the work we have to do is institutional work; otherwise, the bodies that do not reproduce the discipline will just end up doing the "race" courses! We have to use our particulars to dislodge the general.

How influential has Said's critique of Orientalism been on your own work?

I think I probably read *Orientalism* in the first year of my PhD. I think the way in which Said used Foucault to develop the concept of colonial discourse was incredibly helpful. What I appreciated about his argument was the attention to institutional histories that are already in place, such that each text is part of a web or weave that created this thing called the Orient. I think it is a helpful text to teach with because of how it shows how race and geography are impossible to disentangle. I also like the way Said addresses the postmodern virtual Orient as what "strengthens" the hold on the Orient, recreating this figure of the Arab as a menace. He thus invites us to think about what his readings of nineteenth-century texts might mean in terms of contemporary visualizations of the Orient as menace as well as the way in which these constructs can be seen as part of the system, as part of an institution that is predicated on this sharp distinction between an "us" and a "them."

Some of the arguments that are more abstract but still fascinating—those you would get from post-structuralism—for example, concepts of the "constitutive outside" that you might get from someone like Derrida, became in Said's hands so much more concrete and vivid. I learned from Said how the "other" is used to prop up or support a notion of identity, such that the "not" becomes constitutive (I often quip, "Nots unite!"). He shows us how these mechanisms are mechanisms of racialization, how the not-white can establish whiteness. I wrote very early on a small piece on "women and the Orient" and used Said's work to talk about the way in which *Marie Claire* as a fashion magazine used pictures of the

Orient as a background for selling clothes—the Orient as a prop or a vehicle for transporting whiteness. I think *Orientalism* is an exceptional piece of scholarship, and I've engaged closely with Said's work from very early on.

Your body of work engages closely with postcolonial feminism. What do you think postcolonial/black feminism offers women of color, and how do you think it challenges white feminist discourses?

A piece that has been important for me as both a reader and a student is Chandra Talpade Mohanty's *Under Western Eyes*, especially the way in which she examines the constitution of women in the third world as a monolithic "other." Her work made me think about feminist methodology quite differently; it challenges the reliance on a homogenizing notion of women, and, for me, that was very helpful.

I have been more influenced by earlier literatures than that, as I mentioned, including Audre Lorde but also Alice Walker and Toni Morrison. African-American writing and literature was really important to me. I think that is partly because I have an interest in earlier feminist writings, including black feminist and feminist of color writings. It is easy to think about these critiques of white and Western feminism as recent, when actually they were there right from the beginning. So I am very interested in thinking of feminist history and black feminist history as having that long duration and postcolonial feminist critiques as part of that long duration. I think if you place Mohanty's work in that genealogy, it gives it a different kind of ground.

I do think that it is easy to take *intersectionality* for granted as a term. There have been some strong critiques of intersectionality in the works of people like Jasbir Puar and others, and I understand and agree with many aspects of these critiques. Any concept, once it becomes the thing that people organize around, can cease to be doing the work it was introduced to do. I always think of words and concepts as the opposite of muscles. The more you use a muscle, the tighter it is. The more you use a word, the looser it becomes. So I think it is important to go back to some of the earlier work on intersectionality and to think of that term as having a very specific genealogy.

Kimberle Crenshaw's work in critical legal studies and race studies is also significant as a way to think about what intersectionality was requiring as a form of labor. I still think the concept of intersectionality is a major contribution of black and postcolonial feminism, especially when you are trying to think about how these categories—race and gender—are exercised or emerge in everyday institutional situations when we become the "embodied other." So much feminist work, in taking up gender as the primary object, has obscured so much complexity, and it also generalized from a particular set of experiences of gender.

I think it is important to remember that with concepts like intersectionality—even if it now has become somewhat of a catchphrase for black feminism—these concepts have histories that are part of what they do. I cannot now, when I think of experiences of gender, not think about questions of race and other kinds of differences, and that is precisely because black feminism and postcolonial feminism have shaped my horizon. I do think it is worth claiming this as part of the heritage that black feminism, feminism of color, and postcolonial feminism have given us.

In the wake of the War on Terror, there has been a tendency in white feminist discourse to save "oppressed" Muslim women. Was this notion of white feminism as "saving" the "other" also prominent when you started out? Do you still think this narrative remains hegemonic?

I do think that the savior narrative is still exercised. It is evident in popular culture with the amount of white women savior films; there is certainly a preoccupation not only in Hollywood but elsewhere as well. And it is obviously part of mainstream politics, given how white philanthropy and humanitarianism often work through the circulation of images of suffering others. We also come up against it by being positioned as the ones who have been helped or saved. I know of colleagues who, when they have been very critical of foreign policy, have been told by some feminists, "You're so lucky you live in a democracy . . . It is only because you're here that you have the freedom to be who it is that you are."

Although there is a lot of acceptance and recognition of black feminism at one level, on another level there is still a constant desire to catch you out, because it is assumed you got here because of assistance (just the way people can see affirmative action programs but not see the assistance of privilege itself). So the acceptance of black feminism might be conditional on being the "right" kind of black feminist, perhaps the one who is grateful for the hospitality she has received! This comes up in a narrowing of the scripts of what is appropriate to say. So, OK, maybe you can mention race, but you do so on the terms that have been set and defined for you. (We had our report for our diversity project blocked because it was deemed to have too much on race and not enough emphasis on more positive experiences.)

I've had many weird encounters in my time—you learn to expect them. Race triggers such strong reactions; your body, your arrival, and your words remind some of the histories they don't want to admit to. When you use the word *racism*, it can cause such tension! That tension is interesting, intense; learn from it. But it can also be exhausting. When I presented a paper from *Strange Encounters* in Adelaide in 1999, I remember one woman saying during question time, "But what about the white woman?" This was in reference to Audre Lorde's example of the white woman who responds to her with hatred on the subway. And the question was, what about the white woman on the train? Didn't she have feelings too? Questions like this make explicit what is most often implicit—that is, even to focus on racism is to not care enough for the feelings of the white subject; it is almost as if you are stealing their attention.

I've experienced more or less explicit versions of that over a long period of time. In another example, when I was presenting some of my research on diversity, someone came up to me afterward, put her arm next to mine, and said, "Look, we're almost the same color." The physicality of that gesture, putting her arm next to mine as if to perform solidarity, was a way of saying, what are you doing talking about race? Look, look; we are like each other! This is the world in which we've all got the same arms! So there is that sense of absolute denial. And then you get a lot of people who are totally fine with hearing what you have to say, as race becomes something that they're just not implicated in at all, because they think of themselves as critical. That sense of not being implicated produces certain kind of relationship to your work, but if you insist on that implication, you are getting in the way of people's idea of themselves. I think a lot of the trouble that I've noticed recently is the way in which even anti-racism can become a white credential, so that when you as a person of color speak about racism, you become the problem, because you are getting in the way of their capacity to occupy that space.

Could you talk about your main aims of your recent book,
On Being Included: Racism and Diversity in Institutional
***Life*, especially the way in which diversity becomes a key**
mechanism to dismiss institutional racism? Do you see
***On Being Included* as a critique of the "post-racial"?**

That was definitely one part of it. This book began with a research project on diversity that I ended up doing partly because I was the head of women's studies at Lancaster at the time, and I had this opportunity to be involved in funded research. The research was part of a larger project that was looking at diversity within the learning and skills sector. It coincided with being the head of the department and thus attending more faculty meetings. I began to notice how race was and was not being talked about. As soon as you point these things out, you become the person who ends up on the diversity committee and on the race equality committee, which is what happened to me at Lancaster.

Much of the research project involved taking these experiences of being on the diversity committee seriously. I began talking to other diversity practitioners— mainly practitioners who were employed by human resources—about the ways in which this new equality regime was becoming institutionalized. We talked about positive documents that were focused around the positive statements of commitment and policy on race equality and about how these were generating a whole set of techniques for concealing the problem. So you would have a race equality policy, and once you had a policy, you could say that you had "done" race. And so the policies themselves became ways of actually concealing the worlds that they were critiquing. I learned a lot from those mechanisms.

I did think of *On Being Included* as a critique of the post-racial. I was also interested in what I've called "non-performatives." So these documents (race equality policies) are treated as bringing into effect what they name. But the documents come to stand in for the effects, thus creating the impression—one of my interviews called this a "marshmallow impression"—that we have done race. I also explored how race and racism get seen as being in the past, which means that, if you bring it up, you're seen as bringing it back into existence. When you describe a problem, you quickly become the problem. What follows is a practical as well as theoretical problem, and the practical problems are important; we push our ideas when we witness what does not work. Sometimes we have to work with what does not work. I think of institutions as places we need to work *on* as well as *in*. So even though I am very aware that these documents institutions generate can participate in the creation of an impression that race is "behind us," we still have to work with them. This research really made me think in the ways in which we need the critiques of the post-racial, but we also need to think about what follows those critiques in terms of action.

How far do you think the discourse of institutional racism is being invisibilized?

I think it has receded somewhat. It was almost as if to name institutional racism was sufficient to change the condition being named. In other words, because we had critiques of institutional racism, it was on the way to going away. I think we have to keep fighting to retain that language, even though that language can be used problematically.

When institutional racism was introduced as a language, the institution itself got quickly psychologized, so the institution became a bad apple that had to be healed and made better by therapy. And so, although institutional racism is intended to critique the psychological model of race, it can become psychologized. Institutions can be psychologized and given psychological attributes. I think of my relation to these terms as rather like my relation to the word *multiculturalism*. You fight for it when you recognize that it is beginning to recede as a political grammar, even though you had questioned its efficacy as political grammar. You need to keep making a case with these words (there is such a thing as institutional racism), not because you are attached to the words themselves, but because of the histories they bring up. And that makes data quite important. We need to show them, to keep showing them, that whiteness and racism are institutional problems (data becomes important here as a political tool). I think it is vital to keep being the "problem" by naming the problem.

To what extent to you think the humanities and social sciences are dominated by white thought, and how problematic do you find this in contemporary academia?

I think the humanities and social sciences are dominated by white thought. If anything, the feeling that the domination of white thought is no longer a problem is how it stays a problem. This problem of "thinking we no longer have a problem" relates to sexism and racism. I feel like it is getting worse, if anything. I've been very struck recently in virtual encounters and other kinds of encounters about how "identity politics" is used to describe and dismiss any position that names the racial or gendered distribution of bodies. So, when you are pointing to structures (e.g., that all the plenary speakers at this or that event are white men, or all white women, or all white but one), you tend to get caricatured as doing something that is about identity (or even about your own identity, critique heard as a form of self-assertion).

There's a sense that "it's been done"—we've had that, so now we can just be people, and these are the people that happen to turn up or to gather. Those who see who arrives and who doesn't (in terms of categories of social difference) are judged as imposing their viewpoints onto others, interrupting what would otherwise be a neutral, or even happy, occasion. So, in some ways, I think it can be harder now.

I am astonished by how there are academic conversations that almost hijack concepts and ideas that have been circulating among critical race thinkers for generations. It is as if such concepts can only be taken seriously as concepts if they have been invented by a white man; there is absolutely no engagement with that prior history. I noticed this as well in relation to people claiming that Bryan Turner introduced "the body" into social theory. This negates the history of feminist work that went on before that. "The body" can be made into something mainstream when it is reattached to the white male body. There is a politics around who is allowed to introduce what and who is allowed to make something mainstream.

It is possible that postcolonial thought will become mainstreamed if it is attached to a white body! It is depressing thought, but we learn from it. The extent to which words travel can be a sign, not of the inclusion of black or minority ethnic scholars, but of our continued exclusion. Our concepts are more valued if they arrive with somebody else's body. As soon as it is attached to your body (a body of color), you are just the particular; this is your story, and this is just "your" experience. But as soon as it travels through a white body, it becomes something that can be given a more universal and general meaning.

Every now and then, somebody will get through; an exceptional scholar who will be read more widely, like Spivak, for example. This represents an old technique of power, which is that you select a few who come to represent "advancement" in the field. The ideas we introduce as feminists of color—about gender, empire, and race—raise fundamental sociological questions, and the will to keep excluding these ideas is the will to reproduce existing ideas with small differences. And then you begin to realize that your battle with a department or a structure is being repeated everywhere. I think it might be a question of getting more people around to battle.

Can you talk a bit about your "everyday forms of resistance" and "everyday racisms"? What do these concepts offer in debates around racism?

I've had an interest in encounters, and I've often used the table as a motif to describe this—the family table, a meeting table. In my work, I work through everyday encounters and institutional worlds. They are not separate domains. There is a kind of work that I might do as an academic that leads me to have particular kinds of conversations similar to the ones that we've had about what constitutes a discipline or about the institution and its policies. And then there are the encounters you have with those relatively anonymous spaces of intense social exchange, like the street or the bus or the office. There are really important reasons as to why some of the most powerful anti-racist writing has been about experiences on the transport system because they are really intense spaces of interaction among strangers, in the sense of people who do not know each other. And they are intense, compressed forms of sociality. It is not surprising that a lot of the work that is about reclaiming space as spaces for other bodies takes off from what happens there.

I cannot *not* think of Audre Lorde's description of the subway in New York. I just think that was so powerful. It's not so much necessarily about resistance; it is more about the everyday ways in which some people, in more or less violent means, come to feel that this space belongs to them, and that can be just how people occupy that space, whether it is through using their bodies or just speaking loudly or asserting themselves. I remember once, I was on the train going to Goldsmiths to teach my course on "stranger danger," and a group of young black men came into the carriage and then left and went to the next one. There were two white girls next to me, and one of them said, "It's like being with a pack of wolves." So what you hear and how you hear people speak of "others"—creating and relying on long histories of stereotyping—become almost very casual in an "everyday way" in which people assert their right to occupy space by constituting "others" as less than human. It is important to document these incidents and to reflect together on either what they do to you when they happen to you or how they make you feel when you're a bystander, when you say something or don't say something.

I have had so many conversations in taxis about foreign policy. Or I think of those times when you're just in a taxi and you overhear a radio talk station, and it's someone talking about the "Pakis" or someone talking about "too much immigration," and so on. The encounters I've had with my mother, a white English woman, when she has said things that are very problematic about immigration. I think documenting these histories as accumulated histories that really have strong impressions on people's sense of where they can be and where they belong matters. This is an act of everyday resistance, of noticing by describing what it means to not be white in a world that assumes whiteness as a norm. It does mean giving attention to what is difficult and hard. I think there can be a temptation when things are hard to turn away.

Audre Lorde taught me that you have to attend to what makes things hard, which often means magnifying the very situations that you find distressing. It can be a risky strategy, but I think it is important to do the work, because not attending to something does not mean it will go away. Being made into a stranger, one who is out of place, perhaps in the less dramatic moments, can involve a wavering intuition or impression (a sense of something or unease with something). We need to recognize that these impressions as real. Part of this "firming up" of a sense or impression is giving us resources to speak back. I will always remember students saying to me at Lancaster that one of the things women's studies gave them was more tools, more resources, so that they could know what to say when they are challenged like that, when your *being* is challenged.

When thinking about everyday resistance, it is important that we don't make resistance into a requirement. Sometimes you just don't have the resources that enable you to challenge things. It could become another burden that you have to resist all the time, another minority duty! Nevertheless, we have to look at the often small means, the little means that we might have to keep going and find words that can help us be at the table or that might simply help us. I think that is one of the reasons I was very interested in diversity: because *diversity* as a word seemed to offer a way that some people found could allow them to be seated at the table more easily.

Even though *diversity* is a word that can allow organizations to smile, it can also be a word that can allow you to be at that table because it seems friendly. And sometimes the friendly words, the ones that allow you to be sitting at the table because they stop you from being unseated, can give you the room and the time and the opportunity to say other things. I think we have to develop strategies wherever we are, and the strategies and the words we use will depend on where we are located institutionally and on our many histories that we bring with us to the table.

What key insights do you think come out of the articulation of queer studies and postcolonial studies?

I think this is an articulation that is current. I wouldn't say there is a long history of recognizing the articulation of these two areas of study. I would say "queer studies" is still more identified with work being done in the United States. Even though there is a lot of queer theory in the UK, much of this scholarship tends to be framed as sexuality studies rather than queer theory. In the United States, there is a body of scholarship that we could call "queer of color scholarship," following Roderick Ferguson and others. In the last ten years or so, this body of work has been important because it has allowed us to explore how sexuality is implicated in transnational political economies. I think Jasbir Puar's work on homonationalism has been influential for both activists and academics in Europe. She shows through this word/concept (and like intersectionality, the invention of a word should not obscure that the concept has a longer history) how the sexual equality agenda can become a technique of national power by becoming a mark of relative civility or civilization. So it is then the Islamic "others" who are oppressive to "their" gays and oppressive to "their" women, so "we" need to give them our progressive queer agenda.

Even *queerness*, a word that signaled the odd and the strange before it become a word for sexual minorities, can become an instrument of national power. I do feel ambivalent about Joseph Massad's work *Desiring Arabs*, which would be an example of an articulation of postcolonial and queer studies. I think this book is a good use of Edward Said's work, but it carries an implication (if the implication falls short of an argument, it does not mean that it is not there) that the gay or queer is foreign to the non-Western. I am also rather uncomfortable with the use of the term *the Gay International*, which for some can easily generate a homophobic anxiety about those gays who are everywhere, taking over places they should not be. And what follows, again by implication, is that, if you are, say, a Pakistani person who identifies with queer or who identifies as gay, then you are somehow assimilated to the West and its progressive sexual rights agenda. This does not correlate at all with my mixed experiences.

I would say that queerness is very much part of my Pakistani family. It is just not articulated as explicitly or visibly; it is just the unsaid, but it is queer; it is definitely queer. So I think we need to work through a model of queer that does not take Western ideas of sexuality as its frame. Such a model would not rest on concepts of "coming out"—which are very much based on a Western epistemic regime, and it would not necessarily even be based on identity and self-declaration. Such a non-Western queer would not even presume "the public" as where queer happens. I think a lot of the work in early queer studies did generate a model of the public that assumed a certain kind of access to that public, thus assuming along with that a certain kind of white, privileged, able body. In the end, celebrating queer publics can end up assuming certain kind of privileged bodies.

I think Gayatri Gopinath's work is fantastic, as she has shown the way in which in the context of the South Asian diaspora it might be the home that is full of queer potential; queerness as a way of staying at home rather than leaving home. It remains important to think through how concepts of nation and the civilizing mission are predicated on sexuality. We need to think more about how the nation and empire are bound up with reproducing the "right" kind of bodies, a national project that can enlist heterosexuality as reproductive as well as classed and racialized ideas of the "right bodies."

How do you envisage the future of race and ethnicity in the social sciences? What do you hope will be developed by emerging scholars in the field in terms of studying and challenging the dominant forms of whiteness?

It is funny that, when I think of my hopes, I have a sense of exhaustion! There is a sense—that I suspect is shared—that, despite all the work that has been done from the 1970s onward, despite the substantial challenges of Eurocentrism and whiteness, we still have to make the same critiques. And so I think that with that sense of the necessity of repetition is a risk of getting worn down. Is there any point? I call it the brick wall; you just keep coming up against the same thing. If it doesn't move, it is you that gets sore. But I still remain hopeful.

Knowing whiteness and knowing about whiteness has actually given me a lens to interpret so much about how knowledge works, about how bodies work—including social bodies—and about how philosophy works. I think we are philosophers. We are the new philosophers because of our experience of coming up against whiteness. I have a certain kind of optimism about what knowledge can do. The more of us that are there, hitting the wall, the more capacity we have to make connections through each other; it becomes harder for them to keep that wall up. I totally agree with Spivak when she said it is not a body count, but I actually do think more helps. It is important to have more voices, more presence, and just that sense of being among a community—a sense that, even if the problems are the same problems, you can work together to work out how better to describe the problems. I don't think we even have a full description yet.

We need to develop systems that encourage certain kinds of research; we need to make sure that there are routes through the university that recognize and value the kind of work that doing critical race work involves. To some extent, what will happen to race in the social sciences is a little bit out of our hands. Disciplines can be very successful in ignoring people. I mean they have done that successfully for decades. Even if the disciplines seem to remove themselves from our presence, it does not mean our presence will not have an effect. When we develop networks and alternative systems for supporting each other, we are also opening up academic spaces that can be filled by others, those who do not feel at home in the traditional disciplines.

Selected Key Works

Ahmed, S. (1998). *Differences That Matter: Feminist Theory and Postmodernism*. Cambridge: Cambridge University Press.

———. (2000). *Strange Encounters: Embodied Others in Post-Coloniality*. London: Routledge.

———. (2004). *The Cultural Politics of Emotion*. Edinburgh: Edinburgh University Press.

———. (2006). *Queer Phenomenology: Orientations, Objects, Others*. Durham, NC: Duke University Press.

———. (2010). *The Promise of Happiness*. Durham, NC: Duke University Press.

———. (2012). *On Being Included: Racism and Diversity in Institutional Life*. Durham, NC: Duke University Press.

CHAPTER 2

David Theo Goldberg

David Theo Goldberg is a professor of comparative literature in the School of Humanities at the University of California, Irvine.

Can you talk a bit about your biography growing up in South Africa and how you first got into the field around questions of race and ethnicity?

Growing up in South Africa, one could not avoid race, even though white folk very largely tried to. I grew up in Cape Town, which itself is at once both a liberal city and a city in denial of the deeply constitutive racial condition of South Africa in many ways. I grew up under apartheid, during which Cape Town was a very segregated place: whites lived in better-located areas of the city, and often in far better areas, while blacks lived, obviously, in the less well-developed and geographically more vulnerable areas of the city. Even among folks regarded as black or categorized as black, there were hierarchies of privilege and disprivilege, hierarchies of where people could live or not. So people of African descent, or those categorized as of African descent, lived farther from the city, in townships or in shantytowns. Colored, Indian, and Malay in Cape Town lived around the edges of the inner city, and white folk obviously lived in more privileged areas—and even there, there were class differences between and among whites. So civil servants lived in more working-class areas, and the bourgeoisie lived in more privileged areas of the city. On the other hand, white privileged families like my own had people of color living in the home, domestic servants living full-time pretty much in the servant's "quarters" of the house in which they were working. They were both not of the family and of the family at once, which in the scheme of things, is quite a peculiar relationship, not unique to South Africa by a long stretch of the imagination, but at the same time, it played itself out in unique ways.

So I grew up mindful of the fact that the household was not completely homogenous but always understanding that I was privileged. I was called "little master," about which from very early on, I felt awkward. And by the time I was a teenager, I insisted on making my own bed because I didn't think it was right for the maid to be making the bed for me, the woman who worked for my parents for thirty years was of the same age as my mother. Jacklyn Cock wrote a revealing book called *Maids and Madams* about the often intensely close relationship between employers and the employed and the distance, proximity, and closeness within the environment. There was a great confiding between my mother and the woman who worked for her, confiding about family, confiding about grandchildren, confiding about shared lives—but always also a distance. And I grew up with this extended family of mine; the children played together. As I got older, the grandchildren were playing together, so there was this sort of double life, almost Du Boisian, but in a kind of intimacy that was interesting while making one self-conscious about the condition in play.

South Africa declared a kind of independence from Britain in 1960. In 1961, on the very day that declaration was actualized, the white school I was at was given half the day off and sent home waving South African flags and with a commemorative coin. I remember walking home with a friend; I was nine years old. We were actually going to play at his house in this privileged area of Cape Town, and we were walking along the street and a black gardener came along and my young friend said, "Quick, put your flag away." And that was my first moment, probably, at nine years old, of being thoroughly politically self-conscious about the condition of privilege and under-privilege, of exclusion. From that moment on, I began questioning this troubled and troubling condition. Race in South Africa was always present, and one could literally choose to be more or less conscious of it as a white kid growing up. As I became a teenager, there was a group of us who increasingly came to question that condition so that, by the time I got to high school and to university, we were deeply involved in being part of an increasingly self-conscious political project that questioned the condition that formally kept us apart from blacks.

I grew up on a beach; we were kind of beach bum kids. The folks enjoying the beach recreationally were pretty much all whites, occasionally colored or Malay youth, usually young women hanging out with us; those keeping the beach spotlessly clean were black. There was a group of us who were the local variation of the Ken Kesey "Hole in the Wall Gang" crew, which was pretty transgressive. And in South Africa, that transgression inevitably involved the racial component of one's existence. We'd visit the townships to hang out and be invited into a person's home, sitting down in the living room, and what would follow was a conversation. And that then became the condition of realizing that these folks, who were placed apart, had a life like yours; they were interested in things you were interested in, politically or in terms of sport or recreation activity. And that just became—I don't want to call it a "natural condition," because nothing about this is natural—a common condition of the political life that one came to inhabit; and so it also became a kind of self-reflective questioning of that life in deeply constitutive ways that then intensified when I got to college. This was really where I started to engage with more organized anti-apartheid resistance.

How did you go on to develop your political consciousness or activism, and how did your early experiences follow through to your later years?

I got involved in political activity already at high school—I was somehow always pushing back against the way in which the curriculum was imposed on me because curriculum came with a certain understanding of the historical conditions that produced apartheid. And so there was a group of friends who were persistently pushing back. The group I hung with was always multiracially constituted, which in South Africa was in violation of what was expected of you. The boys and girls and some young men and women I hung out with were made up of multiracial constituencies, and that meant we were engaged in conversations that made us aware of the deep injustices concerning where people lived, where they came from, what possibilities were open to them, and what possibilities were open to you.

By the time I got to college, I was involved in the anti-apartheid movement at the University of Cape Town. I think this was partly due to my upbringing in a liberal white Jewish family and partly to my own specific biography. Even in the racial politics of the University of Cape Town, I resisted getting involved in the traditional anti-apartheid student movement, which went by the name of NUSAS, the National Union of South African Students. They were doing interesting and important work, and many of their leaders became national leaders in the wake of apartheid's demise.

However, I took what I thought at the time was a more radical line. In 1976, when I was a first-year graduate student, when the Soweto movement quickly spread to Cape Town, 15,000 to 20,000 high school students marched from the townships right past the university into the center of Cape Town. The position of the group I was involved with was that the university should be closed down in solidarity. That's what we undertook to do, in a clandestine way, because one could have gotten kicked out of the university, not to mention in trouble with the law. We basically mobilized to close the formal activities of the university. We thought the university should not have been teaching classes at this moment because it too was a segregated institution. And so we mobilized, and we were successful in closing down the normal teaching arrangements of the university in favor of anti-apartheid workshops and organizing activities. I was repeatedly looking for ways with others to help move the engagement to a position where privilege would be undercut.

These activities were involved in political consciousness raising, and it worked in the immediate moment. But one couldn't know at the time what the longer lasting effects would be. One should not be naïve that one was transforming the university. But what was interesting was, in order to get the university closed down for the duration of the protest events, there was a mass meeting of about five hundred students and faculty at which a formal vote was taken. Out of that came a resolution to promote the teaching of anti-apartheid workshops during the school strikes as well as to join the march into the center of Cape Town, which then followed.

Cape Town became a war zone, not in any way because of my actions but because of the actions of the really courageous school students from the townships. There were armored vehicles patrolling the city center and tear gas and shootings. The center of Cape Town was closed down in 1976 for about a week. So it had that kind of impact, and in a way, it was the beginning of the movement to render the townships ungovernable, which began to signal the end of apartheid, which would last another almost decade and a half. And all this was a product of the political movement that exploded in 1976.

How did your parents feel about your mobilizations in the movement?

They were ambivalent, to say the least. The way in which Jews became white in South Africa mimicked the way in which Jews became white in America. One can trace this kind of bifurcation in Jewish communities from their arrival from the 1880s to the 1920s. The first and second generations of arrivals included those who became Labour leaders. What followed was the "embourgeoisfying," which was a feature of the 1940s and 1950s and into the 1960s. Second- and third-generation Jewish South Africans who went to college and got degrees became accountants, doctors, and lawyers, and in the process became white and privileged.

My immediate family flourished in the middle of that transformation, both generationally and in terms of how they themselves became wealthy and privileged. At the same time, my father was deeply involved in political life, and part of my family was involved in opposition—in the formal conventional white opposition politics in South Africa. They were members of the Progressive Party and later the Progressive Freedom Party—what grew out of the centrist white United Party. There was always political talk around the dinner table, and the assumption of the middle liberal line. The liberal business line reasoned that, if you get rid of the formal structures of apartheid and its legal apparatus, race would go away. And I was always to the left of that and so had a, let's say, tempestuous relationship with my father as a consequence.

What thinkers would you say have most influenced you and your work?

As a young academic, Hegel and Marx were obviously key influences, and Fanon also. In South Africa, one way of reading of Fanon was engaging with *Wretched of the Earth*, *A Dying Colonialism*, and *The Algerian Revolution*. Interestingly, we read but were less impacted by *Black Skin, White Masks*, which dominated intellectual interest in the United States in the late 1970s and early 1980s. That latter mode of postcolonialism became more impacted by *Black Skin, White Masks* than an earlier generation of anti-colonial works.

The divide between anti-colonialism and postcolonialism can be seen in the divide between *Wretched of the Earth* and *Black Skin, White Masks*. That was palpable for us, as young academics in South Africa. In the mid-1970s, a young lecturer, Jeremy Cronin, returned to South Africa after studying in Paris with Louis Althusser. Now the head of the South African Communist Party, I took a few courses with him at both the end of my undergraduate training and the beginning of my graduate training. He had written a very influential analysis of Afrikaner nationalism, influenced by the distinction Althusser had drawn between repressive and ideological state apparatuses. And then he got arrested and thrown into prison for attempting to foment anti-apartheid revolution. Steve Biko and the black consciousness movement in the mid-1970s were important. I was reading some of the philosophical articulations of Euro-Communism at the time from thinkers like Lucio Colletti.

I left South Africa late in 1977. During my graduate training, I spent a year in Britain and Europe and then went to the United States, to New York, to pursue a PhD in philosophy. While required to read the key philosophers of language and science at the time—Quine, Davidson, Chomsky, Katz, Fodor, and the like—my own influences were Foucault, Stuart Hall, and Said. Some have come to regard me as a kind of Foucauldian voice on race, and I think they read things too literally.

As I matured intellectually through my graduate training, I became less "in the school of" and more looking to thinkers I found generative. The generative thinkers, impacted similarly by the likes of Foucault and Fanon, were Stuart Hall and Said. There were texts with which I was in conversation from which I was deriving something generative. And I always found these figures, along with Arendt's *Origins of Totalitarianism*, more generative than, say, Derrida. You know, even as I came to admire Derrida late in his life when I got to know him when were both at Irvine and we developed a friendly working relationship, I would never say I was influenced by him. I found him more interesting in the latter part of his career than in the formative part. I read and met Achille Mbembe, who has become a very dear friend now; we run some workshop programs together, and I found his work on the postcolony and his more general work today enormously generative. So I look to people for generativity.

At college in South Africa, we were reading Senghor, Cesaire, and especially Ngũgĩ wa Thiong'o, when we could get our hands on their work (they were largely banned under apartheid). In the United States, both during my graduate work and then as a young intellectual, I was in conversation from the mid-1980s with folks like Skip Gates, Anthony Appiah, Houston Baker, and Cornel West. They became collegial friends in the mid- to late 1980s as the analysis of race began to consume intellectuals in the humanities. I was likewise reading and in conversation with Angela Davis and Gayatri Spivak and have remained so. Angela was quite a deep influence in the 1990s on how I thought about the United States and prison more broadly. I co-edited a book on postcolonialism with Ato Quayson in the mid-1990s, and my conversations with him were important in deepening my understanding and analysis of the postcolonial. These were the generative conversations I was involved within that began to shape how I thought about race and the political more generally.

At that time, the fields of critical race theory and postcolonial theory were overlapping but not altogether intersecting, which, given my background, I found somewhat odd. The divide was less pronounced in Britain than in the United States, and I was as much in conversation with people like Paul Gilroy, Michael Keith, Vikki Bell, and others as with American critical race theorists in law and sociology.

Do you think of yourself as a postcolonial thinker, and do you situate your work within this genre?

I've written about and have been influenced by the sets of conversations that have taken place around the postcolonial. And I have always tied the anti-colonial (not the same thing, as I have noted) to my intellectual maturing in the 1970s and 1980s. The 1970s especially were more anti-colonial than postcolonial in disposition and concern.

I don't think of myself as a postmodern thinker, or as a postcolonial thinker. I look for generative influences and impacts that have shaped how I think about the world and then think about their horizons of possibility. And having been involved in postcolonial debates, in discussions with Homi Bhabha, Gayatri Spivak, Lisa Lowe, Dipesh Chakrabarty, Achille Mbembe, AbdouMaliq

Simone, and so on, one gets molded and fashioned by the exchanges with which one is engaged. But I wouldn't want to reduce myself to a political line or thinker, even while I would share many of the presumptions that undergird and underpin the disposition of postcoloniality. Achille Mbembe, among others, has had a formative impact on my thinking. I doubt he would consider himself narrowly, only, or even definitively a postcolonial thinker, and I share that quite deeply with him.

How would you conceptualize the postcolonial, and what do you think is the main significance or contribution of postcolonial thinking?

There are a series of commitments from which postcolonialism starts out, which in turn lead to a range of openings for thinking about the world. One can lay out what those commitments are, starting from a deep anti-essentialism, which does not preclude mobilizing on the basis of something like a Spivakian strategic essentialism to fuel political intervention. The postcolonial opens up new objects of analysis or addresses traditional objects in new ways. Its analytic disposition prompts insights not otherwise available or even possible. For example, oceanic studies, linking societies that in the nineteenth century were constitutive elements in the colonial world order, offers novel comprehension of the sea as a medium of colonial and postcolonial movement and migration, leading to transformed demographic arrangements as much in colonizing powers as in colonized societies.

Postcolonial anti-essentialism in turn is committed to an insistent analytic of historicizing and re-historicizing. This involves recounting the historical conditions of the present, most notably in relation to its conditions and relations of power and their contemporary articulations. This also entails analyzing the emergence of the conditions of power and the possibilities that power opens up or shuts down (in the latter case, what it makes impossible). So analysis of power and its relationalities—conditions of domination and subjugation, resistance, and subversion—become a key constitutive focus of both postcolonial conditions and postcolonialism's logic of analysis, its baseline analytics. What this opens up is a focus on what I call living in a critical condition.

Living in a critical condition is pointedly ambiguous between a focus on structural conditions and the sort of critical focus that takes these structural conditions and the associated practice and expressions to which such conditions give rise as its object of analysis. The structural conditions at issue make living in precarious situations more broadly the condition under which increasing numbers of people around the world are living, some more extremely than others, some for longer periods than others, some in different places—but united by a kind of creeping generalizability of the condition. Those in the Global South have lived with this at the very least since the moment of their anti-colonial resistance and postcolonial independence, and those in the Global North are now, over the past decade, coming to recognize that this is a constitutive condition of our moment.

Living in a critical condition is also how one is critical in relation to that set of critical conditions that have become the generalized condition of our time, and in a way, the relation to it has been flipped. So, because the Global South, or what we identify as the Global South, has been living in this set of conditions for a much longer time than those in the Global North have recognized, they've come to be resourceful in relation to the lack of resources, and figuring out how to survive has become a "normal" part of their disposition about their worlds. And in the Global North, those living in a critical and precarious condition are just starting to realize that what will be required is an agility, a resourcefulness, a resilience relatedly to recognize the challenges and to respond to them creatively and critically—in short, to survive with dignity.

People like AbdouMaliq Simone have been writing now for a good while about civil society stepping into the breach of the lack of state support in post-colonial societies, in the postcolony, which become lessons, primers for how one positions oneself, how you dispose yourself in relation to the possibilities available to you, and then negotiate those conditions over time. And I think that's what we need to attend to in our current moment, analytically as much as politically and in terms of surviving.

Can you elaborate on the key ideas of *The Racial State*? What did you hope to achieve with this book?

So *The Racial State* was driven by a recognition—I'd like to think of it as an insight—that state theory and racial theory had not, for the most part, been involved in an analytic conversation with each other. On the one hand, state theory completely ignored—certainly from the 1960s through the 1990s—the contributions of critical theories of race. Critical race theory in its legal formulation, as it became elaborated in the United States from the late 1980s onward, was very parochial to both the United States and, largely, the law. So what I hoped to achieve was to both raise the question and bring into *being* a way to think about how to theorize that interface between racial and state analysis and how to think about the modern state as a constitutively racial state in the broader historical parameters from the sixteenth century onward. I was concerned with how the modern state is constituted through race and how it constitutes or reconstitutes race at key moments. I was concerned to understand how, as the modern state transforms itself over time from an absolutist state to a liberal state to a post-liberal state, race is configured and reconfigured in those moments and how race configures and reconfigures the state in its modernity across time.

What I undertook was this historical reading of the modern state in and through race, and of race by—or with—the state. So what I was hoping to achieve was to frame how one goes about thinking about race in those key transformations in racial configuration and also to make an intervention in race theorizing, where the main position was an extended critique of the dominant conception that race and racism are really just a product of the sixteenth century. I wanted to show that it has a much longer genealogy but one that wasn't reducible to the specifics of a Foucauldian genealogy either.

Your work emphasizes the relationship between state practices and the production of racism. How significant do you think Western colonialism was in establishing this particular linkage? Do you think it's central?

Oh yes, it's key. The modern state is colonial in its formation and in denial of this formation at the same time. Retrospectively, the modern state wouldn't be what it came to be and what it now is without having been involved in the colonial project, and obviously that transformed over time too. You can trace the historical moments of the transformation in colonial development through the fifteenth, sixteenth, and seventeenth centuries and then the transformation in the eighteenth century to the enlightenment or emancipatory project, which in itself transformed how race was thought about into the nineteenth century.

In material terms, the wealth of the modern European state was a product of its colonial condition; three quarters of the members of the Houses of Parliament in nineteenth-century Britain made their wealth through colonial practices. When you walk around Bordeaux or, for that matter, Liverpool or Bath and places like that, you find the legacies of colonial slavery literally inscribed in the buildings, and one has to pay attention to that in order to recognize how deep this marking goes, even as it's been covered. It hasn't been erased; the attempt has been to erase it, but it's been covered over. These sites have been turned into the material of recreational activity. There's been an erasure of what this stands for. You know, "wasn't slavery cute, right?" For Halloween or Homecoming parties, "wouldn't it be fun to dress up as slaves and slave owners." So the slave museums and things of that kind show how there's been a wiping away from public consciousness of both the horrible historical conditions and their rewriting.

A historian in France a few years back was arguing that slavery benefitted black slaves, and others have argued along the same lines for colonialism—it supposedly brought civilization to uncivilized places. The modern state is a product of its colonial condition, rewritten in every kind of way with multiple layers and sedimentations, and one has to scratch the surface to dig out what those layers are.

Do you consider racism to be a Western phenomenon or a universal phenomenon?

Again, historically, racism clearly emerges out of the West and then gets globalized through colonial spread, migration and counter-migration, movement and counter-movement. If one is to tell a historical story, then one has to understand that race and racism—as ideas, as ways of *being* in the world, as accounts of privilege and disprivilege—are clearly a prompt out of the West and the West's reach. Of course, if you individualize it, you can say that anybody could be racist—that is, they could inhabit the position that privileges themselves in relations and positions of power with respect to others identified racially, either explicitly or implicitly. But that's not to say that the prevailing positions of power are unrelated to the positions of power that gave rise to the initial inscriptions of race and its exclusions, subjugations, and dominations, out of which those racial configurations initially arose, and those have been inscribed and reinscribed over time.

So "can a black person be racist in relation to others?" This is a very conventional question, often expressed from a position of power, as a register of skepticism about dominant modes of expression. Individually, yes, but in terms of positions of power, and relative positions of power over time, it's a much more complex story than that simple inscription or finger pointing.

Can you elaborate on the relationship between neoliberalism and racial logics?

Neoliberals ratchet up to their extreme articulation the central tenets on which classic liberalism rests. And so the neoliberal radicalizes the individual as the centerpiece, insofar as everybody becomes, or is made, individually responsible for the social position he or she occupies in the world. It dehistoricizes the possibilities of an individual's subject position in relation to their horizons of possibility. The neoliberal thus both reinscribes a historically positioned set of conditions of possibility and, at the very same time, erases the possibility of pointing to those historical conditions in order to account for what gave rise to them, in the name of making the individual responsible for his or her own position. One is taken to be responsible, whether as a privileged person or for the failure to achieve certain possibilities out of lack of effort or out of a relative intellectual failure, and so on.

So the way in which the neoliberal and the racial come together is to give a new account—a rationalization—of how it is that individuals occupy the structural conditions, the social positions in which they find themselves, and then make it the individual's own responsibility for achieving or failing to achieve the position in which he or she finds himself or herself or the position the individual claims he or she should be in but was unable to achieve. So it completely erases the possibility, even, of being able to tell a structural story of how it is that the world has come to be what it is, and it completely individualizes those conditions and dehistoricizes them. In *The Threat of Race*, this is what I came to call *racial neoliberalism*—namely, the way in which the racial structures are neoliberal, and the neoliberal retells what's possible in relation to the racial, even as it erases the possibility of invoking race as an account of the way the structural conditions have come to *be*.

A lot of recent academic work has discussed the notion of the post-racial. How do you understand the post-racial condition?

In relation to claims of the post-racial, the usual response is that we're not—that we haven't reached that condition. And my argument is that the logic of the response mirrors the logic of the claim. So you're giving in to the very set of presumptions around the post-racial when you say "not yet." I think the more compelling question is not "Are we post-racial yet or not?" The driving question is "What is the *racial* work that the claim for post-raciality is doing?" And when you put the question in that way, one then has to give a different kind of account of the work that the post-racial is doing to cover over the history and its legacies of the racial in the moment that is being defined as the post-racial.

So the post-racial has a racial logic, just as the postcolonial has a colonial logic. The post-racial, then, becomes a kind of analytic to which one needs to point in order to get an account of it historically and of the racial work that it's doing to reinscribe the racial and its modes of subjugation, domination, and exclusion in these structures.

To what extent do you think the social sciences are largely dominated by white thought? How far do you think postcolonial and black thought have been mainstreamed within the discipline?

Clearly, there is a greater openness, whether it's in philosophy, sociology, and political science on the one hand, anthropology on the other hand, to questions of race. So the mantra of race, gender, and class gets taken up but in two sorts of ways that I think are worrisome. The first is it gets taken up as a kind of mantra, and the analytics that are produced in its name are very flat and superficial. There is a repetitive knee jerk invocation with no depth of analysis and as though new things are being said in its name. It quickly becomes old and predictable. So that's on one side. In more mainstream sociology or the social sciences more generally, what you get almost as a reaction is a quick and much too easy sidelining of racial analysis. This takes the form of either an out-and-out ignoring of racial consideration or a form of racial sociology as just another sociological subfield, with its own journals, its own associational division. But, as a consequence, the mainstream pays little, if any, attention to it whatsoever. So they both go their own ways, more or less happily, but nothing changes—the impact is marginal at best.

One has to ask why that keeps happening, why the repetitive spinning of the wheel that leaves unimpacted, for the most part unchanged, the very conditions of analysis of the dominant strands in the discipline. For modern states, race is not simply a marginal condition that some but not all experience. It is constitutive in variable and changing ways to modern state formation itself pretty much across the board. Modern society is constituted through the racial, even as the category may be made to disappear from state reference and explicit administrative arrangement. You would think sociology in particular, the social sciences more generally, would factor race, like class and gender, into its analytics as a key object of analysis, a complex object not reducible simply to a variable made identical to others wherever it manifests.

What do you hope will be developed by the new generation of scholars in the social sciences in the field of race and ethnicity?

There have been a series of debates that have emerged around race and racism that, as I have said, become more or less repetitive. But what are the challenges that we find ourselves faced by with racial analysis today? And how is it that one has a return of what one can mark socially as essentializing? Why is it that we're facing today the re-emergence of DNA analysis, which has both a cultural component and a biological component? What happens to the analysis of race when we take seriously the challenge from race—as a "natural cultural" articulation, to use Haraway's characterization? How do we rethink racial configurations as a consequence? How do we rethink the conditions of possibility around race and racism in both the Global North and the Global South? In other words, how do we rethink race and racial analysis in relation to the changing conditions of race and racial analysis? How do we rethink the constitutive relations between race and religion?

I think these are the questions of importance and the questions in relation to the rethinking of our historical conditions. I hope that my students' generation is starting to grapple with issues like this in terms of identifying both the historical antecedents from which such issues arise and the socially constitutive conditions giving them expression.

Selected Key Works

Goldberg, D. T. (1997). *Racial Subjects: Writing on Race in America*. London: Routledge.
———. (2001). *The Racial State*. Oxford: Wiley-Blackwell.
———. (2008). *The Threat of Race: Reflections on Racial Neoliberalism*. Oxford: Wiley-Blackwell.
———. (2012, August). "When 'Race' Disappears." Special issue on "Texting Obama." *Comparative American Studies* 2, no. 3: 116–27.
———. (2012, September). "Epistemologies of Deception: Topologies of the Extra/Ordinary." *The Salon* 5 (Johannesburg Workshop in Theory and Criticism). http://jwtc.org.za/salon_volume_5/david_theo_goldberg.htm.
———. (2013). "The Postracial Contemporary." In *The State of Race*, edited by N. Kapoor, V. Kalra, and J. Rhodes, 15–30. London: Palgrave Macmillan.
———. (2014). *Sites of Race: Conversations with Susan Searls Giroux*. London: Polity Press.
Goldberg, D. T., and Quayson, A., eds. (2002). *Relocating Postcolonialism*. Oxford: Wiley-Blackwell.

CHAPTER 3

Catherine Hall

Catherine Hall is a professor of modern British social and cultural history at University College London.

Can you talk a little about your biography and how you first got into the field? What interested you about British history and specifically its relationship to racism, ethnicity, feminism, and colonialism?

Well, I had always been interested in history as a child. I read lots of historical novels; I loved them, and I liked going to historical places. My mother did a history degree at Oxford in the late 1920s, which was very early for a woman, but she then married a Baptist minister so her career became being a minister's wife, not being a historian. But she went on being really, really, interested in history. So there was always an interest in history at home. And then I had a wonderful history teacher at school, as is so often the case—that made such a difference. So I knew I wanted to do history at university.

My parents were very determined that we must all be properly educated. That was the way they'd come to be who they were, so education was very important for them. I just assumed I'd go to university, and I went to Sussex, which I really didn't like at all, as I was brought up in Leeds, so that meant there was a real shift from being a high school girl in Leeds to going to Sussex in its very early days. It was one of the new universities in the 1960s, and it was a place where lots of London kids went if they couldn't get into Oxbridge. So it was very cool, very stylish, and I was a provincial girl from Yorkshire, so I found it difficult.

But meanwhile I'd met the man that I was going to marry, and he had gone to Birmingham to do work there. And so very quickly we got married because, in those days, which were the early 1960s, my parents would have been pretty upset if I'd gone and lived with him without getting married. So we did get married, and I transferred to Birmingham University. There I had one truly wonderful teacher again, who was a Marxist medievalist called Rodney Hilton. He was just a great teacher, and I became completely fascinated by medieval history, which I'd never encountered before and didn't know anything about. It was just really exciting because it was somewhat like doing anthropology. It was so different; it was like entering another world. So then I wanted to become a medievalist, but that was a pretty foolish idea because I'm completely hopeless at Latin. I actually started a PhD in medieval history and then realized it wasn't for me.

This was 1968 and also the time of my involvement in student politics. And then at the end of 1968 I had a baby, my daughter Becky. I had been involved politically from when I was an adolescent with the Campaign for Nuclear Disarmament (CND) and the Young Socialists—left-wing politics. My parents had always been Labour voters; they were very liberal in their attitudes and always taught us that, whether you're African or Indian or English, it didn't make any difference; we're all one under the skin. Of course it was more complicated than that. After I'd had Becky, my life just completely changed. That was the very early days of the women's movement, and together with friends, I set up the first women's group in Birmingham. At this point, I got totally involved in feminist politics, and it was feminism that really transformed my thinking about history.

The reason why I was so interested in British history was because it was where I lived, and I always thought that history was about who you are, where you come from, and what's made the place how it is. So it was kind of natural to me to be most interested in British history. At that time, British history, or particularly English history, was a very exciting area because that's when the Marxist historians were really making an impact. Edward Thompson's book *The Making of the English Working Class* was published in 1963, the year I went to university. It definitely was a formative text, although I've argued with it ever since. Nevertheless, that way of thinking about class, about politics, and about culture was important. That was what really helped me think. Marxist historiography was how I learned to do history, and then came socialist feminism, which was very influenced by Marxism but also very critical of its silence about women. So then I started doing feminist history, which scarcely existed as a subject. In the early 1970s, I started teaching adult education classes in women's history, which gradually became gender history.

After another child, I'd gotten to the point where I wanted to go back to work. I started on a big research project with another feminist historian, Leonora Davidoff. We did a book called *Family Fortunes*, which took years of work and was about the relationship between gender and class, published in 1987. By that time, we'd moved to London, and I became very involved in feminist politics there. The whole critique by black feminists of white feminism really made me think, and I came to understand the limitations of thinking that gender and class were the only two axes that one had to think about. You could say it took me a long time to get to that point because, after all, I'd married a Jamaican, and my children were of mixed-race descent. But questions about race didn't fully enter my consciousness until the black feminist critique. Their critique of white feminists—the assumptions we were making, the ways we were working, the patterns of behavior, the whole lot—were very challenging. It was a very difficult set of things to face because it was one thing to be a kind of angry, white, middle-class feminist, but to have all your assumptions about how you think you're doing things in a good way, and then soon realize that there's actually an awful lot to question in how you're practicing things yourself was really transforming for me. So it was a very tumultuous time. And out of that came a new way of thinking about work. What I learned then was really what shaped so much of my work in the period since.

You were clearly active at quite a young age. Can you elaborate on how you developed this sense of political consciousness?

Well, I definitely grew up knowing about inequality. I mean, as I said, my parents were good, solid, Labour voters. My father was a non-conformist minister, so he had a strong ethical sense and a grasp of inequality and deprivation. He believed it was the responsibility of those who have the education, the knowledge, and the skills to be able to use them for others. My parents were completely committed to the public sector and the welfare state. My mother did different kinds of voluntary work; she never worked for money, but she did work for different institutions and organizations associated with the health service and the welfare state. So I grew up with all that.

And then, when my sister was in the sixth form at school, she had a relationship with a Trinidadian student in Leeds, and that was a real eye-opener because then I saw how difficult this was for some of the people around us, who professed to be so liberal but actually, of course, weren't.

Leeds in the late 1950s early 1960s was one of the places with quite substantial early migration and a lot of students coming in from different parts of the world—the beginnings of a more mixed population. I can remember the Indian and Chinese restaurants opening up and the city just beginning to come out of the period of postwar rationing with its narrowness of life and vision in some respects. Cosmopolitanism was arriving. I also remember at the time demonstrating against the bomb and being really frightened. I can remember very clearly being at school during the Cuba crisis and really being terrified, thinking that maybe we were all going to be blown up and that we'd better get out there on the streets and protest. So that was just part of life, and there was almost an expectation that I'd get involved in student politics, and my sister was also very involved politically, first in Oxford and then in London. That's how I met Stuart, and we started a relationship and then got married. So I lived in a kind of left political world. But then the language that I found, through the women's movement, was my language as opposed to everybody else's language, and that was the language of feminism. This was a language we crafted and a vocabulary we made in the 1970s and 1980s—a collective enterprise. And that was such a rich experience.

Would you describe yourself as a postcolonial thinker and situate your work within this genre?

I wouldn't describe myself as a postcolonial thinker; that sounds too grand. I'd describe myself as a feminist historian working with postcolonial thinking. Postcolonial thinking has been what's shaped my historical work in the last, I suppose, more than twenty years. In the late 1980s, after we'd finished *Family Fortunes*, I began to think about what I was going to do next, and by that time, I was interacting with a group of black feminists, particularly around the journal *Feminist Review*, which we all worked on. That became the site for a big argument about black feminism and its relation to white feminism. It was the women in that group who really forced me to read work I hadn't read but, much more important, to actually think about myself and how I thought about the world.

We also went to Jamaica on holiday, and it was a very important holiday because we were leaving Becky there for a year to live. And as we were traveling around the island, I understood for the first time more of the ways in which colonialism had shaped the island. I'd been there quite a number of times but never thought properly about that history, and I became absolutely fascinated by it and by the connections between England and Jamaica. There was a personal connection that was very important in shaping my work because it gave me a kind of investment in the work and a drive to understand Stuart's family, as well as the left politics that I knew about and also the nationalist politics I knew about in Jamaica.

So there was always a personal drive, but also a political drive, to recover the history of the connection between Britain and Jamaica, which was invisible. It was commonplace to think that Jamaican and Caribbean migrants arrived for the first time after the Windrush, when actually there are more than three hundred years of history. So the process of learning, discovering, and situating all that in that island was deeply engaging. It was inspiring, doing the work, unraveling these connections, and seeing how deeply they run.

How would conceptualize the postcolonial, and what do you consider the main contributions of postcolonial thinking to be?

A starting point would be Said's *Orientalism* and that grasp of the ways in which the West shaped its ideas about the "other." That is so fundamental. The relation between "self" and "other" and how that was translated into a relationship between colonizer and colonized and the power relation, which is absolutely central to that, acts for me as a guiding principle of postcolonial thought. Partha Chatterjee has been terribly helpful; his insistence on the "rule of difference" (Chatterjee 1993) between colonizer and colonized and the efforts to maintain that rule of difference has been absolutely central to me.

I would situate that in the wider context of the recognition that colonialism wasn't finished and that it was not fully grasped until the 1970s. That was relevant to what was happening both in the countries that had been supposedly decolonized and in Britain. We were in Birmingham in 1968, and Enoch Powell's speech was a watershed moment, opening up the deep undercurrent of disturbance about "alien presence" in the heartlands. One's understanding shifts very gradually, and at that time, it seemed to me that Stuart was always working on race questions, and I was doing the gender work. It just took me a long time to truly grasp how those are completely interconnected.

By the 1980s, the sense that this society was in some kind of crisis around race was pretty present. Major riots, talk about race, and huge fallouts were all happening at that time, and it was the recognition that race was "coming home." This is what I'd call the postcolonial moment in Britain. At the same time, there was everything that was happening in countries that had become independent, especially Jamaica, as far as I was concerned. All of it raised a central question about decolonizing the mind, which was my point of entry in terms of work, something I could think about. I was a cultural and social historian, so working out not just how ideas are on paper but how people behave in practice in their everyday lives was something that you could track and understand historically. This gave me a space in which to work.

In your chapter in *The Post-Colonial Question*, you explore histories, empires, and the postcolonial moment. Could you elaborate on these arguments? And do you think there is something distinctive about the postcolonial rising from the experience of British colonialism?

As I was saying, I think the postcolonial moment was the moment of recognition of race being *inside* the society, not outside—and it's only happened in a very partial way. Take the work we are now doing on slave ownership at University College London,[1] it is not unusual to meet people who say, "Slavery didn't happen here, did it? It was all in the US, wasn't it?" That idea of the distance between the green and sceptered island and those tropical places where these nasty things happened is very deeply rooted in the culture. Race did come home, but as I said, only in a partial way.

There was the explosion in terms of black militancy and black and South Asian people organizing themselves, and at the same time what was going on in terms of music, style, and culture. There was a new presence of people of color on the streets and a recognition of how that was changing the society—and that also provoked the excitement of thinking that this country was really going to change.

Do you think the British experience differs from Portuguese or Dutch colonialism, or do you think it's the same across all European imperial projects?

I think there is much work to be done on that, actually. There are very great similarities between the ways in which European empires developed, but there are also important specificities. What's interesting will be, as work gets done, trying to sort out more about what the similarities and differences are. But there are some very striking similarities. So, for example, the ways in which all these European nations tell themselves a story, a national story, of how tolerant they are, how inclusive they are, and how everybody else's colonialisms were worse than theirs. But, at the same time, the British Empire had its specificities. And, of course, the territories of the British Empire were extraordinarily varied and had very different histories. There are ways in which the British tried to impose patterns and regulations across the empire, but the more we know, the more we understand how, in every colonial situation, the relation between official notions of what should be going on and what was actually happening were very varied, and the kinds of colonizers you had in different places varied as well as the kinds of colonial projects. So it becomes richer and more complicated the more we learn. At the same time, I want to hold on to thinking about the major strategies of exclusion and privilege that are in operation, so rather than collapse into just thinking everything is so complicated, try to see the patterns and see what the generalities are that we can understand.

What thinkers have most influenced you in your work?

Well, it is interesting. In relation to feminism, I'd say what lots of women from that phase of the women's movement say that it wasn't about reading texts; it was about talk and discussion and activity, and through that, we all influenced each other. So the idea of gender didn't come from some book or some essay, it came out of consciousness raising. It was the process of thinking collectively about what it meant in this society, to be a woman, and what kind of inequalities we were dealing with, how deeply rooted they were, and what the psychic components of that were, as well as all the broader economic, educational, and legal challenges we faced. So I couldn't say that there were particular thinkers in relation to feminism. My feminism came out of the women's movement itself.

In relation to postcolonial thinking or critical colonial studies, I would say that there have been particular texts that have been very influential to me. So, as I mentioned previously, Said was amazing, and from his work came other writers saying very similar things. But I think Said caught the moment, and he expressed it very lucidly, so it became a beacon for people, just as *The Making of the English Working Class* did in another moment in another kind of politics. Before that—and of course it's what Said draws on—I'd say that Marx, Gramsci, and Foucault are still the sort of base from which I work. We can't look at these authors uncritically though, for none of them were thinking about gender and not much about race; but, for me, it is how one thinks with their ideas, because ideas are there to be used and not to be set in stone. I'll never be a theorist—never—but I do use critical theories in order to think historically.

In your book *White, Male and Middle Class*, you examine the relationship between feminism and history. Could you elaborate on the significance of the intersections between race and gender and the impact that they've had on the formation and constitution of racialized and gendered identities?

Well, I suppose I put together those essays in *White, Male and Middle Class* when I had started the work that became *Civilising Subjects*. It was really about putting together my own family history and Stuart's family history as ways of thinking about British history and Jamaican history. I started working on the missionaries when we were in Jamaica. We were driving around, and we stopped at a place on the North Coast in Jamaica called Kettering. I was born in Kettering, and my father was a minister in Kettering—in England. And so I thought, why on earth is this place called Kettering? And that was the beginning of, as they say, a journey, and discovering those connections was just so moving.

I discovered that the particular missionary who had been based on the North Coast in Jamaica had lived in Kettering in England for a while before he became a missionary in Jamaica. He was called William Knibb, and he was centrally involved in the struggle for emancipation. The missionaries at that time spoke to enslaved men and women, and their congregations were entirely composed of the enslaved. White people didn't go anywhere near their chapels and certainly wouldn't want to mix with their congregations; they were horrified by the message of spiritual equality that the missionaries were preaching. The missionaries themselves never talked about *political* equality, but their message of spiritual equality was interpreted by enslaved men and women as meaning all kinds of equality. So the great rebellion in Jamaica in 1831, Sam

Sharp's rebellion, was led by people who were called native Baptists. They were not orthodox Baptists but had adapted the Baptist faith into a more syncretic version. The planters blamed the Baptist missionaries because it was thought that enslaved people couldn't possibly have masterminded a rebellion themselves. So the missionaries were persecuted, and that was the period just before emancipation.

William Knibb came to England, and he lectured up and down the country, arguing for emancipation. He gave evidence to the select committees on slavery in the House of Commons and House of Lords, and eventually emancipation happened. When he went back to Jamaica, he was greeted as a hero. He then raised a lot of money in England in order to be able to buy land in Jamaica and set up what were called free villages, which were villages where those who had supposedly been freed but weren't really free (they were forced to work unpaid as apprentices on the plantations) could establish new lives. The plantations were associated with slavery, and there was a lot of land in Jamaica that hadn't been settled on and cultivated, so these free villages were set up in those spaces. Some of them were set up with missionary money, and one of them with money from Kettering, so it's called Kettering because that's where the money came from.

Unraveling this story and finding out about connections between Kettering, England, and Kettering, Jamaica, and understanding much better about where my father's faith came from and what his traditions within the Baptist church meant was really fascinating. It was a journey that enabled me to put together these histories as well as see myself inside it all. So the historical work I've done has always come from inside me, which, of course, I think is true of what everybody does; some people are more explicit about it than others. That was the beginning of understanding much more about the varied and complex intersections across race, gender, and class.

That meant grasping the particular kind of relationships between the plantocracy and the enslaved, and between the missionaries and the enslaved, because of course the missionaries—although they believed theoretically in universal brotherhood and sisterhood—did not think that enslaved people were exactly the same as themselves and they [the enslaved] would have to learn to be fully "civilized." The whole paternalistic and maternalistic notion of how they could tutor these newly freed people to become like "us" was very embedded in their thinking. It was quite different from the monstrous forms of racism practiced by the plantocracy, but nevertheless, they certainly had racialized understandings of different peoples and who they were, and this was always also gendered. From this then, all the ways in which I'd learned to think about gender came into play, thinking about the constitution of raced and gendered identities along multiple axes rather than only one.

Did you find alternative voices or spaces through postcolonial feminist thinking?

Yes, I did. I think I absolutely did. One of the most striking examples that comes to mind is, after we'd lived in Birmingham—we lived in Birmingham for 17 years, so all the case studies I did for *Family Fortunes* were on Birmingham—and then I started working on Birmingham and Jamaica because there were so many connections. So I started revisiting some of the same archival materials and printed materials that I'd worked on for *Family Fortunes*, and it was remarkable to see how I'd been thinking exclusively about gender and class. Reading these materials again made me realize how I had not seen questions about nation, ethnicity, and race. It's mind-boggling because it's so clear that whatever the questions in your mind, they shape the way you read. So I don't find it surprising at all that lots of historians go on reading and working and never seeing the gender or race dynamic. It's only when something makes you think critically about those issues that you see it. I've watched myself change a lot, and I'm sure that process is in no way finished. I mean, hopefully you go on being open to ideas and being able to see and self-critique as best you can.

In *Civilising Subjects*, you examine the relationship between metropole and colony and its impact on constructions of Englishness. Could you elaborate on this relationship and the extent to which it became central in narrations of Englishness specifically, as well as the ways in which it regulated and subordinated the "other"?

As I said, I started working on the missionaries, and that got me to really think about their training. What did they already know when they arrived in the Caribbean? What ideas were in their heads about what they were going to encounter? How was that framed by all the discourses that were circulating in the 1820s and early 1830s around slavery, abolition, and Africa? I started looking at materials, which came mainly from men, including autobiographies, travel writing, fiction, and letters, and I began to find out what they were reading before they went. Well, of course, there was *Robinson Crusoe*, the classic encounter between "self" and "other" in which "other" has to be subjugated. Then there were the voyages of Captain Cook. These imaginaries were in the missionaries' heads when they arrived to "save the poor heathens in Jamaica." Looking at missionary hymns, again one can see the way in which the "other" is constructed as "savage." This narrative of the gap between "civilized" and "savage" was embedded, and you begin to understand how a frame of mind was created, which assumed Englishness as normal, regular, proper; it assumed whiteness, temperate climate, and that it was the best model for everyone.

Then came the actual colonial encounter and what they [the missionaries] made of it—particularly how their understandings were already shaped by the discourses that they had grown up with. So abolitionist discourse is itself both paternalistic and maternalistic in its characteristics and is fundamentally about rescuing people constructed as abject. It wasn't about black people having agency, or it being possible for them to have any kind of power; rather, it was about intervention on *behalf of the enslaved* by those who presumed to know them better than they knew themselves. So this work around the missionaries really provided a way into thinking about not only all these relationships of power but also thinking about them [these relationships] in a context where the missionaries were relatively progressive on the question of slavery. They certainly were opposed to slavery, but that didn't mean that they believed in racial equality. Making that distinction between opposition to slavery and a belief in racial equality is a very important distinction to make. The classic Wedgewood image of the anti-slavery campaign, which is the kneeling man and woman, asking, "Am I not a man and a brother?" "Am I not a woman and a sister?" with hands raised to God and to the white knights and ladies who are going to rescue them, carries all these constructions of Englishness, whiteness, Otherness, and the power relations that were absolutely central in such articulations.

How far do you think the consequences and effects of British colonialism have been forgotten in the contemporary postcolonial context?

It's very patchy. The year 2007 and the bicentenary of the abolition of the slave trade was a very significant moment when there was a huge amount of activity. But I think it was much more important for African-Caribbean people than it was for white Brits. And I think an awful lot of what had been done disappeared as soon as that year was over. It was a time, however, when there was much debate, much discussion, and many television programs, plays, radio programs, and exhibitions—but it's a question of how deep it went and how much people took in. We've been having an argument in Britain for the last twenty years, at least, about the impact of empire, and we've won some battles. When I first started doing this work, I think people thought I was just loopy—you know, "Why does she go on about the empire all the time?" Now it is much more recognized that there is an issue.

Look at imperial history in Britain, which has been a subject since the late nineteenth century. It was written without the categories of race or power. When you go through the indexes of huge histories of imperialism and see that race doesn't appear as a category, you think, what is going on here? There's been such a long history of the erasure of race as a significant category in this society.

And that goes back to abolitionism and the ways in which, after emancipation, it was all about the forgetting of slavery in favor of the ideas around—"Look, we're the progressive nation. We're the place that abolished it first. Look at those awful people over there, like in the United States, Portugal, and Brazil where they're carrying on in these terribly cruel ways. We are the tolerant and progressive ones." So, as a result, what is remembered and what enters the collective memory is abolition, not slavery. That erasure didn't just happen, it was made to happen; many people worked to actively forget that Britain had been involved in the slave trade and slavery and had built an empire and become rich on the basis of colonial rule.

And, of course, the end of the slavery didn't in any sense mean the end of forms of racial inequality. New forms of unfreedoms were developed across the empire, now not mediated for the most part through slavery but through forms of indenture, bonded labor, or servitude of different kinds. This legitimated talking about Britain's empire as an empire of liberty and freedom rather than of slavery. Take Gordon Brown a few years ago, talking about the golden thread of liberty. There was a big exhibition in the British Library about the development of British liberty that scarcely even mentioned the empire, and then there are all those deniers or whatever we want to call them: the historians who are so popular and successful and who think that the British Empire was a benevolent institution. There are many battles still to be fought.

What do you think about the critiques of empire and postcolonial thinking outside the Anglophonic context? Have they been influential for you and your work?

No, they haven't really, to be honest. The British Empire is so huge to research; it has totally absorbed me. After a long period of working on Jamaica and Britain, the next project I did was on history writing and [Thomas Babington] Macaulay, the great national historian of England. His father, Zachary, was very heavily involved in anti-slavery and knew a huge amount about the Caribbean and particularly West Africa and Sierra Leone. But Macaulay, who's the historian, just did not want to know about that at all; he wanted to forget slavery, but he did spend time in India. So then I had to start understanding something about India, and for me, one of the weaknesses of the way in which critical postcolonial work has developed has been the huge emphasis on India to the detriment of other parts of empire. One of the things I'm really interested in now is trying to put these pieces together and, particularly, to stop the Caribbean being completely sidelined as a region because it's not seen as important in geopolitical terms. After the death of King Sugar, it was no longer an area of great economic benefit to Britain, so it dropped off the radar. And that's continued; there's an awful lot of postcolonial work that is written as if India is the only place of significance.

Interestingly, as I said, I think Chatterjee is a wonderful scholar and has been very helpful, but his recent book on *The Black Hole of Empire* focuses exclusively on India. The empire wasn't only India; it was an awful lot of other places too. For me, I think understanding the way in which the empire made particular forms of race hierarchy really matters. Take, for example, the hierarchies of race in relation to peoples of African descent as compared with peoples of South Asian descent who "are not so backward" and the idea that they've had a "civilization." All those divisions have been so central to postcolonial histories, whether in Guyana or Trinidad or South Africa or India; we can see clearly the ways in which one lot of colonized peoples are set against another and how different versions of racialization have been used to legitimate that.

As a feminist historian, to what extent do you think the academy had changed in terms of its race politics, and what would you like to see transforming specifically around questions of race, feminism, and colonialism?

I'd like people to understand that both race and gender are absolutely essential categories of social organization and ought to be part of the ways in which we all think and analyze different societies. They are always relevant in one way or another. We're an awful long way off from that becoming common sense. The students I teach are very open to thinking like this, but it isn't there already. It has to be thought about and learned. They are used to living in a cosmopolitan city, and I'm sure they would all think of themselves as without any forms of racial prejudice. But, for the most part, young women, for example, don't think of themselves as feminists. There's a huge distance still to cross in the academy. And look at the numbers of ethnic minority staff in the humanities and social sciences; it's terrible. And it's still very poor in terms of gender; it's still deeply unequal, even after all this time. A lot has changed, though. When I was a student, there must have been about two women professors in history across the country. Now there are an awful lot, but there are still huge pockets of departments with no women in permanent jobs, which I find staggering, never mind anybody of African-Caribbean descent. African-Caribbean women are still subject to gross forms of discrimination in some schools and unequal access to higher education, among other things. So it's hard to be tremendously optimistic because we face a backlash in the sense that people are now saying to me, "postcolonialism—that's old hat," just like feminism was "old hat." I think, well, it may be that it's old hat, but we still haven't righted the wrongs.

It's when things explode that the fissured are exposed. Take the riots in London in 2011—that was an eye-opener. But what's the solution to deep alienation and disaffection and the lack of belief in conventional politics as an answer for anything? I mean, we're all so disillusioned, with very good reason. We see politicians' playing with race politics all the time; it's disgraceful. It seems to me that we don't know how things are going to go, and we really need forms of political engagement that people can believe in and that begin to challenge the organization of the state. So it's a bleak time, but we need to hold on to how much has changed and how much can change. That is one of the strengths of being a historian: think long-term!

Note

1. For details of the Legacies of British Slave Ownership project, see UCL's website (http://www.ucl.ac.uk/lbs).

Selected Key Works

Hall, C. (1992). *White, Male and Middle-Class: Explorations in Feminism and History.* London: Polity Press.

———. (1996). "Histories, Empires and the Post-Colonial Moment." In *The Postcolonial Question: Common Skies, Divided Horizons*, edited by I. Chambers and L. Curti, 65–77. London: Routledge.

———. (2002). *Civilising Subjects: Metropole and Colony in the English Imagination 1830–1867.* London: Polity Press.

———. (2012). *Macaulay and Son: Architects of Imperial Britain.* London: Yale University Press.

Hall, C., and Rose, S. (2006). *At Home with the Empire: Metropolitan Culture and the Imperial World.* Cambridge: Cambridge University Press.

CHAPTER 4

Boaventura de Sousa Santos

Boaventura de Sousa Santos is a professor of sociology at the University of Coimbra, Portugal, and a distinguished legal scholar at the University of Wisconsin–Madison.

Can you talk about your early intellectual formation? You trained as a legal scholar, so how did your broader concerns relate to your interest in law?

Well, very early on I developed the idea—which, in fact, is based on Durkheim's work—that law is one of the privileged instruments [with which] to analyze social relations and the way in which they evolve and get transformed in society. So my interest, probably from the very beginning, was both sociological and philosophical, and I always thought that law could perform that function, even though, at the time, I didn't have the same type of concerns that I developed later. So, when I finished my degree in law in Coimbra, I then went to a different university in Berlin to study philosophy of law and sociology of law, because, at the time, they were the topics that I was most interested in.

This was my first encounter with the philosophy of law in Germany. For many in Portugal, and in Europe in general, philosophy as such, and philosophy of law in particular, was written in German, so if you didn't know German, you were out. That's why I decided to go to Germany and deepen my knowledge of both German and philosophy. It was my first broadening, in intellectual terms, of the perspectives of law that were expanded when, in 1969, I went to the United States to get a degree in sociology of law, working on what was called at the time "law and development." This was a way of developing my understanding of the interaction that I had observed and studied very early on in Durkheim as well as the relation between law and the development of society. From then on, I moved from philosophy of law to sociology. It was this gradual process of expanding my interests that, in the end, got me into epistemological issues, which have become very central for me in the last ten years.

How did you develop your sense of political consciousness?

It developed by phases and in a kind of serendipitous way, very often and very contingent also. I'm a child from a working-class family in Portugal, and I heard—I cannot confirm that, but it was said—that I was the first working-class kid coming to the law school at the University of Coimbra, which was very elitist at the time, and it was a kind of scandal in itself but even more so because I was the best student in class. So there was something rather shocking about my being there. For my family, the most important thing was for the only child of the family to get a university degree, and I indeed was the first in the family to get a university degree. So I was not much involved in political activity; however, I did belong to the progressive Catholic youth movements that existed here.

Portugal was under fascism, or a kind of fascism, from 1928 to 1974, and at the time, it was a period of great repression, but we had here, at the university, a group of progressive Catholic students that were trying to discuss ideas of democracy, human rights, and so on, but we were very much repressed by the hierarchy. We had some support from the chaplains of the Catholic youth, but we suffered repression from the bishop and others, and that was the reason why I abandoned religion—the Catholic religion—very early on. So my political involvement went through various stages.

When I moved to West Berlin, it was the height of the Cold War, so this was really the time of the confrontation between the two worlds. I was very curious about what was going on on the other side of the wall, and since I was a foreigner, I could cross the wall every day. And then on a May Day celebration parade, I fell in love with an East German woman and she became my girlfriend, so you travel, you know, when the passion is at a very high level—I used to travel almost every day, crossing Friedrichstrasse or Checkpoint Charlie, which are the two points through which we would go from the West to the East. And I could see the other side, and the other side was the high time of Stalinism. I used to smuggle products—chocolates, cigarettes, stockings, all kinds of things—to the other side. And I used to bring letters in my shoes: I brought letters from people who wanted to leave East Germany and come to the West.

My political training at the time was strongly conditioned by this, and coming from a dictatorship myself, I was very much impressed by the lively democratic debates in West Berlin. I already had an anti-colonial posture because the critique of colonialism was part of our progressive Catholic movement, so in Berlin, I gave some talks for the students on Portugal and colonialism: Portugal, "the heir of colonialism." In fact, many people from the SDS (Students for a Democratic Society), which later became extremely important, were very curious, and they came to my talks wondering whether I would be defending colonialism. In fact, I did not defend it; I was on the opposite side. They even invited me to join their organization. I didn't, because I was a foreigner, and I was cautious at that time because I didn't know them very well.

This, in a sense, prevented me from moving into a more socialist or Marxist training, inclination, or formation. Because of the impact of the Cold War, the other side of the Wall was a space in which I saw Stalinism and suppression of freedom. It was at this time that a very famous professor, Robert Havemann, was ousted and later imprisoned just because he had written a very interesting book in which he criticized, in a very mild way, the government in the Democratic Republic of Germany, as it was called. I was very impressed by that, and developed some of my democratic ideas there. However, when I arrived in the United States in 1969, it was the time of a radical change in my political activism, political training, formation, and ideological orientation because it was there that I would become a Marxist.

I had already been trained in German philosophy, but it was in the United States that I deepened all my Marxist readings because I arrived at a very crucial moment, at the height of the Vietnam War and of the protests against the war, the civil rights movements, and the Black Panther Party—a period that saw a great radicalization of American society. It was also a time in which we were developing a very deep critique of the conventional structural-functionalist sociology that had dominated the field for so long. Our target was Talcott Parsons, at that time considered the "father" of American sociology.

I was in my PhD program at that time. Some of the students had a sociological background, and some a legal background, coming from Australia, Europe, Israel, and other countries. We started our reading groups, in which we read *Das Kapital* and many other works, and we discussed many ideas among ourselves. But in fact, there was also, at the time, very progressive teaching at Yale University that in fact disappeared five years later when the crisis of the movement came to an end, in a sense. I was a student of a very distinguished Hegelian professor, J. N. Findlay, then at Yale. I took classes with him and took other courses on Marx and Marxism. That was my entry into a kind of intellectual transformation that was also a political transformation for me. Although these readings and teachings transformed me, what really transformed me intellectually, personally, and politically was in 1970, when I went to Brazil to do field research for my PhD thesis, conducting participant observation in one of the favelas of Rio.

I lived in the favela for four months. Spending my days and nights in the community was really a sea change in my life. It was a large community, 60,000 people at the time, and I was trying to analyze the system of informal law and the ways in which the community would solve conflicts inside the community through the residents' association. They had no access to the official legal system because they themselves were an illegal community. And there were lots of problems inside the community, and that was the time in which I learned that, beyond academic knowledge, there were other kinds of knowledge, and beyond official law, there was informal, unofficial law.

I learned that there were ideas of human dignity and respect that were very important and were completely outside our lenses in our academic life; these ideas were coming from people that were considered ignorant, marginal, illegal, and so on, when in fact they were struggling for a dignified life in the most undignified conditions. And I really would spend hours and hours talking with them, in long conversations in which I could see the wisdom of the world as well as different ways of understanding the world and our relation with nature and neighbors and so on, which really transformed me. Most of the organizational work within the community was done illegally, clandestinely, because, at the time in Brazil, we also had a dictatorship that was very vicious in 1970 and 1971. Some of the leaders of the residents' association and the political mobilizations were members of the Communist Party, so it was very dangerous for them to be part of this research.

We developed, gradually, a trust relationship precisely because I was not North American, because if I were North American, they would never have talked to me. They were convinced that all the anthropologists and sociologists that would come to the favelas at the time were North American and, in one way or the other, connected with the CIA. And I think they were right in most cases, even though one of my friends—a great North American anthropologist, Anthony Leeds—had done very important work there, too. But indirectly or directly, such work was often used by imperialistic institutions.

So this was my training in the real politics of the world, and in fact, the embryo of these ideas came to shape my life and interests, particularly in the development of new kinds of knowledge or "ecology of knowledges." These are knowledges born in struggles; they don't come to us through reading other books or reading other people. We come into the context of life situations, sometimes risky situations for your own life, and only through this contact can we have access to other kinds of understandings of reality and other ways of understanding the transformation of reality. So that was a very important moment for me.

Two or three years later, there was also a very important moment in this transformation that moved me away from a more orthodox Western Marxism that I was following at the time to a more cosmopolitan form of political thinking, within which Marxism played a very important role but became one component among others in a broader constellation of critical thinking. This occurred in 1972 or 1973 when I become a very good friend of Ivan Illich.

Ivan Illich was a great visionary and educator from Austria who lived in Cuernavaca, Mexico, where he had a wonderful, very progressive center for popular education for progressive ideas, the Intercultural Documentation Center (Centro Intercultural de Documentación [CIDOC]). In fact, I met many of the political leaders of the left there, including the leader of the peasant leagues in Brazil, Francisco Julião, who was in exile in Mexico at the time and lived there. We had a fabulous time. I even taught a course with a very important sociologist from France, André Gorz, on the topic of law and revolution. So, as you can see, law was there, but I was broadening my interest, and I became much more aware of the diversity of other kinds of knowledge in Latin America and in the world. This led to a certain distancing from the Western conceptions of Marxism. There were core ideas that would be very important, and continue to be important in my work today, but I started to resent the fact that Marxism, in a sense, shared the same conception of history as linear time, and because of that, Marxists had a kind of ambiguous vision of colonialism itself—particularly British colonialism. Therefore, I distanced myself from that, as I always felt that probably the development of the collective forces could not be infinite, in theory.

Ivan Illich played a very important role because he was the one pleading for native technologies and local knowledge. I was not totally convinced by him. There were wonderful debates between the two of us during the night because I came from a very poor country in Europe, and a dictatorship, so I also felt there were some elements of modernity that we would need here, and technological progress and so on, but I was aware that we have to see that technology was never neutral and that there were different alternative technologies.

The 1970s were crucial to me also because, sometime later, the revolution came here in Portugal: the Carnation Revolution of April 25, 1974. This was another big transformation in terms of my political activism. I had been politically active mostly while working in grassroots organizations like the residents' association, and all of a sudden, I found myself in the midst of a revolution in which I had to participate in institution building. After 48 years of dictatorship, everything had to be rebuilt in terms of the university and the social sciences and so on. I was the third member of the Portuguese Sociological Association, which I helped start. I was the founder of the Centre for Social Studies (Centro de Estudos Sociais [CES]) and the founder of the School of Economics with which CES is affiliated. I was also, for 12 years, the president of the Scientific Council of the School of Economics, which at the time was the most important administrative body of the school. So this was a very intense period in which I moved from my more internationally oriented activism to more national activism, because I was concerned about Portugal.

I became very active in the cooperative movement here. I became a member of the peasants cooperatives, and I co-founded one of the cooperatives nearby and became a member. For 12 years, I did the most extensive field research, and because I was a member, I was not studying about them, but I was working with them and studying with them. I learned how to milk cows and helped in all kinds of training that was necessary for the cooperative. They became my good friends; even today, I go there often to have dinner and stay with them, even though the cooperative then had a crisis and collapsed. We had controlled production, but we didn't control distribution, and cooperatives in this context were very difficult to sustain. I also had my school of economics to administer, so I couldn't really dedicate myself fully to both. This was a period in which I was totally absorbed by the Portuguese political and social process. And it was in the late 1980s that I moved again to my international interests of the past.

In 1984, I conducted what was probably the first field research on the postcolonial period in the Cape Verde Islands; to me, this was a very important research project. In Latin America, I engaged in a case study for sociological research, and I did work in Brazil and Colombia. In the latter country, I connected with another very important sociologist in my life, Orlando Fals Borda, who was one of the founders of action-research. So I started again with all my involvement in the social movements across Latin America, which really came to fruition in 2001 with the emergence of the World Social Forum. I have been participating in the World Social Forum since the very beginning, not so much in organizational terms, but mainly in conceptual and political formulations. My activities became more cosmopolitan, and it was then that I could see different traditions of political activism and cultural brandings in political activism that came from Latin America, Africa, and Asia. The World Social Forum in Mumbai was a key transformation, as I became familiar with the struggles in other regions of the world, such as the outstanding example of the struggles and resistance of the Dalits [the "untouchables" in India]. So, as you can see, my political involvement continues to grow along with my intellectual development.

How do you conceptualize the postcolonial, and how would you situate your work within the genre?

I see myself as a postcolonial thinker, and I think that my work has some specificities in that respect, but what we have to start with is how to define what is meant by *colonialism*. Colonialism is a system of naturalizing differences in such a way that the hierarchies that justify domination, oppression, and so on are a *product* of the inferiority of certain people and not the *cause* of their inferiority. Their inferiority is "natural," and because it is natural, they are "naturally" inferior, they "have" to be governed, and they "have" to be treated and dominated. This part of the definition doesn't distinguish colonialism from sexism, so we have to move on a bit further from that.

Historically, colonialism also means "foreign" occupation. This foreign occupation is very important because it is a negation of all the conceptions of *territoriality*, meaning states, political organizations, and cultures that exist within the occupied territories. Even here we could also see a relationship with sexism, which is, in a sense, also a dimension of occupying the body of the woman—that is, the bodies are occupied in very much the same way as the collective bodies of the territories of the colonized. But there are differences, and the main difference is that colonial domination involves the destruction of other cultures, while sexism may exist within the same culture. In modern colonialism, we have deep colonial differences, deep cultural differences, and hierarchies. The destruction of knowledge (besides the genocide of indigenous people) is what I call *epistemicide*—the destruction of the knowledge of these populations and their culture, memories, ancestries, and all the ways in which they relate to others and to nature. Their legal forms, political forms, organization—everything—is destroyed and put at the service of the colonial occupation.

Colonialism also creates a problem for us in relation to postcolonialism; that is to say, there may be a naïve way of thinking that postcolonialism refers to a *post*colonial period, while in fact, postcolonialism claims just the opposite: colonialism didn't end with the end of historical colonialism, because there are other ways through which occupation continues—not foreign occupation, tutelage, and the prohibition of a state formation, but other forms of occupation. In Europe, racism, xenophobia, and Islamophobia are other ways through which you can see colonialism at work. At the level of relations among states, colonialism is also very much present, particularly in the relations between the European states and their former colonies; this is where Nkrumah's term *neocolonialism* (which he coined) comes into being (Nkrumah 1974).

I see myself as a postcolonial thinker because, within the tradition of critical thinking, I cannot see capitalism as separate from colonialism. Colonialism is, in a sense, the evil twin. I'm not saying that capitalism is the good guy. What I'm saying is that much of the Western-centric critical thinking—Marxism included—has looked just at capitalism and never focused on the other side of capitalism, which is colonial domination and also patriarchal domination. Thus colonialism belongs structurally to the modernity of the West and to capitalism, and that is why my ways of thinking focus very much on the ways in which colonialism has been part of capitalism.

In light of that, there are many kinds of oppression or domination other than those that Marxism has dealt with, such as exploitation—that is, capital labor exploitation. What I mean is that colonial domination, oppression, and the relations between the colonizer and the colonized became absolutely key in my understanding of the various forms of domination because the forms of domination never act in pure forms but in constellations of oppression. We still have slave labor today, which demonstrates how the long duration of this underside of capitalism continues to exercise these forms of labor and domination that are not in the "official" script of liberalism or even Marxism.

I'm very much concerned with these matters, and that's why my thinking has turned more seriously to epistemological issues—that is, an engagement with the ways of knowing from the perspectives of those who have suffered in a systematic way because of the injustices, dominations, and oppressions of colonialism, capitalism, and patriarchy. This is the definition I give of "epistemologies of the South," which is a crucial epistemological transformation in order to reinvent social emancipation and to develop a kind of critical thinking that is measured up by the needs of social emancipation on a global scale—not simply based on a Western understanding of the world. We need to develop these epistemologies of the South in a much broader way, and this has been my work for the last ten years. So, in that sense, yes, I do consider myself a postcolonial thinker.

What do you consider to be the main contributions of postcolonial studies? What do you think postcolonial thinkers do to interrupt discourses of colonialism?

In general, what I think of as the main contribution of postcolonial studies, as I understand them, is that they interrupt one of the key narratives of Western modernity, which is the narrative of continuous progress and linear climb within which colonialism performs a certain positive role. On the contrary, we come to the conclusion that there are different colonialisms but that all of them are bad. Additionally, our role as postcolonial thinkers is to show that all the conceptions of Western modernity are truncated forms because they operate on the basis of an "abyssal line" that creates radical exclusions. The abyssal line is the line that separates the metropolitan societies from the colonized societies. The Western-centric conceptions focus exclusively on the metropolitan societies, the societies on this side of the line. The "universal" ideas of Western modernity are therefore based on an abyssal exclusion of the societies on the other side of the line, societies to which such ideas, however supposedly universal, were not applicable. The "other side" is thus abyssally excluded, so much so that it is produced as invisible and therefore not relevant nor considered for the construction of any kind of relevant reality in theoretical or political terms.

Postcolonial thinkers also interrupt the story or the narrative of the progressive law throughout Western modernity. For instance, critical thinking of Western modern Marxist orientation sees labor law emerging at the end of the nineteenth century as the embryonic form of the welfare state—which it was, in fact, in Europe because it was the first time the liberal conception of the equality of the partners (or parties) in a contract or civil litigation was really challenged in light of the evident inequality of power between the worker and the employer. Labor law had to compensate for that inequality in one way or another by somehow neutralizing this inequality. So labor law does develop as a kind of a very progressive body of law, but all this happens in Europe, on this side of the line. On the other side of the line and precisely at the same time, in the colonies, labor law was being developed as forced labor, as a kind of penal law. This double reality is another interruption that I think is absolutely crucial in my way of thinking.

Another interruption, which is even more confrontational, concerns the acceptance by the Western liberal, or Marxist, thinking of the core metaphor of Western modernity as the movement from the state of nature to civil society, which has been developed by all the liberal thinkers since Hobbes and Rousseau and then accepted, in one way or the other, even by Marxist thinkers. From the perspective of the epistemologies of the South, civil society and the state of nature grow together. On this side of the line, we have the civil society; on the other side of the line, we have the state of nature created by the same forces—colonialism and capitalism. These, I think, are measured contributions to the debunking of a story that was told for more than one hundred years without interruption and one that I now think is bankrupt, and that's why postcolonialism is so different from postmodernism.

Initially, I saw my criticism of modernity as what I call "oppositional postmodernism," which was my way of moving to postcolonialism. But I didn't name it "postcolonialism" because my idea at the time was to criticize the postmodern critique of modernity, which in fact made a supposedly radical critique of modernity without criticizing the most basic structure of modernity—precisely the abyssal line. That's why I consider my postmodernism as a kind of opposition to postmodernism, because the conventional postmodern critique in fact wanted, in its supposed radicality, to eliminate even the idea of social emancipation as being another modern narrative. My idea was that, working in Latin America and Africa, I could never have conceived of the idea that social emancipation was no longer needed. On the contrary, it is more needed than ever, and we have to reinvent it. In order to reinvent it, we need a new oppositional thinking, an oppositional thinking that came to fruition with postcolonialism in the last 15 years or so.

What do you think is distinctive about the postcolonial rising from the experience of Portuguese colonialism?

I think that this is where my contribution may also be distinctive. I argue that Portuguese colonialism was very distinct in many different ways, and my basic idea is that, if the colonialisms are different, postcolonialisms also have to be different. I was always very concerned and very much in disagreement with the Anglo-Saxon form of postcolonialism for two reasons: first, because it was based on the British experience, and second, because it was a culturalist program and, from my Marxist training and the realities that I saw in Latin America and Africa particularly, I thought political economies should be part of the discussion. So we should not have a kind of postcolonial culturalist idea, but on the contrary, bring into it the political economy, and in a sense, the Portuguese experience allowed and facilitated that approach for various reasons.

Portuguese colonialism was semi-peripheral, as we call it according to the world-system theory. Actually, both Portugal and Spain, at the end of the seventeenth century, were already out of the game, as they had lost most of their hegemony in the world-system to the Dutch and then to the British, and as a result, some hierarchies within colonialisms and empires developed. Portugal was an informal colony of England, and we see here the very complexity of empires, because Portugal is an imperial center that, in financial terms, is dominated by, or subordinated to, the hegemonic empire of England, the British Empire. In addition, we see a creation of differences within the "Western world." Southern Europe was a periphery, subordinated in economic, political, and cultural terms to northern Europe, the core Europe that produced the enlightenment. This has been my debate with some postcolonial thinkers, particularly in Latin America, and also in Europe, who think that there is just one Europe or one Western modernity.

I think that Portugal and Spain show that, in fact, from the very beginning, from the seventeenth century and probably earlier than that, there is internal colonialism inside Europe, which now is very visible with the financial crisis; therefore, there was no single Europe. In one of my studies, I show that the Portuguese and the Spaniards in the seventeenth century were described by the northern Europeans with the same type of characteristics that the Portuguese and Spaniards attributed to the indigenous and native peoples in the New World and Africa. They were described as lazy, lascivious, ignorant, superstitious, and unclean. Such descriptions were applied to them by the missionaries or the monks that would come from Germany or France to visit the monasteries and people in the south.

I argue, therefore, that there was internal colonialism, and in fact, I believe that we cannot understand the current financial crisis in Europe without the presence of colonialism inside Europe and the way northern Europe addresses the realities of the southern countries. I think that this allows us to give greater complexity to current conceptions of the West, a topic on which I have often clashed with Walter Mignolo and others. I argue that there are other Europes inside Europe even today—for example, the "Indigènes de la Republique" in

France, a very active movement of the second generation of immigrants from the Maghreb with which my collaborators and I work very closely.[1] I believe they are Europe; they are European citizens, as the Roma people are also citizens of Europe. There is the myth of European values, which is something that was created after the Second World War and is really a façade that hides all these complexities in Europe. This has also led me to an even more complex way of looking at the West and at forms of Western modernity that I think could help in our alliance with movements for social emancipation in different parts of the world, but they were suppressed inside Europe precisely because they didn't serve the needs of European expansion, colonialism, and capitalism.

I therefore suggest that there have been many traditions that could have been used in a more cosmopolitan way but that were not found serviceable. They were not functional to colonialism and capitalism because, for instance, they established serious doubts about the existence of the Christian God. How could the missionaries go to Africa and Latin America with those doubts that Pascal formulated so eloquently? They needed certainties, and so this thinking about uncertainty was really left out. Portuguese colonialism allows us to see these complexities.

Portuguese colonialism spread out more than any other form of colonialism; it spread across three continents and for a longer period of time because it started in 1415 and lasted until 1975. It therefore represents the longest duration of colonialism and imperialism, and one wonders how a semi-peripheral country could sustain such an empire. Sanjay Subrahmanyam thinks that there were three Portuguese empires: the empire of the Atlantic, the African empire, and the Indian and Asian empire. They were very articulated but also very diverse forms of domination. Portugal is the only empire in which we have two colonies that became sub-imperial powers within the same empire: Brazil was sub-imperial for West Africa; Goa in India was the center of the empire for the Indian Ocean and for Asia. For me, this diversity of imperialism is very telling.

Some postcolonial thinkers do not attribute very much significance to this difference, but I do. Take the case of Brazil, which is quite striking. Portugal, in order to keep its independence from the Napoleonic invasions, moved the capital to the colony—that is, an imperial power moved its core/capital to one of its colonies in order to preserve its independence vis-à-vis another overpowering, imperial nation (England). For me, this is quite significant in modern history, and it's going to be very important for Brazil, as a settlement colony and probably explains why Brazil is today an emergent BRIC [Brazil, Russia, India, and China] country. These differences, in my view, are quite complex but bring complexity into postcolonial studies because they force us to see better the complexity of the colonized/colonizer relationship that Fanon and Aime Césaire speak about.

All along, there is an extended cycle of colonialism during which Portugal established very different sets of relations with the colonies. At the beginning, in East Africa, the relations cannot even be spoken of as colonial because they were, rather, merchant relationships free from the power of the empire. The native people were not considered inferior; the colonial inferiority of the nineteenth century was not present at the time, so we see these different relationships at play, which again demonstrates the difference of the Portuguese experience, an experience that thus decenters postcolonialism. Postcolonialism was focused first and foremost on the British Empire and second on the New World, which is very clear in Latin American postcolonial studies, as if the New World was the founding structure of Western modernity.

I don't think this is the case, because in 1492, we have Christopher Columbus then we have Vasco da Gama, and the trip to India (1497–1498); in the 1500s, there is Pedro Álvares Cabral in Brazil. Look at the differences between the "characteristic features" of the newly "discovered" territories, which the navigators bring from each of these expeditions. Pedro Álvares Cabral brings some Indians, parrots, spices, and things like that. Vasco da Gama brings ambassadors to discuss in Portugal what the relationships of the Portuguese should be in those areas. What is the difference? The difference is that, while in the Atlantic Ocean, the Portuguese and the Spaniards were very instrumental in creating a new kind of globalization; in the Indian Ocean, the Portuguese engaged in a very old globalization already existing. These are the complexities of Portuguese colonialism and the diversity of situations that brings us more complexity in our postcolonial thinking, and that's where I am.

Who are your main influences, and how have they shaped and impacted your work?

I'm a complex mixture because I have traveled and gone through so many intellectual and political trajectories. I think that one of the most founding influences for me were in fact the favela dwellers. The squatter settlement dwellers were absolutely transforming because of the shock; I had never seen people in such misery. I was coming from Portugal, a poor country, but it was decent in the sense that everybody was poor and there was not the same gap between rich and poor as I noticed in Brazil. All these deep miseries are at the limit of survival—illness, hunger, malnutrition, and violence—which were really terrible, and to see such wisdom coming from these people was very important to me.

I have to say that, on the opposite side, I was influenced by the French and German philosophers. I studied Hegel, as I said, but subsequently, my favorite philosophers became those that criticized most radically the Hegelian tradition, including Schopenhauer, Nietzsche, and Kierkegaard, who still today remain influential in my way of thinking. There were many others that became very influential. Frantz Fanon, of course, and Gandhi were important influences as intellectuals, as well as Ernst Bloch and his work, *The Principle of Hope*.

My work has also brought me together with many influential activists, as in the revolution in Portugal where, for a couple of months, I was the liaison person between the university and the movement of the captains. For me, it was a very interesting role to move every day between the revolutionary discourses of the time and the academic discourses of the university. I tried to bring them together, which was not very easy, as you can imagine.

Your work has developed across many fields. Could you talk a bit more about your current political activism and engagement outside of the academy?

Well, it has been very diversified. Today, particularly with the crisis in Europe, I am very active politically inside Portugal, and I think that my research center represents the source of the resistance against the pensée unique, the idea that there is no alternative to the neoliberal (dis)order. Most of the critical work that is publicized in newspapers and on television comes from researchers from this center, and I myself have been very much involved in the political struggles of the country today.

I've also been very much involved in the struggles in Latin America, particularly with the indigenous peoples. This started with my interest in analyzing social movements across the world. My sociological engagement has led me to actually become part of the movement, where I work with the people and learn through them. That's why I've developed the concept that I'm not a vanguard intellectual but, rather, a "rearguard" intellectual. I go with social movements; I try to facilitate their work; I try to show some of the dilemmas that other movements in other contexts have faced; and I try to bring to the fore comparative density and some lessons of history.

For me, it's very important with my concerns around the epistemologies of the South that they are not just framed as resistances against victimization—that is, it's really about the presentation of alternatives, of new ways of thinking, of transforming society with new ways, new definitions, and new conceptions of dignity and respect. I have learned these ways of *being* from indigenous peoples, particularly from Afro-descendant peoples in Latin America, so now I'm becoming more and more involved with the African social movements.

I've been working particularly in Mozambique and Angola, because they are being victimized by the same multinational corporations I was confronted with in my work in Latin America. There is a Brazilian multinational corporation (Vale do Rio Doce) that extracts minerals in Brazil, Mozambique, and other countries of Africa. It was considered (by the NGO Public Eye) the worst company in the world in terms of human rights a few years ago. I helped bring together peasant organizations from Brazil and Mozambique, all victims of the same plundering of natural resources.

My activism today is very much in line with the lessons of the World Social Forum, and that, in my view, symbolizes the transition from a politics of movements to a politics of inter-movements. What I mean by this is that women's movements have to interact with indigenous movements, human rights with anti-xenophobia movements, and undocumented migrant workers with indigenous peoples. We really have to try to bring in more of these alliances, and for that, we also need a lot of intellectual work, theoretical work—what I call "intercultural translation." In 2003, I launched the idea of "The Popular University of Social Movements," which develops these ideas by bringing together academic knowledge and popular knowledge of the social movements.

As a scholar who works in the so-called Lusophonic tradition, how do you relate to the question of Eurocentrism?

I never use that expression; I think that's part of postcolonial thinking, to criticize all these expressions that are expressions of the colonizer. Nobody in Angola, or in Mozambique for that matter, calls himself Lusophonic. Instead, I bring to the foreground the specificities of Portuguese colonialism and Portuguese postcolonialism to add new layers of criticism to Eurocentrism, and I think we *are* bringing them because, for me, the focus on the British Empire has developed a very naïve conception of Eurocentrism that didn't go deep enough into analyzing "our" Eurocentrism used inside Europe to destroy the "other" Europes. This struggle has to be brought into contact with the struggles outside Europe, and I think that Portuguese colonialisms and empires have contributed to deepen the different layers; the new layers of Eurocentrism.

The fact that Portuguese colonialism lasted until 1975 means that I could still be part of an anti-colonial movement, which is different from most of my colleagues in France or Britain because, when they became intellectuals or scholars, colonialism had gone and they never became postcolonial. In our case, we had to fight colonialism and postcolonialism in the same sets of generations because of the duration of Portuguese colonialism. This duration also allows us to see the seamy side of Eurocentrism in a very different way—that is, how Portuguese colonialism was used to defend apartheid and the gold mines of South Africa, which is very important, and additionally, how Portuguese colonialism was used to defend agreements of the Second World War with the sacrifice of the Portuguese and of the people they were colonizing. So these are very violent and corrupt forms of capitalism that we can visualize through these experiences.

We have projects in our center that are now unveiling even more crudely the forms through which the NATO powers used the Portuguese to fight with Rhodesians and South Africans of apartheid against all the liberation struggles, not because they were interested so much in Angola or Mozambique, but because they were interested in all the natural resources of that region. This is the seamy side that comes to the very foreground through the Portuguese experience, and that's why I think this so-called Lusophone world can't examine adequately all these other forms or Eurocentrism. As such, when we approach Portuguese colonialism, we talk about Eurocentrism, colonialism, and capitalism in a different, more diversified, and probably more profound way.

In contemporary academia, do you think there is a need for a decolonization of sociology, and do you think postcolonial thinking has been acknowledged enough in mainstream social sciences?

Well, they are two different questions. In relation to the latter, I don't think so. This thinking has certainly not been acknowledged; these thinkers are looked at with suspicion in very different ways, and there is even sometimes a kind of a colonial undertone of recognition of postcolonialism in a perverse way. To elaborate, they recognize, or accept, postcolonial studies once they are taught or professed by postcolonial people, and this is a very typical feature of Western modernity. They apparently include, but they do so in an excluding way. I think that postcolonial thinking will take a long time to be acknowledged because there is a weak recognition that, as long as we have capitalism, we are going to have colonialism in one way or the other—so the recognition of postcolonialism is always going to be a contested terrain. There is still a long way to go.

As for the decolonization of the social sciences, this is a topic with which I'm very much involved, and I think, again, that there is a lot to be done. In my work, I try to question the monocultures of knowledge, scale, productivity, and so on because I argue that the social sciences are the very products of those monocultures—particularly sociology, which was the discipline for the "us" study, and anthropology, for the "them" study. If we are to decolonize these disciplines, there won't be disciplines in the end. But there will be something else if we transform these monocultures into ecologies: ecologies of knowledges, ecologies of recognitions, ecologies of temporalities, ecologies of productivities, and ecologies of scale.

We have to profoundly change the curricula of social scientific work in our universities and colleges. Who are the "founders" of sociology? We are content, even today, at the beginning of the twenty-first century, to think that the main thinkers of sociology, of the social sciences, are the theoreticians that developed their work at the end of the nineteenth century and beginning of the twentieth century in a few countries of Europe (e.g., Max Weber, Emile Durkheim, Karl Marx). How can their theories address the realities of the world today? They simply cannot—not only because there were many people (the vast majority of the world population) whose existence was not acknowledged by them and is still not acknowledged today in our conventional curriculum but also because the contributions of "other" founders of social sciences are completely neglected and made invisible. For example, I have considered in my work that one of the main founders of the social sciences is Ibn Khaldun, who lived in the fourteenth century and was born in Tunis, with great influence from Seville and from the Caliphate. His studies on civilization are absolutely crucial to understanding contemporary societies—not just the Arab or Muslim societies but Western societies. So, if you start to unravel this, you will see that Greek philosophy was not Greek, it was Egyptian, it was Middle Eastern, and it was probably Asian. If we decolonize, we will give another value to Joseph Needham's work on science and Chinese civilization, for example.

We still hold onto the inventions and novelties of the West. But I usually wonder with my students how it is possible to go on teaching in sociology that the industrial revolution was the most important event in world history, the event that really transformed the West into the highly developed countries that they are today, whereas until 1750, most of the products that the elites in Europe would buy came from China. Since China accounted, at that time, for 50 percent of the international trade, it is high time to contextualize the role of the industrial revolution. Who invented printing? Who invented gunpowder? I mean, if you go on and on, you will see that many achievements that are attributed to the West, not to speak of the zero, are not Western; they are registered in Sanskrit texts, or they are Arab inventions. So if you start to decenter Western social scientific knowledge and to bring in other realities and knowledges, you will see that the decolonization of the social sciences will be a long task because so much has been made invisible and suppressed, marginalized and forgotten.

Our dilemmatic task in decolonizing the social sciences is that the other realities, knowledges, and entities are today unpronounceable or irretrievable. They are lost forever. For instance, the indigenous people like the Embera in Colombia lost their language and territories, and now they are homeless people in the cities of Colombia; their losses are infinite and final. This is just an example of a much broader phenomenon and a long duration phenomenon inherent to the workings of Western modernity.

Finally, in your work, you have tried to articulate a project of the Global Left, and you are also keen to relate your work in terms of the Global South. Can you talk more about the relationship between what you see as the Global Left and the Global South?

It's a good question. In fact, all the questions are good, but this particular one is a really good one. Why? Because the Global South, for me, is a metaphor; it's not a geographical entity. It's the metaphor for the systematic suffering caused by colonialism and capitalism. Australia is part of the Global North, even though there is a South inside, which are the indigenous people. The Global South calls for resistance and for alternative. The critical thinking and the tradition calling for social transformation against the status quo is what we call, in Eurocentric terms, the Left. But things are much more complicated because the Western-centric Left was racist and ignored or demonized most of the struggles of the people in the Global South in their resistance against oppression and discrimination.

Therefore, when I refer to the Global Left, I am inviting a refoundation of the Left. A refoundation based on an intercultural understanding of radical democratization of social relations among humans and between humans and nature. Such democratization consists of transforming relations of unequal power into relations of shared authority in the family, the factory, the home, the streets, the community, the public sphere, and the research centers and universities and to do so in a way that the means do not contradict the ends—that transformation encompasses self-transformation. So it's this transformation of unequal power relations into shared authority that I'm most concerned with. This transformation involves polarizing or radicalizing differences between oppressors and oppressed and depolarizing or de-radicalizing differences among the oppressed. This is just the opposite of what the conventional Left has been doing in the last thirty years.

The Left has to be global but cannot be the same Left with the same premises of the conventional Left, because it has to be intercultural to begin with and capable of reciprocal translation between different conceptions of a better society. What is common about the different struggles is the struggle for dignity, respect, and a better life that people think they deserve because they are unjustly discriminated against by structures of power. So the struggle against these injustices is what may be characterized as, in a broader sense, a Left thinking.

Why does it have to be global? Because, in fact, capitalism is not a mode of production anymore; it's a global style of life, a global ontology. It's an entity that in fact encompasses all our lives and relations with others and with nature. Therefore, the Left needs a broader idea of our struggle. One may think that the scale of struggle is so big that it is beyond human capacity, and people become cynical. No. I work with people that cannot afford to be cynical because, as I usually say, they are alive today, but they don't know if they will be living tomorrow. They can feed their children today, but they don't know whether they can feed them tomorrow. They cannot be cynical; they cannot afford to be cynics, so they are resisting. They are looking for alternatives, and I think that the Global Left is an unending process; it's always an incomplete process of looking for alternatives of dignity and respect so that humanity ceases to be just an idea.

Today, there is no common humankind in my view because, in our modern world, there is no working humanity without some social groups being labeled as subhuman. (According to the contexts, they may be women, gays, suspected terrorists, enemy combatants, undocumented migrant workers, indigenous or tribal people, Afro-descendants, and/or human obstacles to development such as peasants or others.) The aspiration to a more complete humanity is, in itself, infinite, and that's probably the best metaphor to bring together the Global South with the Global Left.

Note

1. Parti des Indigènes de la République (party of the indigenous of the republic/ Natives of the Republic) is an anti-racist, anti-colonial, and anti-Zionist political movement in France and has been active since 2005. The party was founded by activist Youssef Boussoumah, and the lead spokesperson is Houria Bouteldja.

Selected Key Works

Santos, B. (2002). *Toward a New Legal Common Sense.* London: Cambridge University Press.

———. (2006). *The Rise of the Global Left: The World Social Forum and Beyond.* London: Zed Books.

———. (2007). *Democratizing Democracy: Beyond the Liberal Democratic Canon.* London: Verso.

———. (2008). *Another Knowledge Is Possible: Beyond Northern Epistemologies.* London: Verso.

Santos, B., and Rodríguez-Garavito, C. (2005). *Law and Globalization from Below: Towards a Cosmopolitan Legality.* London: Cambridge University Press.

CHAPTER 5

Vron Ware

Vron Ware is a professor of sociology and gender studies at Kingston University, London.

Could you talk a little about your biography and how you first got into the field? What interested you around questions of race, ethnicity, and feminism?

There was no sort of founding moment or realization. When I was at school, I decided to study Persian and Arabic at university for various reasons. I lived in Iran for three months before I started (this was 1971), and I began to understand some of the ways the world was shaped. Then, the university syllabus, particularly in Arabic, was very safe and taught by ex-colonials. There were only two of us in the Persian class, which was disappointing. The other person happened to be working class and gay, and he was really struggling with the whole experience of being in a place like Cambridge. I was struggling being there too, so it was a very difficult and fraught time. In Oriental studies, if you wanted to talk about the politics of the actual countries, it was all off limits, particularly if it meant criticizing particular regimes.

After two years, I switched to sociology and anthropology, or what was then a new department called Social and Political Sciences. It was very intense, like a crash course, as the terms were only eight weeks long, and I was absolutely unprepared, having only read medieval texts in Persian and Arabic for two years. I preferred anthropology and distracted myself by wondering what happened to the anthropologists themselves when they immersed themselves in other cultures. So I would read Evans-Pritchard and various people and think, how did their fieldwork change them and the way in which they saw the world?

At that time, I was also encountering the beginnings of the women's movement in Cambridge, which was emerging out of anthropology. There was a whole critique of anthropological knowledge because it was so much derived from the perspective of male investigators. It was very exciting to be part of that radical questioning, although terrifying in some ways as well. I remember being in my supervisor's study and realizing that his great wall of books were all written by men, and at that moment, I felt like they were going to fall down and crush me—a bit like Alice in Wonderland.

I decided to take the sociology of religion module as one of my options, partly because it meant I could write a longer paper instead of taking an exam-based course. I wrote my essay on the connections among migration, racism, and religion. I knew quite a few Iranian and Iraqi refugees in Cambridge and had noticed the way in which my Baha'i' friends in particular organized themselves as a community with their faith as a focus. I wanted to explore the way that religion became more important for migrant individuals and groups, partly because of racism, loneliness, and a sense of isolation, but also because of the solidarity and mutual support it offered.

Of course, there were almost no books on that subject, and my supervisors were either useless or disinterested. But I had a friend whose father was in the Community Relations Council in Birmingham, so I went to see him to do some more fieldwork. I had another friend working for the Workers Educational Association (WEA), who suggested that I contact a group called All Faiths for One Race (AFFOR) based in Handsworth. I only appreciated later what an important organization this was; at the time, they were a bit hostile to me as a student from Cambridge, understandably perhaps. As a result, I had a lot of different experiences and conversations and was really provoked to think about what I was doing, but that didn't happen in Cambridge; that was outside.

I got my degree, and I was out of there. The first thing I did was save up enough money to go to India. It sounds a bit naïve now, but I really thought I could work against the impact of British imperialism. I suppose I thought vaguely that I would do some kind of development work (whatever that was). During the three months I was there, which was a life-changing experience, I met a lot of amazing people, and particularly some Marxist activists who basically said, "You really don't need to be here. We're quite fine without your help." Anyway, the experience helped me see that it would be far more productive to go back to the UK and work on the problems of racism there—on the basis that racism was directly connected to that colonial history. Eventually, by the summer of 1977, the summer of Lewisham and the rise of the National Front (NF), I had moved back to Birmingham.

In the meantime, I had worked out that, essentially, I wanted to be a writer and to work for an anti-racist publication. My friend in Birmingham said, "You should meet Maurice Ludmer, the editor of *Searchlight*,"[1] and he introduced us. I remember going to meet Maurice for the first time in my dungarees and him saying very kindly, "Now what can I do for you?" He basically warned me that the work could be dangerous and demanding, but we really got on well and I started working with them immediately. At first, I was just shuffling magazines and sorting out the subscriptions, but Maurice also encouraged me to write and to take photographs as well. My experience with *Searchlight* was very profound because I was really doing what I wanted to do. I was looking at the NF and their ideology, reading all their work, learning how they organized, and exploring all the international links. At the same time, I was getting friends to show me how to put a magazine together: how to do copy editing, layout, and other really useful skills. Meanwhile—particularly during the run-up to the 1979 election—I was involved in community anti-racist groups and going to Anti-Nazi League and Rock Against Racism events.

There was a very active women's movement locally in Birmingham too. In 1978, the last national women's liberation conference was held there. It was quite tumultuous, with huge arguments between the radical feminists and the socialist feminists. I remember vividly the moment where a group of Iranian women were trying to talk from the platform about the situation in Iran, and no one was listening. Then a group representing Third World Women (as they were known then) said, "If you don't let us speak, we will never ever come to any of your conferences ever again." But there weren't to be any more national events like that. A couple of years later, I went to a socialist feminist conference on imperialism in London, but even so, a gendered analysis of racism and colonial history was quite absent.

I guess in those days I was not ambivalent about feminism but perhaps choosy as to where I got involved. But some women at the Birmingham Centre for Cultural Studies (CCS) started a group called Women against Racism and Fascism (WARF), which was fantastic, a really positive experience, and fun as well. We organized events to raise money, painted out racist graffiti, and made a beautiful banner for demonstrations. We wanted to campaign with leaflets that explained why women should be against fascism, which was relatively easy, comparatively anyway.

Early in 1978, Maurice Ludmer had asked me to write a pamphlet about women and the NF, and it turned out that the Birmingham CCS group was also writing about women and fascism. It was a very productive and supportive conversation, but explaining in a snappy way why women should be particularly critical of racism was more of a problem. Because I was scouring fascist literature all the time, I kept noticing the recurring figure of the white woman in their propaganda. The NF was obsessed with what they called "race traitors" and had stickers that said, "Race mixing is treason," with a picture of a black man and white women. White women were also represented as the main victims of black crime as well. This was the period when the police were really pushing the idea that young black men were disproportionately responsible for what they called "mugging" or street crime. The recurrence of this pairing—the predatory black criminal and the white female victim—really got me thinking. Recently, I was watching one of Stuart Hall's early programs about racism in the media, and it brought it all back. He was showing two different newspaper reports on street crime, and the instigator who was arrested was black, and the victim was white and female in both cases. They were quite close together in terms of the date, but in the second one, the thief had become the "mugger." This was central to the *Policing the Crisis* project, the idea of a "moral panic" around black street crime. The figure of the vulnerable white woman was an integral part of this racist, fear-mongering discourse.

I began to try to write something about the issue of racism and violence against women, but it was really difficult. In Birmingham, we had a "reclaim the night" march because there had been a series of rapes locally—it was really horrible, and it was a red-light area anyway—so the march was about women reclaiming the streets. But if you tried to say, "Hang on a minute. What does this say about white women in relation to ideas about the black mugger?," you were kind of shouted down. In a way, I thought it wasn't really worth having those arguments anymore because either you got it or you didn't, and there were lots of issues like that. Nonetheless, I really was enjoying myself on many levels at that time. There were a lot of groups, things to do, and music—being young, taking pictures, and working on a magazine. It was really an amazing time. I had just met Paul [Gilroy], too, so it was romantic as well. It was just such a transforming period, being involved in those social and political movements.

Also, I'd had experience of teaching English as a second language, and I did that as well to get a bit of extra money. I ended up teaching in a local doctor's office in Balsall Heath, an area mainly inhabited by Pakistani migrants and also Bangladeshi and Sikh families. I'm sure I was crap at teaching, but it was really interesting to do something like that in the neighborhood. I suggested to other people in the WARF group that there was this opportunity to teach but nobody in the group seemed to want to do that. Perhaps it seemed like spying on Asian women or exoticizing them, but to me, it was just simply about saying that we all live here and are all interested in gender and race politics. I made a lot of friends and still have loads of photos of my students from that time. When you're young and in your twenties, these things really continue to shape you.

I suppose the thing that made me want to try to write a book about women and racism was the emphasis on white women in NF propaganda that I mentioned. It wasn't just about women's role in relation to the family—as wives, mothers, and breeders—but the way in which the figure of the vulnerable white woman was used to underpin the idea that society was fundamentally threatened by immigration. In the meantime, I had started to think about all these things in terms of the history of empire. And then there were certain moments like when I went to the United States in 1981 and bought Adrienne Rich's book *On Lies, Secrets and Silence*. I don't remember who tipped me off, but I read her essay "Disloyal to Civilisation" on the subway and was completely riveted. Then learning about American women abolitionists made me want to know all about British women's role in the anti-slavery movement. I went to see Catherine Hall, the historian, whom I knew from the women's movement, and she told me about the Birmingham women who had been engaged in local campaigns against slavery in the early nineteenth century and where I could find their records in the library. No one had really written about this phenomenon at that time. So I had to really become a sort of a historian and go to all these libraries and archives. Eventually, ten years later, my book *Beyond the Pale* was a direct result of that political struggle to understand and articulate the links between race and gender. It was informed by all those experiences and more.

How did you develop your sense of political consciousness?

As a young adult, it was partly through my travels in Iran and my sense of alienation in Cambridge, as I said. I think that accounting for the development of political consciousness is part chance and part contingency. I can think of several books I read as a child that shaped the way I learned about injustice, cruelty, and racism. It also has quite a lot to do with generation and the political climate. I grew up in a small village in Hampshire in the period immediately after the war. It was the 1950s and 1960s. I was ten when the Beatles had their first hit, and I was delirious. Pop music changed our idea of what was possible; American hippy culture and anti–Vietnam War vibes reached our corner of England as well.

Meanwhile, a number of people who were neighbors or my parents' acquaintances had lived in the colonies. In the village, there was also an elderly English woman who was a real old "memsahib" from the Raj. Her husband had been the headmaster of a boarding school for young Rajas in a remote part of India. Anyway, this woman was obsessed with India. She used to have tiffin in the mornings, and she made curry lunches for people at the drop of a hat. She was always trying to marry off my sister and me and matchmake us with her friends. She had a semi-adopted son who was Indian who would come and stay regularly. So, even within a very small place, there was always this sense of nostalgia for a colonial past. As we began to come and go a bit more, we began to notice racist attitudes from people who were quite close to us, awful views on things like immigration or apartheid. I got really sick of hearing that the system really worked in South Africa and that if you hadn't been there you had no right to criticize it. I've tried to go back and reflect on that cultural and temporal enclave by writing a book about the village called *Where Was I?* (as yet unpublished).

I also made a film in 1988 with my friend Mandy Rose called *Hilda at Darjeeling*, which was shown on Channel Four. The idea was to try to catch that generation of Englishwomen who lived in the Raj and to explore the stereotypes that were popular in fiction and also films like *Passage to India* and *Heat and Dust*. We also wanted to engage with women who had had a critical relationship to colonialism and who were aware of their position as white English women; I was writing *Beyond the Pale* at the time as well. We tried to find people who weren't comfortable living there with tons of servants and a nice big house and who attempted to object to the racism around them. In a way, the inspiration came from the memsahib in my village, although she was definitely not a candidate for our film. When we interviewed her, she went on and on about how much she loved Indian people but that she agreed with Albert Schweitzer that black people in Africa were savages. I don't think I spoke to her again after that.

And then there was a neighbor who lived next door, whose first husband had run a rubber plantation in Sri Lanka, and she had grown up in Ceylon. She was much more interesting because she told us all about the workers' strikes. Anyway, we used a lot of home movie footage from the archive in Cambridge, in the Department of South Asian Studies, to evoke the texture of peoples' lives. The aim was to capture oral memories of that colonial past while there was still time. But it was also about getting our contemporaries to think about the salience of imperial history in the present. For me, this was a political project and an important part of the research for writing *Beyond the Pale*.

Which thinkers have most influenced you and your work?

I've had the incredibly good fortune to be part of an extraordinary circuit of people—whether here [in England], or in Europe, the United States, or South Africa—who are all broadly part of a larger political conversation, particularly on race and postcolonial questions. It would be impossible to name all the thinkers and writers whose works—and friendships as well—continue to influence my own.

At that time, when I was writing *Beyond the Pale*, I was both inspired and provoked by the interventions on racism and feminism from the United States. I remember when Angela Davis's book *Women, Race and Class* came out, for example, and bell hooks's *Ain't I a Woman*, both in 1981. Hazel Carby, who I had known in Birmingham, was also important, and her book *Reconstructing Womanhood* was a real landmark. Then, of course, there was Adrienne Rich, who was possibly the most inspiring of all. I always cite her "Notes toward a Politics of Location," which she published in 1984 and in which she positions herself as writing in the context of the Cold War in the United States against the backdrop of nuclear proliferation. Some of this feminist work really shaped my own writing style too. One of the things I've always found difficult is tone of voice—knowing whom you're writing to. Because I wanted to be a writer above all, that was very important to me and still is. I think there's a way of connecting different kinds of experiences that writers like June Jordan and bell hooks did particularly well. I liked Sara Evans's book *Personal Politics* about her experience of the civil rights movement too. Their voices always helped me get into a certain frame of mind for writing.

At that time, Richard Dyer's amazing essay "White," which first appeared in *Screen* in 1988, was one of the few texts that talked directly about the representational power of whiteness. David Roediger's book *The Wages of Whiteness* was published in 1991, just before *Beyond the Pale* and by the same publisher. We contacted each other soon after that and still keep in touch. I first spoke to Ruth Frankenberg on the phone when my book was in production, and we did our first joint seminar together at University of California, Santa Cruz not long after *White Women, Race Matters* was published in 1993. I liked John Hartigan Jr.'s work, although the book *Racial Situations* wasn't published until 1999.

There were so few of us working on questions of whiteness that, for a while, it was possible to have a conversation about where we were all coming from and experience a sense of solidarity. I remember "meeting" Matt Wray (co-editor of *White Trash,* 1997) on the airwaves during a BBC radio interview, and we had a very engaged and productive dialogue for a while as well. None of us had any idea that there was going to be this splurge of interest in whiteness, let alone that we were implicated in the birth of something called "whiteness studies," as it was first called.

In your groundbreaking work *Beyond the Pale*, you examine the complex relationship between black women and white women. Could you elaborate on the way(s) in which this relationship/connection links to the discourse on racism?

When I began working on *Beyond the Pale*, there was still a residual notion that "sisterhood" transcended all boundaries, so feminism was very much understood to be a resource available to everyone: to refugee women from Chile or Iran, for example, or to working-class women, lesbians, middle-class mothers, and black women. But it didn't really work like that. Having an analysis of gender oppression that applied across all kinds of different situations and backgrounds was hugely contentious, and it took a while for people to figure that out. Once you start representing or speaking to the experiences of women as a kind of homogenous group, without recognizing all the other dimensions of their lives, it has the effect of silencing, patronizing, or excluding anyone who is not like you.

The book began as a commitment to a politics of gender, race, and class that took account of those differences and didn't try to speak on behalf of anyone. It might sound obvious today, but in the early 1980s, a lot of white feminists did have a problem understanding that they were implicated in racist ideas and practices because there wasn't a sense of their "whiteness" or their "femininity" being an issue. Then, of course, there was the perennial excuse that "race" was the preserve of black folks and that one shouldn't overstep boundaries by having something to say about it. There was certainly a lot of policing and guilt-tripping.

The penny dropped for me when, after a couple of early unsuccessful talks where I was hammered for suggesting that there was a value in deconstructing white womanhood, I realized that the emphasis should not be on white femininity *per se*, but that the very idea of making distinctions along racial lines depended on a web of relationality. In other words, our ideas about blackness were developed historically in relation to the idea of whiteness—or white supremacy—in a hierarchical system of race thinking. The task of deconstructing identities or constructs that are racialized as "white" is inseparable from deconstructing those that are classified as "black" or "Asian" or "Oriental." They derive from historically formed ideas that make sense in relation to each other, not as abstracts sitting out there on their own. Meanwhile, gender is crucial to understanding the representational power of all racialized constructs. I'm simplifying, of course, but I hope the point is clear.

So in *Beyond the Pale*, I tried to approach this relationality from many different angles, looking at contemporary media representations and feminist politics, alliances and quarrels between women in different historical periods, and finally, its implications for feminist theory as well. The concept of relationality is perhaps easier to understand in terms of gender, but when you introduce race into the equation, it becomes clearer why certain racist tropes are so powerful and so enduring. I examined the representation of vulnerable white femininity, for example, tracing it back through the colonial context, to show how powerfully it fit with a certain trope of threatening black masculinity. Yet this pairing isn't fixed in stone. You could also see how ideas about modern white liberated femininity—seen in opposition to subjugated (often veiled) non-Western women—highlighted the belief in civilizational superiority in Europe and North America. After 12 years of war in Afghanistan, I think most people are familiar with that particular message now, as they were in the nineteenth and twentieth centuries.

Could you elaborate on the relationship between the production of whiteness and colonialism? And what do you think is "critical" about critical whiteness studies?

I'd like to talk about the book I subsequently wrote with Les Back, called *Out of Whiteness*, published by the University of Chicago Press in 2002, ten years after *Beyond the Pale*. We both felt uneasy that, as the 1990s progressed, the analysis of whiteness coming out of the United States was losing its radical potential. There were too many books and articles that accepted the basic premise of racial difference, as though whiteness was an unassailable racial identity that could be purged of negative associations. It often seemed as though focusing on whiteness—particularly as an aspect of identity—meant entrenching racial categories rather than trying to dismantle or undermine them.

Meanwhile, historians like David Roediger and Noel Ignatiev were arguing that the category of whiteness could and should be abolished altogether. For a while, I was on the editorial board of a journal called *Race Traitor,* which they set up, and it felt as though there was a political project that was attached to the intellectual one. The other problem was that the literature was dominated by what was happening in the United States and spoke to very specific US concerns where you couldn't really dislodge the idea of what "race" was and wasn't.

So *Out of Whiteness* was our attempt to argue for an anti-racist ethics and politics that might emerge out of an analytical approach to whiteness, if not an abolitionist one. It addressed what we called ethnographies of whiteness, ways of knowing about race and racial difference. I had become interested in the genealogy of anti-racist politics and the notion of being a "race traitor" and wrote about people like John Howard Griffin—I had been very affected by reading my older sister's copy of *Black Like Me* in the 1960s—and Lillian Smith and the concept of non-racialism in South African anti-apartheid struggles. Les wrote wonderful essays about music, fascism, and racism; in one of them, he wrote about the impact of the Internet on the cultural networks of racist skinheads and cyber-Nazis, for example. We certainly covered a lot of ground. When the book came out, we were both unhappy with the title, which the publishers insisted on, and we didn't like the cover either. We didn't want to produce yet another book on whiteness *per se,* but the editor insisted that this was how we should market it. Even then, in 2002, the notion of critical whiteness studies (CWS) hadn't really taken off.

Now I am not so involved in what CWS has become as a coherent anti-racist intervention. If you stick "critical" in front of anything, it's supposed to trouble the idea that there is such a thing and so on and so forth, but then you gradually get a canon, which means certain people will always be cited and others left out. The danger is that the original force of the intervention gets dissipated as it becomes incorporated into a more mainstream way of doing routine academic work. Having said that, you could have knocked me down with a feather when I discovered that CWS was a significant component of my daughter's sociology undergraduate course in race and ethnicity in 2008. On the positive side, I realized that all that work in the 1990s really had helped open up new ways of approaching the study of racial categories and racial injustice. In a way, I suppose I think of it as offering a method, a particular angle of vision, or an ethics of what Les and I thought of as bearing witness to racism, not being complicit. It was a way of thinking about things that were previously unexamined, regarded as "normal," and therefore invisible.

Could you talk a bit about the main arguments in your book *Who Cares about Britishness?*, particularly the ways in which you think colonialism impacts and influences the construction of national and cultural identities?

I think that's the interesting thing about twentieth-century Britain: the fact that the 1948 Nationality Act made everybody into a British subject throughout the empire, or what was left of it, so that the concept of Britishness was a global category at that point, and a symbolic one as well. Since then, we have seen the relentless and often quite abrupt retraction of what this definition of Britishness meant in its formal terms. But the imprint of colonial rule and imperialism provided a cultural orientation to Britain as the mother country, which has strong residues in all the former colonies—not least in legal and political systems, culture, and education.

The book [*Who Cares about Britishness?*] was commissioned by Counterpoint, a group in the British Council back in 2006, when Gordon Brown resurrected Britishness as a politicized topic. It was a great project, to be asked to write a non-academic book that reflected the way young postcolonial citizens in a variety of countries, including the UK, thought about the concept of national identity on one hand, and what they understood by "Britishness" on the other. It started with a weekend conference with about thirty young people who had either come to live in Britain as children or grown up with migrant parents, all of whom had very strong opinions about what they thought Britishness was or wasn't—mostly the latter. The project was linked to about five other countries, so I then went on a whistle-stop tour to attend similar events—in India, Bangladesh, Pakistan, Kenya, and Ireland as well as a video conference with people in Poland. What was amazing about that project was being able to listen to the participants talk about their lives in different cities, like Nairobi and Dhaka, and to hear how their generation negotiated all sorts of political and social issues, including nationalism. What we found was that people tended to say the same sort of things; they had the same sorts of struggles; they came up with the same sorts of truisms or thoughtful interrogations of where they were and so on.

At first, I wasn't sure how to write about this, but then you realize that the fact that people were saying similar things from all these different backgrounds is really interesting. I wanted to draw that out as well as keep the historical and local specificity. I wrote the book like a travel narrative, or like a documentary, in fact, with a lot of different scenes showing how the young people participating in the research were making sense of their lives, often in difficult circumstances. Their views on Britishness were actually the least interesting aspect—although, of course, most of them were very angry about Iraq (this was 2006), and their image of the UK depended on whether they had been there, what kind of music they liked, or things like that.

Your recent work, *Military Migrants—Fighting for Your Country*, is the first book to critically explore the role of migrant soldiers within the British Army. Could you talk a little about this research and the way in which Britishness, memory, and militarism relate to questions of racism and citizenship?

The first thing I would say is that the British Army, as the oldest of the three services, is a repository of empire. You go to any officers' mess or any garrison town, and it's saturated with the material culture of empire—absolutely saturated. It's not surprising when you think about it, but it's kind of a shock when you get there. In the military academy at Sandhurst, which is probably the most extreme example I saw, they have these cannons by the front door that were captured in India in the eighteenth century with Islamic calligraphy all over them. I was shown what they actually call the "bling" room, with all these diamond-encrusted swords and so on, evidently "presents" from colonial subjects. British military history is predominantly about capturing, consolidating, sustaining, training, and losing empire, so it's quite shocking to encounter that history in its material and mundane form.

The second point is that the country's military institutions have an important domestic role as well as representing the country abroad in terms of organized violence. I learned so much about the country while writing this book, which actually was an indirect result of the Britishness project. I realized that the question of who volunteers and who gets to be recruited into the army is really critical, as it connects with deeper and more complex issues around who belongs and who doesn't. So, for example, in 2009, eight years into the wars in Iraq and Afghanistan, the British National Party (BNP) started pushing the idea that being a soldier fighting for this country (especially in the First and Second

World Wars) was the ultimate test of belonging. They represented the people who fought for this country as being all white and English, Scottish, or Welsh. Plus, they claimed Winston Churchill as a would-be BNP supporter. Even the military leaders balked at this and made a public statement refuting the idea that the British Armed Forces were all white—both now and in the twentieth century—and made it clear that they were as committed to representing the country as a multicultural national organization.

I began this book because I was so angry about Iraq and fed up with feeling so ineffective trotting along to demonstrations and vigils. I wanted to know how politicians like Tony Blair could order the armed forces to go and attack another country without UN support, let alone the support of the electorate. It just so happened that I met somebody who was very senior in the human resources department of the army who told me about the presence of Commonwealth soldiers who were having a hard time because of their status as migrants. I think there was a concern too that, as a British institution, there was something wrong in employing so many "foreigners." So I went to see him about it, and he was very welcoming, and I was able to get permission to write a book. Afterward, I realized that in 2007 there was a crack in the façade of military public relations, and I was able to slip in more or less unnoticed.

The book took me two years to research as I soon realized that I wasn't just looking at Commonwealth soldiers as migrants but had a chance to tell the larger story of institutional reform—and to interrogate the place of the armed forces in society more generally. In terms of racism in the organization itself, imagine going into any authoritarian institution or workplace that has a predominantly white male workforce and a strong sense of both national and regional tradition; that sums it up, really. But how you begin to have a debate about levels of institutional racism in the army, which is such an opaque organization, so off limits to the public is the issue. I am still working on the connections between militarism and racism, as there are all sorts of implications and political avenues to pursue.

Could you elaborate on how you understand the postcolonial?

I find the postcolonial useful for my work on soldiers particularly, although I still go between postcolonial and post-imperial. I see the Commonwealth as being a structural legacy of empire, whereas *postcolonial* captures the way in which the migrant soldiers are affiliated to Britain through cultural and social routes as well as political agreements. I am also interested in how the postcolonial relates to the idea of historical memory.

Another point I would make about the postcolonial, especially in our contemporary times and in the context of war, is that it's absolutely crucial to engage with and have a deep awareness of questions like the following: Which parts of the world are being bombed? Who's doing the bombing? Where is the money coming from? Where are the resources? Where are the scarcities? Where are the complicities? And where is the ignorance being fostered? The geopolitical shape of the world in the current climate is very much defined by European colonialism and the United States, and as postcolonial thinkers, we should never lose sight of that.

Note

1. *Searchlight* is a British magazine founded in 1975 known for its anti-racist and anti-fascist positions.

Selected Key Works

Ware, V. (1991). *Beyond the Pale: White Women, Racism, and History*. London: Verso.

———. (1996). "Defining Forces: 'Race,' Gender and Memories of Empire." In *The Postcolonial Question: Common Skies, Divided Horizons*, edited by I. Chambers and L. Curti, 142–56. London: Routledge.

———. (2007). *Who Cares about Britishness? A Global View of the National Identity Debate*. London: Arcadia.

———. (2010). "Whiteness in the Glare of War: Soldiers, Migrants and Citizenship." *Ethnicities* 10, no. 3: 313–30.

———. (2012). *Military Migrants: Fighting for YOUR Country*. London: Palgrave Macmillan.

Ware, V., and Back, L. (2002). *Out of Whiteness: Color, Politics, and Culture*. London: University of Chicago Press.

CHAPTER 6

Ash Amin

Ash Amin holds the 1931 Chair in Geography at the University of Cambridge, UK.

Could you talk a little about your biography growing up in East Africa and how you first got into the field of geography? What subsequently interested you in questions of race and ethnicity?

I was born in Uganda but lived in Kenya until the age of 16, when in 1971, our family, including my radiographer mother, my pharmacist father, and my elder brother, left for Britain. The transition was exciting but also a shock. I was a boy from a privileged but cruel Kenyan public school catapulted into an East London school, which was refreshingly ordinary but wary of immigrants.

I remember arriving in London on a rainy August evening, ferried in a taxi to digs in the east end, where we lived for some six months before buying a house in Seven Kings. This was at a time of immense racial tension in East London: white xenophobia was raw and denigrating. It was not uncommon to be called names, to be told to go back where you came from, to be pushed around, or to be treated like an undesirable alien—interestingly, less so at school than on the streets. Public culture and public space were decidedly color-coded. This is when I started to see and experience through the skin, though this had never been far from the surface, growing up in a racially conscious and ethnically divided Kenya. After the mid-1970s, race receded into the background in my personal experience, when I went to university, where the milieu was much more cosmopolitan and forgiving.

The story of my disciplinary background is equally contextual. I studied physics, chemistry, and biology at school in preparation to pursue pharmacy at university but did not achieve the required grades. Having never found the sciences to my liking, I ended up starting out in linguistics at university and then switched to Italian studies, a degree I thoroughly enjoyed. After writing a dissertation on the Italian Mezzogiorno, I realized that, much as I liked literary studies, it was a further degree in critical social science that I wanted to pursue—a rather checkered disciplinary journey!

Much to my delight, I was offered a UK Social Science Research Council studentship in 1979 to pursue a doctorate in regional development studies at Reading University. I worked on the class and economic consequences of inward investment into the Italian south during the 1970s. My conceptual preparation involved understanding the political economy of uneven development, the sociology of work, and the spatial consequences of modernization. Building on my PhD, I worked as an economic geographer on problems of regional development in Europe until the mid-1990s, largely from a Marxian perspective.

Then came another disciplinary break, an unshackling if you will, that coincided with my taking up a chair in geography at Durham University in 1995. I had had my fill of working only on the political economy of regional development. Running the risk of amateurish foray into new fields, I decided to work on issues and sensibilities that had malingered in the store cupboard of underexplored interest. These included critical social theory beyond political economy, post-structuralist insight into the situated asymmetries of race, theorization of the city as post-human, open interest in communities of practice as sources of innovation, and framings of belonging and citizenship sensitive to the genealogy of lived material practices. My work in all these areas has continued into the present. My thinking became more sociocultural, and my writing more overtly political.

How did you develop your sense of political consciousness?

I grew up in a Left-leaning family, and the experience of being an immigrant in Britain further sharpened my political antenna, as did my interest in the counter-hegemonic. A particularly significant moment was the year in Italy I spent as part of my first degree. This was in Bologna during the 1977–78 academic year, when the city exploded with the protests and occupations of a student and autonomist movement campaigning for direct and egalitarian democracy in Italy. Although I was on the margins of the mobilization, it certainly shaped my thinking and political orientation. It sparked an awareness of the power but also the fragility of direct democracy, the centrality of affective politics, and the power and obduracy of embedded political institutions. This awareness has been sharpened by subsequent political experiences and observed developments, all prompting further reflection on the fine grain of power and its uneven settlements and on the strengths and trials of subaltern and autonomist politics.

Which thinkers have most influenced you and your work?

As I embarked on my graduate studies, my head was full of Dante, Petrarch, Leopardi, Pavese, and Gramsci, and only Gramsci survived—in a nontrivial way—to help me make sense of my doctoral studies on the Italian south. From literary studies, I was thrown into the deep end of Marxism, laboring through the writing of the founders, but especially Althusser and Poulantzas, to understand state, capital, and class. At the same time, the efflorescence of Marxist thinking in geography in the 1980s helped me locate space and place in the theorization of modernity and its inequalities and oppressions. In turn, and arguably because of my interest in Italy, the thinking of the workerist and autonomist movements, especially ideas relating to the labor process and its social consequences, became immensely important in my attempt to read the Italian south through the lens of the workplace, especially the transformations and possibilities ushered in by the rise of mass production. Here, the writings of Toni Negri, Mario Tronti, Renato Panzieri, and Sergio Bologna were very influential.

Subsequently, a host of critical theorists shaped my thinking, depending on the nature of the work I was pursuing and the questions I was asking: David Harvey, Doreen Massey, and Nigel Thrift on space; diverse writers in heterodox political economy, institutional economics, and cultural economy thinking of the economy as both instituted and culturally assembled; Henri Lefebvre, Georg Simmel, and Walter Benjamin on the simultaneously lived and ordained city; many critical race theorists but especially William du Bois, Franz Fanon, and Stuart Hall on the genealogy of race; and Bruno Latour, William Connolly, John Dewey, and William James on pluriversal politics.

There would be many more thinkers to add, but I suppose the general point is that my thinking has been shaped by ideas across the full range of critical social theory, never in the interest of constructing an elegant, systematic theory of everything but as a set of provisional ideas helping to illuminate particular problems.

Do you think of yourself as postcolonial thinker, and would you situate your work within this genre? And how do you understand postcolonialism? What do you consider as the main contributions of postcolonial thinking?

I have never thought of myself as a postcolonial thinker, primarily because I do not write about the colonial or postcolonial condition: the critique of hegemony, the entanglements of rule and resistance, multiple hybrids of modernity, or developments in Latin America, Africa, and Asia. My field is somewhat distant from that which postcolonial thinking was honed, although my thinking owes a huge debt to the sophisticated ways in which this thinking has freed the mind and knowledge from the vices and seductions of master narratives.

Postcolonial thinking liberated the periphery from the center without reducing either to itself, and it has engaged in historical explanation without crude judgment or generalization, revealing the labor involved in sustaining the colonial and colonizing project, the intersections and distances of hegemony and resistance or tradition and modernity, and the narration of counter-histories. I am drawn to the sensitivity in postcolonial thinking toward the never straightforward machinations of power as well as the intricate crossings of the hegemonic and subaltern, without any loss of clarity regarding the possibility of decentered and parallel modes of being and thinking. The debt of this postcolonial thinking to Gramsci is of obvious appeal to me, and its commitment to re-narrate modernity, nation, power, and subjectivity echoes mine in relation to space, city, race, and political economy.

Could you elaborate on your culturalist reading of the economy in relation to the postcolonial city?

It is an attempt to make more and less of political economy in making sense of the contemporary city. Less can be registered in the way of revealing the economy as cultural practice, such that the economic significance of what elites do, how cities are symbolically characterized or ranked by rating agencies, and how leaders and citizens shape civic culture and social orientations, can be registered. For me, such factors have real bearing on the shape of an urban economy: a city's investment potential, international attractiveness, knowledge dynamics, consumption patterns, and distributional outcomes. No account of urban economic performance, wellbeing, and inclusion can be complete without consideration of such factors normally ignored by mainstream economics and political economy.

Equally, a cultural reading should add to, rather than subtract from, a political economy's attentiveness to power by expanding on the practices involved in maintenance and resistance. If embedded structures and institutions play to particular economic interests, so do everyday routines of organization enjoining technologies, industrial standards, civic norms, and cultural orientations—coalescing around distinctive distributions of economic reward. At the same time, and echoing postcolonial thinking, such attentiveness to the everyday moorings of urban political economy also uncovers the unruly and the hidden in the city—for example, the world of informal economic practices, improvised innovations, and hybrid economic arrangements—such that the political economy of urban order is shown to be much more unstable and temporary than it seems.

You have been a pioneer around the intersection between urbanism and ethnic diversity. Could you elaborate on the relationship between the postcolonial and the urban form—that is, how far do you consider the urban to be a postcolonial phenomenon?

I am not sure if *postcolonial* is the right term to describe the city that interests me, although I accept the gesture toward hybridity. Most cities, in the North and South, have ceased to be territorial entities conforming to singular logics of development (if they ever did). I think of the city as a relationally constituted entity, an assemblage of heterogeneous networks of varying spatial stretch and composition. This makes the city the product of its combinations, juxtapositions, and diversities with many forces—contemporary and historical, local and global—forming city life on the basis of their interactions. As such, the city must also be recognized as thoroughly post-human, and this includes seeing sociality itself as the product of entanglements among humans, the built environment, technologies, and infrastructures, with all these reciprocities thoroughly altering embodied experience and, indeed, the very meaning of what it is to be human in an urban environment.

To take the city to be an open and hybrid assemblage prompts a very important question: Is it legitimate to characterize the city in holistic or essentialist ways, to reduce its multiplicity to a master narrative? My view is that it is not, and the best we might do is develop a provisional and constantly modified reading of urban multiplicity based on "following the networks" as Bruno Latour would argue, attending to the combined effect of the myriad of relational links between humans, institutions, technologies, nature, and matter in the city. This is not an easy task, one that requires a willingness to work through the detail, opacity, and complicatedness of realities that defy abstract diagrams of cause and effect. Thus matters of race, rights, or rewards in the city, for example, cannot be reduced to formulaic explanations or singular logics of composition. I would like to think that this kind of openness is close to the ethos of postcolonial thinking.

Do you think the emphasis on the cultural distracts and diverts political and analytical energies from the problems associated with socioeconomic deprivation?

If we treat the cultural as a realm that is separate from the political, then the answer has to be yes, but not if we take cultural practices to lie at the heart of political economy. As I have already implied, I find it impossible to understand power without understanding the cultural practices of elites, the ways in which orders of justification settle, the habits of bureaucracies and political leaders, and the relationship between public sentiments and corporate or political orientations and strategies. It would be impossible to understand deprivation without taking stock of such cultural practices, because they explain how particular forms of exclusion are justified; how the poor and other marginalized groups are discursively framed; how the cultures of states, markets, and elites reward some and not others; and how the excluded come to see themselves. The cultural is no diversion but the staple of addressing deprivation, although I suspect many sociologists, economists, and political scientists might disagree.

Do you think the concept of the "third world" is still useful in helping people understand the persistence of inequalities that operate at both the global and local level?

Contemporary globalization is producing geographies of connectivity and difference that challenge received wisdom on the world's regional configurations. We can no longer speak of three worlds, each with its own developmental logic and operating as separate territorial blocs. The "second world" fragmented and realigned after the collapse of communism. Powerful cities across the world are forming ties with each other and seceding from their national territories. All national societies are locked into variegated global geographies of connectivity and flow. Neoliberalism is producing sharp inequalities within all nations. New rankings of prosperity are arising that cut across the old blocs, and elites have more to do with their counterparts globally than with local populations. And finally, a series of world-level forces (e.g., transnational corporations and banks, international organizations, global agreements, virtual domains) affect individual cities, regions, and nations in distinctive ways.

Globalization has thoroughly punctured the logic of territorial or scalar organization, of spatial proximity equating to relational proximity. If we use the term as shorthand to denote the rise of network society, any clear-cut distinction between the three worlds disappears. This does not imply a flattening out of the world or the disappearance of stark contrasts between the North and South, even though their geographies have become entangled and more than territorially organized. Though the names and positions of countries within each bloc change, there is also considerable continuity and the persistence of distinctive imbalances between the two blocs. The differentials of wellbeing, inequality, and social justice remain stark, and the ties between North and South over trade, technology, and expertise; ownership of assets; corporate and financial interdependence; and bargaining influence are still stacked against the South.

Witness also how the North, unsettled by globalization, austerity, and the emergent powers, still manages to exercise phenomenal world influence through its control over the media and cultural industries, international organizations and agreements, military and diplomatic relations, and various forms of discursive and symbolic power. These are interventions that continue to ensure returns to the North, maintain Western hegemony, and discursively present the power of the South as anomalous despite the rise of China and India. So a term that acknowledges this hierarchical relationship between North and South, and the stark differences between them, is worth maintaining, including "majority world."

Can you elaborate on the factors that are responsible for the high incidence of inequalities in areas with large concentrations of ethnically marked populations? And how far do you think these urban spaces have become constituted by a racialized grammar of "slums, ghettos, and segregation"?

If things are bad in areas dominated by minority ethnic groups, it is because of poverty, unemployment, degradation, and inadequate services, but it is also because of cultural isolation and social desperation within the areas. Deprivation is the composite of available opportunities, household capabilities, neighborhood qualities, institutional offerings, connections with the rest of the city and beyond, and local cultural and affective orientations. Poor people in poor areas face similar circumstances, suggesting that reducing their prospects to race or ethnicity is far too simple and ultimately inaccurate. Both ethnic majorities and minorities stuck in deprived areas confront the same conditions, and while there may be differences of experience and expectation between them, to resort to a racialized grammar to explain the character of place or social subjectivity is to exclude a host of processes—local and non-local—responsible for inequality and deprivation.

Political and media commentary, sometimes also loose academic work, is prone to ignore this, with its racialized grammar of slums, ghettos, and segregation standing in as received wisdom on the problems faced by the color-coded poor living in poor places. Thus the habits and cultural practices of minorities who have become majorities in an area get cited as the cause of social and spatial decline, fanning endless, irrelevant, and damaging speculation on the religious habits that stand in the way of secularity, the slothfulness of particular ethnic groups, the reluctance to live by the values of mainstream society, the lack of ethnic variety, and whatever else can be dreamed up about the otherness of the other. Before you know it, the grammar of racialization takes on a life of its own, leading to resentment or resignation among the marked communities, policies set on ridding the areas of their ethnic excess, and forms of typecasting that stave off investment, attention, and hope. Deprivation becomes a problem of ethnicity, and its solution, the disciplining of ethnic minorities.

You have examined questions around clusters of civility and the management of ethnic diversity through an engagement with the biopolitical model. In what ways do think the state regulates ethnically marked bodies in the age of the War on Terror?

Very closely indeed. Europe, on the tide of the War on Terror, is going through a time of obsessive scrutiny of strangers and immigrants. Everywhere you look, you find a culture of hyper-vigilance, close up monitoring of the figure of the stranger, and accounts of nation and community based on racialized bodily evaluation. The hyperbole on who does and does not belong has created a situation in which almost every aspect of public and social life is phenotypically tagged, with bodily characteristics standing in as measures of social worth. The result is that Muslims, asylum seekers, dissidents, or the poor all get swept up into the same category as suspicious, undesirable, or ill-fitting subjects. If ever there was a time of filtering nation and belonging through a politics based on judging the qualities of the body, it is now, ill at ease with abstract principles such as freedom, liberty, or solidarity as the measure of community.

In *Land of Strangers*, you examine the complex relationship between majority and minority communities. Could you elaborate on this relationship and the various ways in which ethnically marked communities occupy a "stranger" status? And following from this, what are the main points you would like a reader to take away after reading *Land of Strangers*?

A significant part of *Land of Strangers*—following on from the previous question—is about the punitive biopolitics of our times, feeding on rituals of aversion toward the imagined stranger. This kind of biopolitics is not new, but it is not historically constant, so one question that interests me in the book is why the biopolitical present is so punitive, much more so than even 10 or 15 years ago when multiculturalism and qualified tolerance of the "other" were part of the biopolitical landscape. I find the answer in the jostle between three modes of bodily judgment that shape mainstream public culture and policy practice toward the imagined stranger: state/media framings of nation, community, and their outsides; everyday habits of encounter (physical and virtual) between strangers; and deep-seated vernaculars of racial coding of difference. The always finely poised balance between the latter two modes is regulated by the intensity of the first mode—at least this is my argument.

To elaborate, on the one hand, the multicultural society characterized by everyday mixity develops a kind of "civility of indifference to difference" born out of the co-occupancy of public space and public culture. Here, aversion is tamed, not out of any special regard toward the other, but through an unconscious of cohabitation. On the other hand, there lingers another form of bodily judgment, equally unconscious, based on automatic coding of the other as a racialized, gendered, sexualized body, tapping into deep-rooted legacies of bodily judgment triggered by sensory perceptions, almost always hostile toward the marked stranger. Where this balance settles in public culture depends on the tenor of state-sanctioned biopolitics—until recently, generally tolerant of diversity and difference in Europe and less focused on bodily form as the measure of belonging, but today, exactly the opposite.

Today, with the state, political movements, and the media clamoring to discipline the stranger and link the health of the nation to bodily traits, any shame or reservation attached to racialized bodily judgment has evaporated, with everyday conviviality called into question as majorities are urged to become more vigilant on the street. Without a radical overhaul of biopolitics, of which there are few signs, the escalations of xenophobia and racism that we are witnessing today will continue to mount, normalizing the absurdity that the multicultural society and multiculturalism are incompatible.

During your time in the field, how far do you think the social sciences have been dominated by "white thought," and to what extent do you think postcolonial/ black thinking has been acknowledged in the field?

I am wary of this kind of question because it runs the risk of essentialism and of blunting changes within the academy. Of course, the history of the social sciences is the history of Western canonical thought, with all its white (and gendered) overtones. That said, we cannot deny that feminism, queer theory, postcolonial and post-structuralist thinking, and the albeit slow incorporation of knowledge from the Global South have forced disciplines such as sociology, anthropology, cultural studies, and geography to become much more decentered, cosmopolitan, and hybrid. In this regard, you could say that they have lost some of their whiteness.

There is still a long way to go. For example, there remains the need to open up theory in economics and political science, to raise the profile of non-English writing, and to better the ethnic mix of the academy, but there can be no denying that postcolonial/black thinking has altered thought in the social sciences in very significant ways. How far this is fully acknowledged, and at what expense to canonical thinking, is another question and very much a matter of altering the institutional structure of the academy so that novel practices, theoretical innovations, and new faces can acquire grip and momentum.

Selected Key Works

Amin, A., ed. (1995). *Post-Fordism: A Reader*. London: Wiley-Blackwell.

———. (2012). *Land of Strangers*. London: Polity Press.

Amin, A., and Cohendet, P. (2004). *Architectures of Knowledge*. Oxford: Oxford University Press.

Amin, A., and Thrift, N. (2002). *Cities: Reimagining the Urban*. London: Polity Press.

———, eds. (2005). *The Blackwell Cultural Economy Reader*. Oxford: Blackwell.

———. (2013). *Arts of the Political: New Openings for the Left*. Durham, NC: Duke University Press.

CHAPTER 7

Avtar Brah

A vtar Brah is an emeritus professor of sociology at Birkbeck College, University of London.

How did you first get into the field, and what was the journey that led your work to where it currently is?

Actually, my movement into the field of race, ethnicity, and postcoloniality was partly accidental. I came to Britain for a visit from the United States where I had been a student from Uganda. While in Britain, I became a refugee when Idi Amin, the then president of Uganda, expelled Asians from Uganda in 1972. I had never actually planned to settle in Britain, but suddenly, when I became a refugee, I started looking for a long-term job. It just so happened that there was a post going at Bristol University for a project exploring ethnicity and youth identities, and because I could speak Punjabi and Urdu, I applied for that job and got it. Subsequently, that post, which was initially based on interviewing, developed into a research assistant position and then into research associate. So I walked into this field rather accidentally.

How did you develop your sense of political consciousness?

Well, this really goes back to my teenage years in Uganda. My family was not particularly political, but I had a family friend, a young woman, who introduced me to the work of a Punjabi novelist, Nanak Singh,[1] and a female poet, Amrita Pritam,[2] and these were radical intellectuals. Amrita Pritam was a feminist who, among other things, wrote a very famous poem about the position of women during the Partition of the South Asian subcontinent. Nanak Singh wrote novels that provided a window into the social inequalities that existed within Punjabi society, so he looked at questions of caste, class, and gender; he was very concerned about women's equality. I read a lot of his novels at a very young age and became strongly influenced by his work so that by the time I went to California as an undergraduate, I was already fairly politicized.

When I arrived in America, it was the late 1960s, a period of student radicalism, as well as black politics and the Black Power movement. That experience really galvanized my political sensibilities, and later, when I came to Britain in the early 1970s, the feminist movement was on ascendancy, and I became involved in feminist politics. So, by the time I started working around race and ethnicity, I was already involved in various social movements. In America, there was a lot of racism against African-Americans and other groups, but during my time in America, there were not that many so-called "foreign" students of color at the University of California in Davis, and the racism I experienced in Britain was quite different from the orientalizing exoticism that I experienced in America. Racism really politicizes you, and my experiences carried me forward and further into my political activism.

Which thinkers would you say have most influenced you and your work?

At different stages, different thinkers have influenced my intellectual trajectory. Malcolm X's autobiography was quite formative in my undergraduate days when I was a science student. I did my PhD in Education in the late seventies, and the seventies and the eighties were crucial years when Marxism was a strong intellectual and political presence in the academy. During this period, I was influenced by Marxist thought, particularly by Gramsci's concepts of common sense and hegemony. Gramsci, for me, really offered a way into thinking about race and how common sense becomes racialized. Louis Althusser was also influential, particularly his notion of ideology and interpellation. Those aspects were quite important in the early stages of my work.

Then, of course, there was a lot of internal critique within Marxism, as well as critique from outside, and for someone like me, who was interested in questions of racism and gender alongside class, Marxism was too class-centric. It was very difficult to think about these other axes of differentiation within classical Marxist frameworks, and at that time, there were also many debates among socialist feminists that really helped me develop my thinking. I still find Marxist insights important because you can't really understand capitalist structures without some recourse to Marxism. Moreover, Marxism's commitment to equality and social justice remains compelling. But there were other ways of addressing questions dealing with race, gender, class, and sexuality through which feminist thinkers influenced me greatly. Feminist debates were hugely productive in ushering new intellectual and political agendas.

Who shaped you in terms of postcolonial thinking and black feminism?

Stuart Hall has been a huge influence on me, as were figures such as Edward Said and Foucault, and of course the Black Power movement in the seventies and eighties, when it was quite strong. That's how I first became involved in black feminist politics in Britain: because it was a movement that enabled people to say, let's look at color, not in its chromatist sense but, rather, a political one. It deconstructed chromatist discourses and infused the word *black* with a different kind of meaning, a positive meaning, and if you are subjected to racism on the basis of color, you can be black, irrespective of the hue of your skin color. I was one of the founding members of Southall Black Sisters, and we actually called it Black Sisters back in 1979,[3] although it included African-Caribbean origin black women, as well as women of South Asian heritage.

Post-structuralism has also had a significant impact on my thinking, especially in relation to dealing with questions of subjectivity and identity, though my work on "difference" combines insights from both post-structuralism and materialist analysis. Black and postcolonial feminist debates also influenced me greatly, and I think my work is centrally located within these debates. There is a long list of scholars whose work resonated with my concerns. Figures like Angela Davis, Chandra Talpade Mohanty, Lata Mani, Ruth Frankenberg, Ann Phoenix, Gail Lewis, Nira Yuval-Davis, Floya Anthias, Inderpal Grewal, Caren Kaplan, Donna Haraway, Jacqui Alexander, Gayatri Chakravorty Spivak, Joan W Scott, Catherine Hall, Judith Butler, Irene Gedalof, Nirmal Puwar, Sara Ahmed, and others—their work has played its part in helping me along my intellectual and political journey.

Did your Sikh heritage impact your intellectual trajectory and way of thinking? Is that important to you in terms of the kind of work you engage in?

I think my Sikh heritage has been important in relation to my politics. I think we are lucky that we have a heritage where, at least in theory if not in practice, there is a commitment in Sikhism to gender equality, social justice, class equality, and anti-caste politics. I was strongly influenced by such ideas and notions within Sikh scriptures, although I found that, in reality, that wasn't always the case on the ground. I remember when I was quite young, I used to have arguments with the Sikh priest in our gurdwara (temple) about why what was said in the scriptures was not actually practiced. My Sikh background and my Sikh heritage have both certainly marked my understanding of ethical issues, but I have had a troubled relationship with organized religion. In terms of the relationship between religion and state, I am quite secular, though simultane-ously, I am attracted to spirituality. Of course, questions of religion and secular-ism remain very complex, especially in the contemporary world.

In terms of my research, I have worked on the overall category of Asians in Britain, rather than Sikhs *per se,* although when I was working on my PhD in Southall, a substantial number of my respondents were Sikhs because Southall at the time was predominantly Sikh. But I didn't look at them as Sikhs; rather, I saw them as Asians, and that again has to do with the politics of the time because the category "Asian" actually had a political purchase. It was based on solidarity among different Asian ethnicities. It has since fractured across differ-ent religions and ethnicities.

What were your main aims and goals in *Cartographies of Diaspora*? What did you hope to achieve with this book?

I didn't have a clear-cut plan as to what I wanted to achieve with it; it gradu-ally developed. I had empirical as well as theoretical concerns, and I wanted to produce a book in which theory, empirical work, and political practice came together. So that was one aim. And of course theoretical and political debates around "difference" were pretty central in framing the book.

I think another aim was to address gender because a lot of the work on class, racism, and ethnicity in those days didn't, in general, look at issues of gender, and work on gender didn't much look at issues of race and ethnicity. That, I think, has changed now, but at the time, there were all those exclusions, and so I wanted to produce something that would examine closely questions of gender, class, race and ethnicity, nation and nationalism, sexuality, belonging, identity, and culture. These were some of the themes that attracted my attention, and I worked around them as they developed. I didn't actually have any grandiose idea about *Cartographies of Diaspora* as such. The concept of diaspora provided a grounding and generative theme for these concerns. Diaspora as a concept provided a critique of racialized, essentialized, and nation-centric work.

In much of the literature on South Asians in Britain, readers are still confronted with the recycling of frameworks such as the "culture clash,"[4] yet you broke away from reproducing these tropes. How dominant were these themes during the early period of your research?

Yes, this paradigm of "culture clash" was dominant in the academy and the media as well as in political discourse. There were all kinds of newspaper articles and tele-vision programs that focused on this theme, and I wanted to disrupt such a narra-tive. This was one of the first things I really came to grips with when I was writing my PhD thesis. Questions of culture were of great interest to me, although when I was finishing my PhD thesis in the late seventies, the study of culture was not as yet such a big element in the sociology of race and ethnicity, then commonly termed *race relations*. There were, of course, anthropologists working in this area for whom the concept of culture was central. However, there was a tendency in some of this work to be "culturalist." For me, the work that came out of the Centre for Cultural Studies at Birmingham University was exciting.

On the whole, sociology of "race" in Britain was focused on class; class was the big axis of analysis, and I was among the minority who were foregrounding culture and identity within the field of race and ethnicity. When you analyze culture, there are some very complex issues to be handled, and it wasn't always easy to articulate certain non-culturalist perspectives. Debates on ethnicity and culture were highly politicized and polarized. The important book *Empire Strikes Back*, produced by scholars form the Centre for Cultural Studies, provides a glimpse into the nature of the debate. Overall, it was difficult to challenge and disrupt the dominant paradigms and to think about these issues critically and differently.

What makes your engagement with diaspora distinctive, and why it does play such a big role in the work you do?

My engagement with diaspora emerged out of my research agendas. I was doing research in relation to British South Asian, Caribbean, and white groups, and I was interested in understanding the ways in which social relations between differently marked ethnicities were impacted by questions of migration and globalization: What kind of life-worlds are constituted in and through the encounters between dominant and minoritized ethnicities in postcolonial Britain? What kind of power dynamics would be entailed? What effects would positioning along various social axes have on social relations on the ground? I began to consider how migration might be thought of in new and different ways, and diaspora was a concept that attracted me. It seemed to offer new possibilities for making sense of mobilities in the late twentieth century.

When I went to the University of California at Santa Cruz for a sabbatical (1992–1993), I spent my time thinking about diaspora and how to theorize: on the one hand, movements of people, cultures, commodities, capital, and technologies in critical ways, and on the other, how to tackle the issues of borders, home, and location in relation to movement. So there were global mobilities, but I didn't want to privilege movement at the expense of questions of belonging and questions of "staying put." I started exploring these concerns through the concept of diaspora and diaspora space and attempted to differentiate between diaspora as a concept and diaspora as a historical movement. I also brought into play the relationship between time and space in the formation of diasporic identities. I am always grappling with and trying to explore non-essentialist ways of constructing politics, which is a difficult but essential task. So the concept of diaspora, diaspora space, and intersectionality—of location and borders, changing temporalities and spatialities—all came together in my work on diaspora.

You also talk about your East African–Asian background in *Cartographies of Diaspora*. How does your African experience interact and interplay with the British Asian experience?

Well, the East African–Asian experience is very important in my life trajectory. Uganda was home throughout my childhood and teenage years. It was an experience of racial and economic privilege compared to that of black Africans, and it made me very uneasy. I was already reading things about inequality, so although I didn't know theories about colonialism as a system, I could see that there were inequalities in Ugandan society, particularly in relation to the Africans and the way in which the society was divided into white people at the top, Asians in the middle, and then Africans at the bottom. A growing understanding of these aspects of society was an essential element in my politicization. I saw myself as a Ugandan of Asian heritage, and my relationship to India, the place of my birth, has always been marked by this.

Coming to England was such a different situation because, among other things, it was an encounter with Asians from the subcontinent with which I didn't have much previous experience. I had visited India once or twice as a child, but I didn't actually have any kind of long-standing experiences with Indians from the subcontinent. East African–Asian culture and social life had its own specificity. In time, I found myself becoming part of a broader British Asian scene, and this was a new diasporic reality.

Could you elaborate on your specific use of intersectionality? And to what extent do you think it is an important category for the social sciences?

Understanding intersectional processes is important, although we didn't use the term *intersectionality* until the late eighties and the nineties. I became engaged with the idea through feminist debates around the category of "woman." These debates challenged the notion that "woman" could be addressed as a homogeneous category. We argued that it was not possible to talk about "woman" in the singular as there were many different groups of women. So questions of intersectionality—of race, class, gender, sexuality, age, disability, and so on—are essential in thinking through the multiplicity of power dynamics in and through which differentiated bodies are produced.

I do not see these axes of differentiation as identity categories but, rather, as modalities of power implicated in the historically specific processes—economic, political, and cultural—that underpin the constitution of what we name as a specific category or as a specific identity. Intersectionality is not, in my view, a grid on which you can map different subject positions. It might more appropriately be construed as a continually shifting, interchanging, kaleidoscopic constellation of multiple flows of power.

Cartographies of Diaspora is an attempt to try to think about these different processes of power. Intersectionality threads throughout *Cartographies of Diaspora*. The book is less about theorizing intersectionality than about one way of doing intersectionality. Intersectional analysis, in my view, can be done in many different ways, depending on the nature of the problematic to be addressed and the disciplinary analytical tools at hand. I would suggest that there is no single, overarching research method that is relevant to all situations. I like Nirmal Puwar's designation of intersectionality as "analytic sensibility." Intersectionality has become a very significant feature of analysis within feminism, though probably not so much outside feminism. Within feminism there are a number of critiques of the concept of intersectionality, some of which are productive and others not. It remains a contested terrain.

Post-structuralism has clearly been influential to you and your work. What do you think post-structuralist thought offers, and why do you think those of us exploring postcolonial identities are increasingly drawn to ideas of post-structuralism?

Stuart Hall has been especially influential in Britain in this turn to post-structuralism. This theoretical, political, and analytical perspective is attractive because it raises certain important questions that, in part, relate to the debates on intersectionality in that it actually critiques the power regimes through which subjects and bodies are produced and differently marked. The "European subject" has often been seen as the center of the universe, and I think post-structuralism puts forward a convincing critique of this idea, and so, for postcolonial thinkers, it is really quite important.

Foucault's notion of discourse has been rather productive in this regard and allows us to rethink in creative ways the play of power and constellation of identifications, as has been Derrida's concept of *différance*. I found post-structuralist ideas and concepts helpful in enabling me to analyze certain problematics. Located as I am within feminist politics and, more specifically, within black feminist politics, I realize that some feminists do not favor post-structuralist perspectives, partly because people tend to assume that such an approach might be apolitical. But I would say that it is not necessarily the case. To critique particular hegemonic discursive practices that underpin subject and meaning formation is not to undermine the importance of the subject or the body. But I respect their reservations.

I am eclectic, and I use ideas that I find are helpful in analyzing the issue at hand. So I have found post-structuralism quite productive in many ways, but I also know that there are questions raised from within Marxism, for instance, and other materialist feminist perspectives that are crucially important to address, especially the ones about local and global inequities and inequalities. And so I don't want to place my analysis within just one theoretical framework. I prefer to draw on and integrate the range of different subject disciplines, theoretical frameworks, and political movements to help me think through the various concerns that have come to inform my work.

Feminism is central to your work and activism. How do you think black and/or postcolonial feminism challenges and unsettles conventional white feminist thought?

I think this is a very important question. Just to give you a terminological context—postcolonial feminism and black feminism, particularly in America, concluded that it was perhaps better to use the term *women of color* rather than *black* to refer to the coalition of different categories of non-white women. Here in the UK, we used the term *black* to refer to women with African, Caribbean, South Asian, and other postcolonial racialized heritage. Subsequently, these politics fractured somewhat along different ethnicities. I understand that there are currently efforts being made by a younger generation of feminists to revive politics around the signifier *black* along lines developed during the seventies, eighties, and nineties. I watch these developments with great interest, although I have started using the term *women of color*.

I think both postcolonial and black feminism offers us a way of thinking not only about racism, which is very important, but also about the global power relations. Black feminism and postcolonial feminism critique the global system as a way of looking at structures of authority and power that continue to govern unequal relations between countries and between regional blocks. This type of feminism plays a very important role in that sense: they foreground and challenge the machinations of neo-imperialisms that stalk the globe today. This is not to say that these questions are not important to white feminist thought, which is not homogeneous at all. Many white scholars tackle these issues, but black and white subjects and subjectivities are different and differentially positioned within and across racialized networks of power. Everyday social experiences are different, and these differences matter.

In the earlier years, there were a lot of debates around the question of white feminism and black feminism. Hazel Carby's influential article "White Woman Listen!" and the Special Issue 17 of the British journal *Feminist Review* epitomize central tenets of this debate. There were also questions of how racism was understood and how the black experience was understood and theorized. So all those issues were discussed and debated, and the question of subjectivity then became very important, the argument being that racism was not simply just an epistemological feature; rather, there is a very deep psychic investment in particular ways of *being* and particular ways of relating to the world. Recognition of this is important to the politics of coalition and solidarity across ethnicities, religious groups, and class fractions.

When you were first in the academy, was there a space for black thinkers to engage within and unsettle that space?

It was difficult for us; it was a struggle to introduce different ways of thinking about issues of race, ethnicity, and feminism, especially in the field of race relations. Leaving aside individuals such as Stuart Hall, the most support I got was from feminists. Overall, we had a huge struggle initially to foreground the ways in which racism was deeply implicated in all forms of social relations. A smile, a look—those things can convey a lot of racialized sensibilities and meanings, so it was difficult; yes, definitely. It was difficult to construct certain types of courses. It has been, and I believe to an extent continues to be, a struggle about the very nature of knowledge produced in our universities.

On the whole, the hegemony of white thought continues to persist in the social sciences, though some positive changes have undoubtedly taken place, not least that there are more scholars of color now in the academy and that the course content has shifted in some universities. We were able to introduce some important curricular changes at Birkbeck College, and I know colleagues who have done the same in other universities.

What do you hope to see developing in the social sciences around questions of race, ethnicity, and the postcolonial?

Sometimes I worry whether these areas or topics might disappear from the curriculum, so I would like to see the study of these subjects continue in schools and universities, partly as a way of challenging the idea that we are somehow already "post-racial," if by this there is a suggestion that we no longer have racism. We do not as yet, unfortunately, live in a post-racial world, though we may hope for post-racial/non-racial futures.

I would also like to see teaching around race and ethnicity to be approached differently than it is. These issues should be integrated across the range of courses and modules offered, although it is still important to look at specific topics and themes separately and in depth. So, for example, if you are doing a course on gender, it should be axiomatic that you integrate throughout the entire course the experiences and contributions of women and men of color and how discourses of race have marked Western knowledge formations. But on the other hand, it is important to maintain the specialist study of such subjects. These issues can no longer be neglected in the social sciences. There is a major imperative to address questions of postcoloniality, neo-coloniality, and new imperialisms if we are to have better worlds.

Do you consider yourself to be a postcolonial thinker, and what do you think has been your main contribution to the field?

I've never actually thought about that. My work is quite eclectic, as I said earlier, and I'm certainly looking at questions of postcoloniality as well as new colonialisms and new imperialisms in the current global order, so I suspect that my work could be situated within postcolonial studies. My particular way of thinking about feminism, and questions of diaspora and difference, marks my contribution; these are the three main areas, and within these, there are a specific set of critiques relating to postcolonialism, ethnicity, and race, which I hope have made some difference.

Notes

1. Nanak Singh (1897–1971) was a prolific Punjabi poet, novelist, and essayist whose work was critical of British colonial rule in India. Key texts include *Pavitar Paapi* (Saintly Sinner; 1942) and *Chitta Lahu* (White Blood; 1932).

2. Amrita Pritam (1919–2005) was a prominent Punjabi poet and novelist. Her important poem on partition is titled *Aj Aakhaan Waris Shah Nu* (Today I Invoke Waris Shah). Other works of significance include her novel *Pinjar* (The Skeleton; 1950).

3. Southall Black Sisters (SBS) was established in 1979 and based in Southall, London. It is a non-profit black organization, and its politics remain committed to race and gender equality.

4. The belief that South Asians in Britain have to navigate between two distinct cultural formations and this navigation informs and explains much of their behavior and outlook. Cultural conflict then is inscribed in the body and circumstances of South Asian settlers and is continuously mobilized to give an account of their experiences (Anwar 1998; Sian 2013).

Selected Key Works

Brah, A. (1993). "Re-framing Europe: Engendered Racisms, Ethnicities, and Nationalisms in Contemporary Western Europe." *Feminist Review* 45: 9–28.

————. (1996). *Cartographies of Diaspora: Contesting Identities; Hybridity and Its Discontents: Politics, Science, Culture.* London: Routledge.

————. (1999). "The Scent of Memory: Strangers, Our Own, and Others." *Feminist Review* 61: 4–26.

————. (2002). "Global Mobilities, Local Predicaments: Globalisation and the Critical Imagination." *Feminist Review* 70: 30–45.

————. (2003). "Diaspora, Border and Transnational Identities." In *Feminist Postcolonial Theory: A Reader*, edited by R. Lewis and S. Mills, 613–34. Edinburgh: Edinburgh University Press.

Brah, A., and Coombes, A., eds. (2000). *Hybridity and Its Discontents: Politics, Science, Culture.* London: Routledge.

Brah, A., and Phoenix, A. (2004). "Ain't I a Woman? Revisiting Intersectionality." *Journal of International Women Studies* 5, no. 3: 75–86.

CHAPTER 8

Howard Winant

Howard Winant is a professor of sociology at the University of California, Santa Barbara.

How did you first get into the field of race and ethnicity, and how was this linked to the development of your political consciousness?

My involvement with these issues really goes back to my childhood experiences. I was born in New York in 1946. My parents were Jewish refugees from Hitler and had just made it out as teenagers. They had not themselves been in the camps, but they had lost family members. They were progressive, democratic, and tolerant liberals in the US sense of that term: center-left. The legacy of Nazism was a big part of my childhood. We lived in a lower middle-class refugee community, and many people I knew had the tattoos on their arms, so I was always around Auschwitz and Belsen survivors as a child.

When I was growing up, it was the time of McCarthyism and the Cold War, a reactionary period. Eventually, we moved to the suburbs; we were part of the "white flight" from the cities. So a racial dimension was very much a part of my experience, in positive ways (I had black and immigrant friends) and negative ways (my parents were fearful of the right wing). So all those things together I think really helped give me an early sensitivity to race and racism issues.

Then there was the movement, the civil rights movement. From the early 1960s, when I was still a kid, I was involved in some of the demonstrations and protests. This came from liberal Jewish influences and from having black friends more than through my parents. They were quite nervous about getting "out there" politically, having seen pretty bad things happen in Europe. Over time, I became more involved in the civil rights movement, a bit in high school and certainly in college with all the black struggles (and anti-war mobilizations) that were taking place at the time. I did not go south as many I knew did, but

I was active in other ways. I think all these early experiences were quite consciousness raising and formative. I finally figured out that race was all around me when I was at university. You can see white privilege there; kids of color understand that a lot earlier than I did.

What thinkers have been most influential to your work?

I was a new leftist. I resonated with Marcuse, and I really learned my Marxism from the Frankfurt School, C. Wright Mills, and other Western Marxist thinkers. I actually studied in a very peripheral way with Marcuse as both an undergraduate and a graduate student. I had opportunities to take courses with him and got the chance to know him a little. He had students who were much more central than I was, but he was particularly influential for me. Marcuse was rather unique among the Western Marxists because of his openness to the black movement. I think Angela Davis played a big role in that.

I didn't really encounter W. E. B. Du Bois in a serious way until much later on. Now, however, I think of myself as very much situated within the Du Boisian tradition, but when I was younger, I really only knew Du Bois through *Souls of Black Folk*. I still see that book as an absolute treasure, an amazingly crafted piece of work. (Don't get me started on *Souls*; I could go on for hours about Du Bois!) But it was only quite a bit later on in my life that I really came to understand the depth and breadth of Du Bois's contribution, his masterpiece *Black Reconstruction in America* in particular, but so much of his other work as well.

I was a graduate student and an anti-racist activist, so I looked to the work that was taking place in sociology and philosophy around race, which at the time was a burgeoning field. The journals *Telos* and *Radical America* were important to me, and I was a member of the editorial collective of the new left journal *Socialist Review*. My learning and scholarship were therefore very much located within a Marxian context, and that remains influential to my thought and work today.

Could you talk a little about how your co-authored book *Racial Formation in the United States* emerged and what the main aims that you'd hoped to achieve at the time were?

This book is something that my co-author Michael Omi and I have recently returned to. It has been more than 25 years now since we wrote that book; it really came out of the age of Reagan, and it reflected the resurgence of racism—"coded" as anti-welfare statism, "law and order" politics—during the anti-Reagan years. We wrote the book as graduate students. It took initial form in a series of articles that we published in *Socialist Review* that was quite influential for a while.

More than anything else, we wrote the book because we were dissatisfied with our own movement and its orientation. Although new left or neo-Marxist politics and understandings were great advances in the United States in many ways, with their stress on "participatory democracy" and so on in relation to issues surrounding racism, they were inadequate. This was ironic because the new left owed its existence to the black movement as much as it did to Western Marxism. So we were unhappy with the sort of analysis that reduced race to a product of the indirect rule of capital, to the divide-and-conquer strategies of the capitalist class. These ideas were deeply connected to the Communist Party and other left organizations, which were largely focused on the notion of "black and white unite and fight." Racism, in their understanding, was the bosses' tool to divide the workers. In other words, race consciousness was "false consciousness," drawing attention away from the "real issue" of class. We saw this as woefully inadequate to not only everyday struggles against racism, which were ubiquitous and could hardly be dismissed as unimportant, but also a deeper understanding of the United States as a country built on conquest and slavery as well as democracy and revolution.

And then there were other variants of that kind of reductionism or determinism that we also didn't like. For example, there was a very strong ethnicity-based reductionism too, a "moderate" and gradualist anti-racism that equated race with ethnicity and saw blacks as equivalent to European immigrants. There were many famous articles and books about this at the time: "The Negro Today Is Like the Immigrant of Yesterday" was the title of an article by Irving Kristol (1972), the founder of the so-called neoconservative political current that helped shape Reaganism. This type of thinking is still influential. Underlying racial "moderation" is a great fear that the comfortable feel, consciously or unconsciously—a fear of radical democracy and the full inclusion of people of color in the United States. White supremacy is utterly fundamental. Since the country is moving inexorably toward a "majority-minority" demographic profile (California is already there, as are many other areas), the concept of "the American people" is being drained of its implicit whiteness. Yet it remains almost impossible to imagine the United States as a non-white country.

Of course, back in the day, Omi and I were not yet in touch with these trends. What we really wanted to do was critique class reductionisms, ethnicity theories, simplistic nationalisms, and calls for "moderation" because we felt they implied that racial democracy had been achieved or could be achieved within the US system of liberal (now neoliberal) capitalism and that it could somehow coexist with worldwide empire.

We were also critical of nationalism—not just US nationalism, for its implicit white racialism, but also black and brown and yellow and red nationalisms (to use the always absurd color categories). Of course, we felt solidarity with such movements as the Black Panthers and the American Indian movement, but in the United States, black people, Latinos, Asian Americans, and Indians need allies: blacks are 12 percent of the population, Latinos about 16 percent, and Asian Americas about 7 percent. We were concerned about the narrowness of radical nationalisms and about their exclusionist tendencies.

Our main concern back then was to challenge class, ethnicity, and nation-based reductionisms of race. We argued against the temptation of reducing race to something else. The book had what we (at least) thought was an elegant structure: first, to critique the existing paradigms of race as reductionist; then to offer our own account of racial formation; and then to apply our account to the post–World War II trajectory of racial politics, the rise of anti-racist movements, and then their containment by incorporation and rearticulation (as well as repression). Our aim was really to question, in a deep and critical way, what was meant by, and what constituted, racial formation in the United States. To do this, we had to dispense with the three main reductionist paradigms of race and recognize it as a central feature of modernity.

In my later work, *The World Is a Ghetto,* I have tried to offer a broader global account of the postwar trajectory of racial politics. There, I argue that the United States was just one case, although a large one, of a worldwide racial "rupture" that began with World War II and ended more or less with the downfall of the apartheid system in 1994. I attempt a comparative historical sociology of race, looking mainly at the United States, Western Europe, South Africa, and Brazil, and I also provide a genealogy of race that links it to the rise of the "modern world-system" (Wallerstein 2004).

In *Racial Formations,* you have a particular reading of the significance of race and racism in society that owes a lot to the Gramscian paradigm, particularly the notion of hegemony. How do you understand Gramsci's significance in analyzing contemporary American society?

I'm an old fossil who really likes Gramsci. I'm still quite a committed Gramscian. I think his understanding of fascism and the way in which capitalist states manage oppression and domination are elements that remain very central for us and for politics today. In the book, we were concerned with the cyclical, trajectorial notion of politics that Gramsci describes as "the life of the state." He characterizes this as a process of "formation and overcoming of unstable equilibria." We saw this state-society confrontation, this "movement versus state" dynamic, in US racial politics. So these cycles of political confrontation and hegemonic absorption were really important for the book in that sense.

Since the onset of the trajectory the book discusses—that is, the post–World War II movement upsurge and subsequent containment—it has not been possible to craft or sustain a new racial hegemony in the United States. While there has been a great deal of incorporation, it is no longer possible to undo "identity politics," not only in respect to race, but also in regard to gender, sexuality, disability, and other matters as well. This is the real achievement of the black movement: the "politicization of the social." However, it is not without its contradictions. There are also rearticulated, right-wing identity politics focused on possessive individualism, exclusionary rights, the "right to life," and so on.

The closest thing we have in contemporary America to a new racial hegemony is this "color-blind" regime that we are dealing with now, but it's really hard to consolidate color-blindness in the United States. The United States has a number of contradictions in its relationship to race. For example, the state claims to be post-racial and color-blind, and then at the same time, it practices a very overt form of racialization through repression and racial jurisprudence. So what's our story about race? The current hegemonic story says that it used to be a terrible division in society but that now it's been overcome. But I think that this story is really very hard to swallow, in just about every way.

What do you think the significance of race is in the formation and maintenance of the American Republic? In other words, why does race matter so much in America?

It's hard to understand the United States without acknowledging the centrality of the race concept, and of racial practices and structures of various kinds, in every sphere of life. The country is the original anti-colonial society, yet it was based from before its beginnings on settler colonialism and African slavery. The United States likes to imagine itself as this pioneering democracy; the first modern anti-colonial revolution; life, liberty and the pursuit of happiness; enlightenment conceptions of popular sovereignty; and so on and so forth. It's quite interesting to look at the Declaration of Independence and the Constitution of the United States—the founding documents. Look how Indians, the "savage" Indians, are portrayed and how slavery is dealt with there. Slavery is everywhere in the US Constitution, but it's never explicitly mentioned; it's always euphemized. Roughly half the "founding fathers" (great patriarchal term, that) were slave masters. So the incomplete nature of this democracy, the incomplete nature of the foundational structure; and the Constitution of the country are all based in race.

Just on the legal and jurisprudential level, the effort to recognize and to manage race is fundamental. But it goes way beyond and way beneath that too, to the political and the economic. The White House was built by enslaved black hands; the Capitol building as well. More than that, the entire economy was built by slavery and the slave trade. The slave trade is its very foundation! It's not just the cotton; it's also the shipbuilding and the cooperage, the trading, the mercantile classes, and so on. So race has always been pretty fundamental to America. And that's just black people. We haven't talked yet about land seizures or territorial expansion and their early colonial venture, or about Asian and Latin American immigration (and Irish immigration too—the Irish used to be a race in the United States). So race is what America is built on; it's inscribed in the law, the economy, the political system, and the national culture—it's everywhere. Du Bois made all these points long ago.

How do you understand racism in relation to colonialism?

The imperial enterprise is built on systems of domination and exploitation that we would now label as racist (sexist too; see Ann Stoler 2002 on this). I think the whole edifice of the modern world-system has a fundamental racial dimension. Supposedly, we're postcolonial now, but in practical terms, colonialism is not really over; there are new forms of colonialism and imperialism to be found all over the globe. What is Palestine? What is Bangladesh? Of course, there is no British flag flying in Lagos or Nairobi or Singapore or wherever we want to talk about, but on the other hand, the Global South and much of the Global East are still, in some sense, giant plantations from which multinational and state-based corporations still extract resources from and recruit labor for exploitative purposes. The enforcement of those purposes is every bit as brutal as it was in the officially colonial years. From Rosa Luxemburg to Giovanni Arrighi, we have a steady analysis of how the periphery (both external and internal, so to speak) is forced to subsidize the core. So how postcolonial or post-imperial can we really say the world is today, in the twenty-first century?

A recent figure I saw was that the United States has 144 military bases in other countries. They are not all labeled as bases; many of them have euphemistic names (e.g., missions, supply centers, forward operating posts), but bases is what they are. So a US military presence can be seen almost everywhere, and the imperial metropole maintains order everywhere, or at least tries to do so, anyway. In the modern world, empire is always a racial regime.

How do you think the idea of the post-racial has impacted studies in race and ethnicity?

After World War II, we see the beginnings of arguments for non-racialism, color-blindness, and post-raciality. Before World War II, in large measure, those critiques came only from outside the system, from dark voices. During and after World War II, a tremendous racial transformation, a worldwide racial "break" occurred, overdetermined by many forces: the war's general democratic ideals; the vast demographic shifts it engendered; the arming of people of color throughout Asia, Africa, and the Americas (e.g., in Alabama); and the competition of the Cold War that took place in those same places. Given our recent racial history, and given the vast aspirations that persist across the world for democratic and egalitarian change and for citizenship and cultural recognition, there's no reason to think that race could ever be consigned to some kind of less significant status. This is perhaps the most important subject of our anti-racist work today. We have to confront and reconfigure these concepts of "post-racism," "post-racialism," and "color-blindness."

I mean, *color-blindness* is a horrible term; it's really a neologistic term that goes back to a particular famous Supreme Court decision in the United States in 1896: the *Plessy v. Ferguson* case, which enunciated the principle of "separate but equal" as a supposed "solution" to the "problem" of all these now-emancipated black people wanting freedom and equality. I repudiate the term *color-blindness*; not only is it really disparaging, but it's doubly misleading. You can't be "blind" to race, at least not all the time; and race really isn't about "color" either. Sure, race is phenomic, but it's also performative. That's what we mean by the "social construction" of race.

Underlying the post-racial or color-blindness concept is the central idea that it is necessary to consolidate the idea that race is a thing of the past but that, today, people are suddenly and finally individuals. And as a result, we don't see race anymore. My students often say those things to me, mostly my white students: "I don't see race. A person is just a person to me; everyone is an individual." The obvious practical consequences of this are the ratification of the racial inequalities and injustices that they are thus claiming to have transcended.

This constitutes an ongoing dilemma for us in the field. These statements are superficially appealing to the kind of low-calorie anti-racism on some level. And at the same time, "I don't see color" also means "I don't have to deal with it; I don't have to worry about that; and in fact, I don't have to consider my neighborhood or my own proclivities in social life or who my friends are, who I employ, or who I work side-by-side with because I don't see any of that." Even on an academic level, we see versions of this, often argued by people who actually see themselves as profoundly anti-racist, and you hear them saying, "Let's get beyond this stuff and get back to class, or biopower, or homophobia," or something like that.

How would you explain the significance of civil rights reform in the American landscape?

Civil rights reforms were a very important achievement of mass political action. They also had fundamental cultural and economic consequences. They resulted in a set of political accommodations that were achieved in the racial state, reforms that were transformative but, at best, partial and deeply unstable. Civil rights reform permitted discriminatory practices to operate in new, more modern, and more disguised versions. The limited, negotiated character of civil rights reform was critiqued from the outset by black radicals such as Malcolm X and also, in a somewhat different way, by Martin Luther King Jr.

In practice, civil rights remain compromised, especially for the great majority of people of color in the United States. Black and brown elites, however, have made substantial gains during the post–civil rights era. This is very important for the racial regime: that the "black bourgeoisie," as E. Franklin Frazier called it (and today the Latino bourgeoisie as well), be maintained as loyal as the voices for and tokens of reform and racial democracy. But the larger structures of racism remain in place; pick any social indicator you wish—wealth/income inequality, mortality/morbidity, economic returns to education, indices of dissimilarity in residence—and you will find that little has changed.

In some areas, like incarceration and police profiling, and in wealth distribution by race in the aftermath of the 2008 economic crash, structural racism has dramatically increased. Repression of all types is on the rise; this is not only a racial problem, though it is inordinately so. Surveillance and electoral disenfranchisement are particularly worrisome. In many ways, beneath a certain socioeconomic level—at the strata where most blacks and browns live (and quite a few whites too)—the United States is a police state of a "soft" kind. There are millions of fugitives, most of them people of color: 12 million undocumented people; about 2.5 million incarcerated; and about 5 million on probation or parole. A huge ex-felon class, disproportionately black, is excluded from most employment, from the franchise, and from such welfare state benefits as still remain. This does not even begin to address the informal economy.

The outcome of this is that, in a very deeply structured way, civil rights are increasingly compromised, or nearly non-existent, in practice. This is the country that dares to present itself as a model of color-blind democracy!

What do you hope to see emerging from the new generation of scholars engaging with questions around race, ethnicity, and the postcolonial in the social sciences?

The social sciences have always had a very important role in both fortifying and containing political challenges. In the US context, race has always been more central than class in the social sciences. It is out of racial upheavals that we get the modern social sciences in the United States, in the same way that it's out of class upheavals that we get the social sciences in Europe. European sociology (e.g., Weber, Durkheim, Simmel) emerged as a response to class struggle and a riposte to Marx. American sociology (e.g., Social Darwinists, the Chicago

School, Parsons) came out of slavery, abolition, and mass immigration, so it has always had a racial subtext.

I think, in the social sciences, across such disciplines as economics, political science, and anthropology, as well as in sociology, we are still helping the state manage structural racism. For example, sweatshops and *maquiladoras* are defended as entry points to the industrial working class for the peasantries of the world. Military interventions in the Global South and East are supported as the perhaps unpleasant but necessary defense of civilization against the "barbarians at the gates." The racial genealogy of these social science disciplines needs to be de-rooted and re-rooted as a way to overcome their particular ways of thinking, and particularly their allegiances to the state, capital, and white supremacy. As scholars in these fields, we really have to extend and deepen our theoretical and intellectual capacities. Let's return to the eleventh thesis on Feuerbach. Fundamentally, we need to realize that the invention of racial meaning and the creation and understanding of race comes from everyday life and self-reflexivity.

Selected Key Works

Winant, H. (1994). *Racial Conditions: Politics, Theory, Comparisons.* Minneapolis, MN: University of Minnesota Press.

———. (2002). *The World Is a Ghetto: Race and Democracy Since World War II.* New York: Basic Books.

———. (2004). *The New Politics of Race: Globalism, Difference, Justice.* Minneapolis, MN: University of Minnesota Press.

———. (2006). "Race and Racism: Toward a Global Future." *Ethnic and Racial Studies* 29, no. 5: 986–1003.

Winant, H., and Omi, M. (2014). *Racial Formation in the United States.* New York: Routledge. First published in 1986.

CHAPTER 9

Heidi Mirza

Heidi Safia Mirza is a professor of race, faith, and culture at Goldsmith's College, University of London.

Could you talk a little about your biography and how you first got into the field of education as well as what interested you around questions of race, ethnicity, and postcolonial feminism?

I guess it all came from the heart, really, and from very personal experiences. I have this theory that nobody does what they do by accident; it's like our path in life is driven by a deep need to find answers to our burning questions. One of the things about academia is that we can hide our search behind grand theories, but really, my academic work is about my own identity and then using theory to find out how it fits in to the wider picture. How this fits into my own life is that I grew up in Trinidad in the Caribbean. I was actually born in Britain but as a very young child in the 1960s moved with my parents and was brought up in Trinidad. My father is Indo-Caribbean, and my mum is Austrian—hence why I am named Heidi! So being of mixed-race heritage triggered many identity issues, both growing up in Trinidad and when we came back to Britain.

When I was 16, we came back to England in 1973, and it was a time of incredible overt racial expression on the streets. There was the massive clash between the anti-Nazi league and the National Front. Brixton was really at the center of a lot of this strife, and it was the place I went to school. So it was a huge shock for me—it was like being slapped in the face—because I had grown up in rural Trinidad and went to a secondary school that my grandmother had founded, so it was really, I suppose, a relatively sheltered experience. You don't question your right to exist, but that is what happens when you become a racialized "other."

I remember my first encounter with school in the UK: I had a very strong Trinidadian accent, and the school actually didn't want to let me go there because they didn't understand me and thought the only way I had passed all the entry exams was by cheating. They thought I couldn't possibly be doing that well because I came from Trinidad—because, of course, all the Caribbean children at the time were being put into the "educationally sub-normal" (ESN) schools. So when I did get into the school, on my first day, I remember there was this gang of white girls who made monkey noises and threw peanuts at me, and I remember thinking it was incredible. I just didn't get it because I had a really strong sense of being me; growing up in the Caribbean gave me a strong sense of centeredness.

I came from a family of strong Caribbean women. My grandmother taught Sunday school, and my aunts and cousins were teachers, so I had a sense from early on that education was a "calling." My grandparents were indentured and converted by Canadian missionaries, and my grandpa was of the first local people to be a minister in the Presbyterian Church. So they were well known; my father had a good job in the oil fields. Then in the UK, I found myself in a place where I was considered nothing, a nobody, so it was a huge transition in terms of my personal journey and then how I had to learn to cope with that. By the time I left, three or four years down the road, I had learned to speak the "queen's English," and this experience really signaled my move from one world to another world. The way that collides in your personal experience is difficult, but I wouldn't be me without it.

I went to the University of East Anglia in 1977, and again, this was another huge life changing experience. It was the time of the anti-apartheid movements in South Africa, and Zimbabwe was just becoming independent of Rhodesia, so there were many students from the armed struggles in Africa. I was doing development studies and "third-world development," which at that time was a way to think about how to change the world. I found myself in this world of freedom fighters, radical thinkers, and people from the trade union movements, and we were talking about and engaging with socialism. In the 1970s, there was the anti-Western uprising in Iran led by the Ayatollah Khomeini, and then there was the Palestinian struggle, so there was so much going on in terms of various postcolonial upheavals in the world, and there was a sense of finding an anti-imperialist voice where we could actually say, "These are our movements for self-determination!"

Perhaps one of the most interesting things at East Anglia was that any student of color, even those who were British born, were all put in the same halls of residence in the same building; we were literally separated off, so there were these "ghetto" blocks for only black and ethnicized students. But that's how I met my husband: he was from Pakistan, we got married in my first year, and I had my daughter soon after my final exams. So it was quite an interesting space, and even though it was a very male world and white institution, at the same time, there was this bubble of students with these common interests. So both my earlier and my later experiences really shaped and cultivated my interests around education, race, ethnicity, and feminism.

How did you develop your sense of political consciousness?

When I was about 13, there was a military coup in Trinidad,[1] and it was a Black Power coup. (It was the time of Angela Davis and the Black Panthers in the United States.) I remember we were under curfew; we couldn't go out at all. There was a real sense of danger but, at the same time, also excitement, as there were these armed guerrillas hiding in the hills and all around us in the bush. We would listen to snippets on the radio or gather around the black-and-white television we shared, and I just remember this realization that there was another world out there where a lot of things were going on, there was a lot of turmoil, but there was also this other voice for black liberation. Things were not right with the world, so even though we lived a relatively sheltered life, at the same time, there was this other tumultuous happening in the Unites States. This, for me, was really the beginning of my politicization or conscious awareness.

My father was one of the first nationals to return post-independence to Trinidad. In 1963, he came back to work in what became a nationalized oil industry, and I saw his personal struggles working with both British and American global corporations and how he was positioned as a black man. We lived on expat camps in the bush—a bit like *Out of Africa*! They were white-only enclaves, and with my father being one of the first nationals married to a white woman, we were inserted into this world, so I saw that division and separation of color as a young child. So, even though we were in a "black" country, there were still these enclaves of whiteness that certainly contributed to my sense of black politics.

Another turning point in my politicization was during my time in university. As I mentioned previously, it was the time of Ayatollah Khomeini, and during this period, I converted to Islam in my first year of university. This really was a huge transition for me because I went from being a Christian Caribbean girl to becoming a Muslim, wearing the Hijab and dressing in a conservative way. The transition was not just a psychological or physical shift but also a spiritual and intellectual journey. Converting to Islam really gave me my voice as a feminist, and it was the time when I felt the most in control of all that had happened to me in my life, all my sexualized and racialized experiences from primary school right through to coming to university; it really empowered me. What I learned was the sense that, by covering myself, I wasn't seen simply as a woman but, rather, that I was seen first and foremost for my intellect—not for my sex or for my gender, but as a person—and that was a major step in the direction of my feminist journey. In the 1970s, sexism and institutional abuse were rife in universities, so as a young woman in the university, Islam gave me a strong sense of protection, and it politicized me. It was an incredible journey.

What thinkers have most influenced you and your work?

Frantz Fanon has probably been the most influential thinker on both me and my work. I remember doing a reading class with my students, and a student said to me that what is amazing about Fanon is that he writes so unselfconsciously, as if he is speaking to you directly. I think what happens to us as academics is that we are always thinking about our audience or being worried about saying the wrong thing, but for me, Fanon just says it like it is, and he says it from the heart; there's a driving sense of purpose, there's anger, there's indignation, there's power, and there's intellect. He also uses storytelling, so there's reflexivity; he just captures all those elements as a postcolonial thinker. I think, with Fanon, there is also a really personal sense of pain about how he is constructed as a black man in a white world that resonates with what I saw in my father, and what Fanon does so well is show us the tensions within the black psyche and how ultimately that colonial mind-set translates into whole economic systems of complete racial subjugation.

But then, in *Black Skin, White Masks*, Fanon also talks about the mulatto woman, which is a very problematic chapter for feminists in the way that the woman is constructed as this objectified entity that can use her feminine wiles to attain social mobility in a white racist social structure, without actually placing that social structure in the wider understanding of power in a patriarchal world (Fanon 2008). There is his own masculinity and his own sense of frustration with love and rejection that really comes through—so I have to pull back and see how he has situated himself in terms of his own emotional attachment to that story.

In terms of female voices, I think I have to say Patricia Hill Collins and her book *Black Feminist Thought*; again, she has a real power. She is subversive in the way that she uses white male social theory and their search for the "truth" to build her case by bringing in the notion of marginality, empowerment, and resistance of African-American women as an "other truth." It is really quite remarkable: by taking up the social construction of reality as her position, she is able to develop an argument from a black feminist standpoint, which is to say, "This is our reality as black women, and this is how our world has been constructed by others." So what I like about her work is that it is not just saying, "I am a black woman, this is my experience, and look how we have been oppressed as a group." Instead, she says that there are ways we can systematically understand it through the deconstruction of ideology; we can break it down through time. She brings in the history of African-American women intellectuals and social movements to develop a set of compelling arguments that show how gendered racial struggle is a powerful, binding force.

Of course, I also love Gayatri Spivak's *Can the Subaltern Speak?*, which is seminal but also challenging. I like the way she uses a Marxist framework and the way in which she pulls out the historical to explain the contemporary "third-world woman." I especially like the way she problematizes agency and asks if we can ever truly hear the many voices of those written out of history. She looks at sati (or suttee, widow burning) in India,[2] and she describes the way in which there was this erasure, this total wiping out of human life, and that when the woman puts her hand into the mud to leave her imprint as her only mark of existence before being put on the funeral pyre, you just feel the intense disempowerment of that one act and what it really means to have no voice. And when she talks of "saving brown women from brown men," it just sums up everything about the civilizing project of colonialism, especially now around the way in which women and the veil have been constructed in the contemporary climate and the Islamophobic narratives circulating today—that one phrase sums it all up!

My other favorite person is Paulo Freire. Now, Paulo Freire, for me, is probably on par with Fanon in the way he writes from the heart. He talks powerfully about the pedagogy of the oppressed and uses love, indignation, and hope to express that. He was totally dedicated to the idea of education as transformation through literacy for the poor and marginalized in Brazil. What I find really significant about his thinking is his work around "conscientization"—that is, how through education you can build an intellectual class and how you build education as transformation through pedagogy, because it matters how and what you teach. In other words, how you make education meaningful to the learners, how that meaning then translates into cultural knowledge, and how that knowledge translates into liberatory social movements that are owned from within is important. Now, when you think about when he was writing, and when you read it now, it's almost like he had a crystal ball to talk about the way in which the state and technology and the neoliberal impulses that we see now frame the conditions of the masses and how we still need education as the means to bring about radical social change.

How do you understand postcolonialism, and why do you think this type of thought is important?

For me, postcolonialism is about the historical linking of the past with the present, examining the historical trajectories to understand the contemporary space. It gives you that dimension to explore the complex connections between the past, the present, and the future and the way certain kind of knowledges are produced about "the other" through time and space.

I often think about what postcolonialism means for the current generation. I remember having a conversation with a student about ideas around the diasporic condition of home and belonging, migratory spaces and the way in which we form new contested spaces, and the importance of our sense of rootedness, and this student said to me, "Well, that's only true to your experience because you did that journey, but we're kids. We're here and now, so what do ideas of home and roots have to do with people like us, who were born here and now?" So, in that sense, and as a response to these kinds of arguments, I really think there is a need to understand the postcolonial as a timeline—not as a chronological timeline but, rather, as a journey through time that demonstrates that, as discourses shift and change the manifestation of race and racism and in that sense, colonialism remains intact, and although it comes in different forms and the racist technologies of concealment get more and more sophisticated, it still shapes the experiences of people of color today, whether or not if they were born "here" or "there."

You have made a significant contribution to British black feminism. Do you think there is a distinction between black feminism and postcolonial feminism? And do you think of yourself as postcolonial thinker?

For me, postcolonial thinkers are iconic; they've transformed three generations of thinkers who have gone on to become political leaders and anti-racist activists. I think black feminism is a distinct form of postcolonial thinking; however, the two relate to each other at the same time. The work that male postcolonial thinkers have been doing is about precisely exploring issues of colonial identity and the diasporic condition that people of color have encountered. I think black feminism is linked closely to this because it is about that marginalization in the context of imperialism, but then it looks at the particularly gendered nature of that displacement and how patriarchy then manifests itself in that colonial and postcolonial trajectory.

Black feminists tend to center their lived experiences to understand the raced and gendered condition, and there is a sense in which this is problematic for some postcolonial feminists when the impulse within postcolonialism is to de-essentialize the subject. It is possible to be both a postcolonial scholar and a black feminist—like the wonderful and imaginative Sara Ahmed, who crosses so many boundaries in her queering work. I love it when she says that being in our white institutions makes us necessarily "sore and angry black feminists!"

I was recently reading through *Black British Feminism*, and I was reminded of just how energetic I was all those years ago; I wanted to change the world, and I felt that black feminism gave me the voice to do that because it opened up the possibility of relocating the marginal through the idea of the outsider within, which is what I felt. Maybe, in my experience, it seemed that I was always on the outside looking in and could see the dynamics of race and gender as they played out in my own life, particularly around issues to do with sexuality and race. So, for example, I have written about honor crimes and violence against women, and this comes from a place of silence and a need to name it in our communities. In Trinidad, at school, many girls disappeared when they reached puberty; some never came back, like one girl who sat next to me in class, and many years later, I heard that she had died.

So, for me, black feminism gave me a voice to speak about the unspeakable by reconfiguring the marginal space as a place of resistance and activism so that it becomes a place where you can talk about things that just don't exist in everyday language, social theory, or any of your traditional and cultural knowledge that has been passed on. Reading people like Fanon and Spivak, who talk about that psychological condition and the way in which subjectivity is formed, and then reformed, and then how we live it, was really transforming.

What black feminism did for me was center the black female experience. If you now look at the world and the way in which capitalist accumulation and globalization is unfolding, for example, it's done so on the backs of women in the garment industry, or sex tourism or trafficking, so in that sense, the ethnicized woman is the fulcrum for capitalist accumulation. Without these apparently "docile" bodies, the system would not work. Critics often say black feminism is dead, past its sell-by date, and so on, but I think that actually it has never been more relevant than it is today, because our lives have never been more structured by feminized labor that comes in the form of black women—whether they're Turkish, Egyptian, Indian, Chinese, African, Caribbean, South American, Mexican, Filipina, Sri Lankan, and so on. It's their labor that is the main stay of this globalized system, so how can anyone say black feminism is dead? We need to look at the world from where these women are located and hear their stories of resistance and agency. For me, what black feminism is precisely about is voice and agency and trying to see the ways in which we are always locked into this hegemonic battle for freedom against the state, the globalizing super-states, and the transnational capitalist forces. More than ever, black feminism is significant.

What I find interesting about black feminism and postcolonial feminism is the way in which *black* is still so contentious a category. Some black women prefer to be called postcolonial feminists because it's often seen as a safer space, and that's really interesting to me because I've never thought about it that way. I always thought black feminism was a trajectory rooted in a postcolonial experience, so the heart of this argument is around the color signifier *black* and its epidermal identification. Although it's a troubled essentialist space, I still think it's an important unifying space, and it has a lot of political power—like when, in the 1980s, Asian and African women came together in unity under the umbrella of OWAAD (Organisation of Women of African and Asian Descent).

So whether one identifies as a black feminist or as a postcolonial feminist doesn't really matter. The forces shaping a woman's life in Mexico are the same forces shaping a woman's life in Africa, whether we understand it through labor and capital, representation and construction, or patriarchy and sexuality. Their lives are structured by the same thing, which is a black and female condition based on the forces of neo-colonial globalization fueled by the desiring machine of capital that continues to eat at their female bodies.

Can you elaborate on the idea of "embodied intersectionality" in relation to white feminism and how you think this notion shapes "difference" and the experiences of the "other"?

To give you an illustration, I will use the example of the discourse around the veil and Muslim women. The idea of the veiled Muslim has become so popular in recent years because it is very visual and you can deconstruct it. Even though there are Muslim women critically writing about it on the one hand, I notice many white feminists also are on the other. And so, in this sense, the veiled Muslim women has become a safe "object of desire," a symbolic object of the ultimate oppression, and therefore in need of the ultimate "saving." So you have white politicians' wives saving women in Afghanistan from the Taliban, calling for their rights to education while, at the same time, their politician husbands are involved with armed conflict and the American and British military killing machines out there.

Chandra Talpade Mohanty—who, by the way, is another iconic postcolonial feminist on my list—in her seminal essay "Under Western Eyes" speaks about the way in which the "third-world woman" is represented in Western feminism as a passive and oppressed monolithic "other" without any regard to the specificity of her circumstances or sensitivity to her agency and culture. So, although I think there is some interesting work being done theoretically on intersectionality, the Muslim woman and the symbol of the veil represents the new monolithic objectification of the "third-world woman."

Now, I myself have written a bit around women and the veil, partly in response to some of the white feminist discussions and critiques, and partly because I felt that there was a strong need to theorize it from the women's voices, and I do so beginning with this notion of embodied intersectionality. For me, embodied intersectionality moves intersectionality as a concept beyond the way in which some white feminists have seen it—as the burden of the never-ending list of crosscutting "isms"—to really saying that it is not simply about including a long list of the protected characteristics such as racism, sexism, classism, disability, religion, age, and so on, and picking and choosing which issue we think is most important; rather, if you start with the embodied experience of any woman or man, what you have is the bringing together of all those complex multifaceted elements in a lived life.

So the notion of embodied intersectionality starts with the lived experience, which is very much what black feminism is about. I therefore find embodied intersectionality really quite powerful because the way we embody our "difference" and how that difference is written on and experienced within the body tell a very complex and textured story. That story is about the coming together of all the diverse structural and institutional elements in which we live, in which we work, and in which our inequalities are played out.

Furthermore, to what extent do you think Islamophobia has been inscribed on the body of the Muslim woman in the context of the West?

The figure or the body of the Muslim woman has come to embody Islamophobia and the entire Western fears of the Muslim barbaric "other." It is so popular to talk about it that it's over-analyzed in the press and on TV; we see the same tropes being repeated again and again. The circumstances and places may change, but the stories are always the same. You have a veiled Muslim woman who can't teach in the classroom or be a doctor because she can't be seen and trusted, but then on the other hand, she is seen as a victim and has no choice in the matter because she is forced to wear the veil by her "backward" family and religion. So the account that follows is that she is either a heroine struggling against her backward family and in need of saving or she is a pariah and a dangerous terrorist threat. Her overdetermined body has become the key way in which the deep fear of the Muslim "other" is played out and represented by this black, formidable, dark shadowy figure. So that's the story, and it's circulating in different ways—in politics and academic circles, from student theses to papers and books, and so on.

What I would want to say about this is that, while it is being over-examined, it is still out there, and it is has real consequences for the women concerned. For example, the banning of the hijab across Europe is spreading like wildfire, because in the battlefield against Islam, it is the faceless woman who has come to represent the face of Islam. So, even though we are examining it too much, these are my questions: What are we doing in terms of human rights? What about their agency and voice? What are we doing to counteract the majority population that does have a fear of the veil? The long and the short of it is that there is a mismatch between what we are doing and saying as academics and postcolonial thinkers and the way in which the media, the press, and public perception are untouched by our work. So the question is, what are we doing as public intellectuals to disrupt this hegemonic discourse?

In your book *Young, Female and Black*, you examine the various challenges and obstacles faced by women of color. Could you elaborate on your key findings and the ways in which such inequalities continue to perpetuate in contemporary society?

Young, Female and Black—now that was quite a while ago! It was based on my PhD thesis that I did at Goldsmiths, and I would still say that a lot of the things I found in that research are still very much true today. I know we might say that young women are living in a different kind of media-driven, technologically savvy society and that the tentacles of commodification through music and style are very different from those times (there wasn't that much style in the 1980s), but there are still some striking similarities. What I found in *Young, Female and Black* was that the young African-Caribbean women were very strategic about how they navigated opportunities in the racist education system, and we still do that today—education by any means necessary!

What these young women were doing was drawing on their Caribbean female identities rooted in slavery, survival, and gendered migration in order to succeed. They would defy expectations by strongly identifying with credentialism by getting more credentials and passing their exams but doing it in a resistant kind of way. They would navigate themselves into the world of work and find backdoor ways into further or higher education and then move up. So what they were doing was actually taking advantage of the segmented labor market that was becoming increasingly feminized at that time—and it still is, as I was saying before—and profiting *on the backs of women*. These women, then, were strategically negotiating and using their abilities with what might be considered conservative-with-a-small-"c" ideology, like doing well.

In my later work on Caribbean women in black Saturday schools, I found something similar going on. Here the mothers were engaged in exhausting educational activities in order to "raise the race," and they were working with mainstream schools to subvert racist expectations by educating their children. So all these women were resisting not in masculine ways (e.g., by rioting on the street or leaving and walking away); instead, they were actually doing well in order to achieve, and by achieving, they were then actually resisting and counteracting racism in quiet, subversive, feminized ways. To be successful as a black person is actually to undo the system of racist signification in which you are expected to not be successful or not be clever—"educationally subnormal."

Even though that was 25 years ago, I still think strategic negotiation of gendered racism is going on. For example, there are so many black women's organizations that are about being mainstream entrepreneurial business leaders or life coaches and inspirational speakers in the workplace. Now, it might seem counterintuitive to say that is a form of resistance, but if that is a way of negotiating a racialized system, then so be it. What we then need is a form of conscientization, which is where Freire comes in for me, to build feminized black intellectuals in those spaces of professionalism and corporate culture.

Your work around racism and inequality in education has been significant. What do you think the main barriers are that ethnically marked communities face within the education system?

Racism in the classroom is endemic; our intellectual and academic knowledge is quite robust on the evidence of racism in schools. We have achievement statistics that continue to show that Turkish, Pakistani, Bangladeshi, African, and African-Caribbean students are underachieving, both boys and girls, despite the mythology of girls doing better. And yet, in the face of all that evidence, which I've been working on now for thirty years, we still have teachers coming into our schools that do not feel equipped to teach in multicultural classrooms. And even with all the training, they have no confidence in dealing with racial issues. So again, we see a mismatch between our work as academics theorizing race and the teacher educators who are educating the next generation of teachers and our children. What has happened to anti-racist teachers that reflect on their praxis? There's no time for them! The bureaucracy, the discourse on standards, and the targets and educational league tables means there is very little time for teachers to engage with anti-racism, and they have no career investment in teaching it or understanding it. So there is a sense in which inequalities continue to play out in education as there is no discourse in schools to capture it.

Education is the most interesting space to see change. It can be the place where we can evolve critical pedagogies and knowledge that can actually rock the system. As Paulo Freire says, if we can make education meaningful, it's the true terrain of struggle for social justice and against unequal power relations. Ironically, at the same time, it's the space where inequalities are more rife than ever. Take the way in which the gaps between wealth and poverty are growing in society; inequalities in schools are growing in the same way because the same class distinctions are superimposed on education and play out quite explicitly in the classroom. It's raced and gendered as well. Teaching therefore continues to be the main barrier for students of color in the system.

You are one of the UK's first black professors. Could you talk a little about your experiences and the challenges that you as a woman of color have faced in the academy? And what would you like to see change in academia?

I just think, how many times can we say the same thing about these issues? I think there are about 85 black professors in the UK now, compared to more than 18,000 white professors. We are so marginal. I get upset when I talk about it. You're despised then needed; you're reviled then important. I'm sure this is true for most academics in many ways, so I don't want to say that my experience is different from anyone else's, but it's a hard and lonely space to be. For solace, I was reading bell hooks, and she eloquently describes how white people in the system would say, "Well, we wanted a black person for the job but nobody came forward, or if they did nobody was good enough." This is the constant trope that is still out there today; there's always this story about how *they* tried but *we* failed—they tried, but "we," as the black "other," are lacking. When they do give us an opportunity, it's under the cosh of equality and diversity policies, so in this way, our black bodies become mere "targets" to fulfill their needs, not ours. We bear that burden to show how diverse our institutions are, and in the end, for us, there is always a question mark on us and our ability.

When I first got my chair position, a white male professor said to me, "Well, they are giving Chairs to anyone for anything these days." That is what they are thinking: we are always seen as not quite good enough. So the fact that we are not there in large numbers is justified because of who we are, not because of their privilege. There is no reflection on white privilege in higher education, and that is very interesting because these are places of so-called learning and reflexivity. But it's probably the place of least reflexivity because everyone has too much at stake; they have their own careers and self-interests. I've been caught up in it, and I've had to leave in order to go back so that I can think and be under new conditions of my own making.

We have a more diverse student body than ever, with more black and international students, but little effort is made to actually host international students or welcome black and minority ethnic students and treat them with dignity and respect. So higher education is in crisis because their pedagogy and their identity haven't shifted to the new market. It's twenty years behind the times. Academic institutions are white, elite, and out of touch. I don't know what's going to happen in the future, but race, gender, and class inequalities are still rife across the education system. It's a complete and utter disgrace, but nobody is doing anything about it, and I think it's a scandal.

In terms of looking forward, what I find really interesting is that, in times of austerity and high fees, black and minority ethnic students are still choosing to take race courses, and it's not a vocational subject; it's considered a luxury. These are not students who are privileged in terms of class background, and studying a subject like race often has bleak job prospects, but despite that, they are still coming, which I find amazing and inspiring. Racism is alive and well, and these students are aware it; it is their lived experience. They are angry about racism, but at the same time, they are strategically engaging with it to bring about change. They are a body of new intellectuals, and there is a real sense of this conscientization going on, which is exciting. But what we don't currently have are collective movements in order to then bring these fragmented individuals from different universities across the country into some sort of space to share that collective voice. We need to navigate through our many voices and come together in order to collectively empower ourselves and fight racism and gender discrimination because they are as strong as ever in the system.

Notes

1. The 1970 Black Power Revolution in Trinidad and Tobago was heavily influenced by the US civil rights movement as an attempt to bring about social and political change.
2. Sati refers to a practice carried out among some Indian communities whereby a recently widowed female would set herself on fire on her husband's funeral pyre. For her critique of colonial interventions around the Sati practice, see Spivak 1998.

Selected Key Works

Mirza, H. (1992). *Young, Female and Black*. London: Routledge.

———. (1997). *Black British Feminism: A Reader*. London: Routledge.

———. (2009). *Race, Gender and Educational Desire: Why Black Women Succeed and Fail*. London: Routledge.

———. (2013). "'A Second Skin': Embodied Intersectionality, Transnationalism and Narratives of Identity and Belonging among Muslim Women in Britain." *Women's Studies International Forum* 36: 5–16.

Mirza, H., Bhavnani, R., and Meetoo, V. (2005). *Tackling the Roots of Racism, Lessons for Success*. Bristol: Policy Press.

Mirza, H., and Joseph, C. (2010). *Black and Postcolonial Feminisms in New Times: Researching Educational Inequalities*. London: Routledge.

CHAPTER 10

S. Sayyid

S. Sayyid is a reader in rhetoric in the Department of Sociology and Social Policy at the University of Leeds, UK.

Could you talk a little about your biography and how you first got into the field? What specifically interested you around questions concerning race, ethnicity, postcolonialism, and Islamism?

In retrospect, one can always kind of narrate a certain degree of seemingly necessary development from one thing to the other, although at the time, you don't really experience it like that. There was certainly the consciousness of being Muslim, which was there for a very long time, but there was never any special claim for piety; rather, I understood it as a marker of a historical sequence, though I would not have phrased it like that at the time. How I actually started working with questions around race, ethnicity, and postcolonialism was very much to do with the fact that I was dissatisfied with much of the existing literature, which I found very—to coin a phrase—"ontic," and I was really interested in the ontological, so for me, postcolonial thinking gave me the tools to do that kind of analysis.

The condition of being ethnically marked, matched with an idiosyncratic impulse that sought to deflect, refuse, and reject attempts to be fixed and framed in particular ways, was what perhaps helped cultivate my interests around these questions. How or why that led into one particular direction and not another, I don't really think I can know that. More often than not, it is when you look back on it and reflect that you see that there's a certain kind of regularity to those decisions that probably didn't *knowingly* occur at the time.

How did you develop your sense of political consciousness?

I don't think that I'm particularly politically conscious; certainly, I am not affiliated to any party or organization. Whatever political consciousness I have comes from a vague but persistent sense of being out of place. This sense of being out of place helped make me an ironic citizen, not able to find consolation in the prevailing narratives of national belonging. I think this ironic experience is corollary to one of the effects of racism. In these circumstances, many of us who become over-educated find alternative realities to cover up the gaps produced by the confrontation between the nationalist-racist imaginary and irony.

I like to think that my fascination for history was really an attempt to connect with the counter-factual. Maybe it was a recognition that the world as it is doesn't have to be that way. So, for me, it was about seeing how things came into *being* and recognizing that, if things have come into being this way, then they can come into being another way. As such, I would say that I've always been interested in transformations and changes. So maybe that's what makes one politically conscious: a sense that you deem the world around you as denaturalized, fabricated, and forged; you don't think things are the way they are because they have always been that way, but rather, they came out of a particular struggle or sequence of events. Things happened to make things the way they are now, and as a consequence, things can unhappen. It's the possibility of this *unhappening* that has always interested me. My interest in history meant I had an interest in speculative fiction, and as a consequence of that, my political consciousness was really about a sense of the recognition of the contingency of the way the world is; so if the world is this way, then why can't it be better?

Can you talk about the political and social climate that you found yourself in during your academic development? And to what extent did this influence your thinking?

I think that there were certain kinds of moments of crystallization where suddenly your history and biography meet for brief moments, for example, urban unrests and "uprisings" like in Brixton and Southall, and so on. You kind of become conscious watching them on television. At a more mundane level, the social and political climate I recall was far more polarized. This polarization was public; it was part of the culture. The Left and the Right (overdetermined and imprecise) were metaphors around which one could hang a description of the world and position oneself. The Cold War was not just to be found geopolitically; it was also a capstone of an edifice that included social, cultural, and political dimensions.

The end of the Cold War was the backdrop to my entry into academia. It was odd because, one year, you are listening to lectures on Soviet foreign policy, and next year, the Soviet Union is no more (though the lectures on Soviet foreign policy continued for a while longer). This polarized world reached a degree of intensity with the election of Margaret Thatcher and the undoing of the Keynesian welfare settlement that basically governed the Western plutocracies since the end of the Second World War. This unraveling, however, not only had an effect on the organization of the economy and the reconfiguration of the political agenda but also meant the undermining of a distinct sense of Britishness.

The thing about Margaret Thatcher is that, for someone who was an old-fashioned British patriot, she fought tooth and nail against Britain's integration into the European Union—but she was also willing to concede almost everything to the Americanization of Britain. And I don't mean that just in a crass sort of sense of "oh, there are MacDonald's everywhere," but actually, many of the key institutions that gave Britain a sense of being distinct (for good or ill, and sometimes for both) were hollowed out or lost, and with that loss, a kind of particular way of life also began to fade. As usual, the "immigrants" got the blame, but it was not the ethnically marked populations that gave up on the idea of a cultivation of a distinct sense of Britishness that was not forever anchored in the visions of the 1950s or enamored by a burning desire to become a neoliberal "little America." The people I went to school with, and my friends, were at the cusp of this transition. We were witnesses to the time when the idea took hold that, to make Britain great, you had to make it a "little America."

There's a very interesting story that you can tell about Britishness through popular music. Anglophonic popular music was perhaps considered predominantly an American medium, but despite this, there was a kind of specific British inflection to it, which was able hold its own often, and it emerged mainly around the Beatles and the Stones, and then from there to Bowie—Bowie must be one of the first singers to sing in an English accent rather than an American accent. And then there is punk, which is a uniquely British phenomenon (The Clash particularly), which is again the highlighting of some form of a globalized Left sensibility linking it directly to popular music.

When the Berlin Wall fell, I think a particular world came to an end, and we're now living in a new world of war and terror. There's a new sensibility, but perhaps it doesn't have that same kind of mobilization of cultural responses to it in a way that unifies all these different points. It may come or may not come; I don't know. But certainly there was this sense of a kind of Left anti-colonial chic, which I don't find in the same way anymore. So these changes and processes were important to my political thinking and how we account for these shifts and what they represent.

I think that there has been quite a profound depoliticization, which has, in many ways, led to the depoliticization of cultural formations. Consider athletes like Muhammad Ali: an exceptional figure but one willing to sacrifice three years of his prime athletic life to resist going to war. He may have been jailed, and he did not know what could've happened to him at the time. Think of the critiques that he made of white power and white authority in his "trash talking," and now watch all the heavyweight boxers who've come after and imitated that style. It's vacuous now; it means nothing because it doesn't carry that same energy. There's no investment in it, and the gestures are halfhearted.

While Ali was exceptional, he was not unique, in that many athletes of color were willing and able to use their "cultural capital" in the service of political goals that were transnational. The international cricket boycott of apartheid South Africa would not have been sustained if it wasn't for the domination of West Indian cricket. The refusal of elite cricketers from the West Indies (for the most part), Pakistan, and India to succumb to the temptations of the rand was crucial in maintaining the cricketing boycott even when the establishments in England and Australia were unenthusiastic.

The end of the Cold War was also the beginning of the end of apartheid, so in a sense, the end of a lot of the anti-colonial struggles coincided with the demise of the Soviet Union. These transformations, I believe, really heralded a kind of consummation of neoliberalism. This is where Francis Fukuyama's book *The End of History* resonated with the zeitgeist. History did end, and part of that was this idea that questions of race were over, so we saw the movement from, let's say, James Brown to Michael Jackson—not that Michael Jackson had to pretend to live like a caricature of an African-American performer, but simply how a clear transformation in culture and politics took place.

The election of Obama is significantly and symbolically important. This, however, was the culmination of a war of position in which, as a direct result of the civil rights victories, African-Americans were able to win elected offices throughout the country. Perhaps this long march came at the price of the Americanization of the African-American experience, by and large, rather than the decolonization of the American experience. Subsequently, we can see that there is a real commitment, in the contemporary context, to the idea that there are no more racists and that the racism that exists is now kept hidden, institutionally and structurally.

What thinkers would you say have most influenced you and your work?

I think, at different points and at different periods in your life, there are people who speak to you with a greater urgency and a greater poignancy than others. Looking back on it, you can construct a kind of lineage, but at the time, it's not like that. When I first came across Edward Said's *Orientalism*, I was still at high school. I didn't think that I would ever return to that book, let alone return to it time and time again. Clearly, my graduate studies were a period in which many intellectual influences and currants were consolidated. I was fortunate to be in a department that had a very large postgraduate community that included a research program based on the articulation of continental philosophy with the study of politics and the political. So many of the thinkers and writers who I have ongoing conversations with are those I first encountered in regular seminars associated with my postgraduate studies. I am not sure that I have been attracted by thinkers *per se* but, rather, conversations and projects that are associated with some people.

Then you go through different writers along the way. For example, I was always taken by Richard Rorty's style, especially in his later phase. The first book I think I read of Richard Rorty's was *Contingency, Irony and Solidarity*. And then I began to excavate his work, not that I agree with him on certain things—in many ways he's an American nationalist, or at least an American patriot of kinds—but at the same time, I enjoyed the way he said what he said.[1] While I don't share his American dream, I had always liked the way he expressed himself, and I thought that was quite useful. Similarly, people like Jorge Luis Borges for example, really helped me through his writing. There's something about it that just speaks to me; it's kind of a world that is all made up, and at the same time, he also shows the contingency of the world. More recently, I've really become fascinated by Wittgenstein. I think there's certainly something about the economy of his expression that compelled me: the way that you actually get it without being able to explain why you get it.

Do you think of yourself as a postcolonial thinker, and would you situate your work within the genre?

For me, disciplinary categories are not banners of allegiance but flags of convenience. My academic training has been eclectic—from international relations and discourse theory to continental and political philosophy—but my employment in the academy has always been in sociology departments. I mean, it's a very, very, odd thing: I did a BA in international relations and an MA and a PhD in a government department, but my entire academic career has been within sociology. Having said all that, I am happy to include myself as someone who works in the field of postcolonial thinking. Perhaps I may be more inclined to talk about the decolonial rather than the postcolonial, but as a broad generalization, I wouldn't refuse this classification.

How do you understand the postcolonial?

For me, the postcolonial is quite specific to the aftermath, but not in a chronological sense, of European colonialism. I do not consider colonialism to be a generic phenomenon; European colonialism is very specific, and I think what makes it specific is to do with the invention of racism. Not every imperial project is akin to European colonialism. I am not making any particular claims that European colonialism is more venal, more corrupt, or crueler compared to other imperialisms; rather, the significance of the imperial venture of Europe is that the world in which we live now has been largely formed and framed by the European colonial enterprise.

The postcolonial is about the weakening of the violent hierarchy between the West and the non-West. It's important, then, to acknowledge the centrality of the colonial enterprise in laying the foundations of the contemporary world. The very shape of the world—our comportment toward it, its cartographies, its economy, and its culture—are all products of the colonial enterprise that emerges in what has been called the long sixteenth century (1492–1798). You can call this the second axial age, as it is pivotal to the formation of the world as we know it. The postcolonial, as such, is really about the disruption of the philosophical, political, and socioeconomic foundation of this order. I believe that, if people have a postcolonial perspective, whatever that may be, they will be able to tell more interesting stories about the life and the world in which they are in. The postcolonial alerts you to the pure contingency of the way that we frame all the questions around the world; it broadens your horizon and it makes you aware of the world you live in. That's all it does—but perhaps that is enough.

Throughout many of your works, you deploy an anti-foundationalist perspective. What do you think this type of theorizing enables others to develop in relation to questions around the formation of ethnic, racial, and postcolonial identities?

I'm more and more inclined to agree with Stanley Fish right now about that: anti-foundationalism doesn't have any special claims to truth or knowledge; it's just how the world is. This is where I find the positivist critique of anti-foundationalism so amusing. First, they make a caricature of anti-foundationalism (post-structuralism or postmodernity, etc.) as stating that "there is no truth," and second, they exclaim that "there is a logical fallacy because if there is no truth then anti-foundationalism cannot be true." Well anti-foundationalism *is* true. The interesting question is not "what is true?" but rather, "what is truth?" Positivists and post-positivists have different ideas of what the truth is and how it works. Anti-foundationalism alerts you to the contingencies of formation and how things have come into *being*. It shows you that there is no particular ground for any formation.

In relation to questions around race and ethnicity specifically, the thing with anti-foundationalism is that it simply makes you aware more quickly about the fact that, for example, the division into races and the construction of race have whole sets of politics around them. These are processes and not simply the transparent transcription of a transhistorical reality—they are formulations, and it's important to see that. One of the things that continues to strike me is how the question about race and ethnicity still continues to be haunted by the nineteenth-century conception of what a "race" is and what racism is. I find these conceptions unhelpful as they attempt to naturalize our understandings—so "race" is somehow real. In this sense, for me, anti-foundationalism radically breaks, or at least puts into serious question, this narrative by allowing one to see such formations as part of a wider set of complex political processes.

Could you elaborate on your main arguments in *A Fundamental Fear*?

The book sets out to explain the emergence of a Muslim political agent. I was dissatisfied with the accounts that privileged urban rural migration, or the failure of nationalist elites, and so on, as accounting for "Islamic fundamentalism" or, as I prefer to call it, Islamism. What was missing from most conventional accounts was the link between social upheaval and the reactivation of Islam. It was assumed that social upheaval would axiomatically lead to "Islamic fundamentalism" in societies historically dominated by the Islamicate. Such assumptions were essentialist, Eurocentric, and most importantly, unpersuasive. So *A Fundamental Fear* was motivated to tell the story about the emergence of Islamism without resorting to essentialism or succumbing to Eurocentrism.

There is a common belief (perhaps less common than it used to be) that there is a kind of universal sociology or a universal social science that can explain all social phenomena in all places at all times. Opposed to this is the belief that there is a need for a more attuned analysis in which every culture of society is unique; therefore, you can only explain things through a very grounded historical examination. I guess my position is somewhere in between, because it seems to me that you need to have a sense of the textured nature of human societies and, at the same time, recognize that the tools of the social sciences were forged in the smithy of European presumptions of cultural and racial superiority and therefore may not be fit for purpose in helping us understand a world that is rather different. At the minimum, we need to at least ask the question of if these tools are adequate. Maybe they are, but perhaps they are not.

A Fundamental Fear, when it appeared had an odd reception, with some white anthropologists demanding that I should have written an auto-ethnography. There was an expectation for an anthropological understanding and a discomfort that the empirical was refused. Perhaps within that there was a challenge to the very common division of labor in which the role of academics of color was to provide ethnographic descriptions while theoretical work was the preserve of whiteness. The book interrupted such considerations, and I'd like to think that its ontological analysis is what continues to mark its contribution.

How does the question of Eurocentrism fit within the book?

At the heart of the book is the idea that Islamism is a critique of Eurocentrism in a profound way. At the time, I argued that Eurocentrism was something that sought to pin universal values to Western history. It is important to note that Eurocentrism is not a euphemism for Europeanness; Eurocentrism is really a set of practices that establishes that the future history of the world is nothing but an upscale history of the West. Islamism then becomes deeply troubling, because it doesn't simply operate at some kind of level of—for want of a better term— political ideology, so it's actually very disturbing because it questions and inter- rupts the deep rootedness and centrality of Western discourse. In other words, Islamism at its most rigorous is simply a stepping out of that historical narrative.

Could you talk a little about the Muslim question? And how far do you think this occupies the Western imaginary in the contemporary context, particularly in the wake of the War on Terror?

The reference to the Muslim question describes a sort of fascination with the Near Eastern question or the Jewish question in nineteenth- and twentieth- century Europe. It's the idea of "what is to done with this group?" Take the Near Eastern question, where we had a discourse around "what is to be done with the Ottoman Empire" and the Jewish question of "what is to be done with Jews." So the Muslim question really asks, "What is to be done with Muslims?" Such a question presupposes the existence and salience of a Muslim subjectivity, and the very idea of Muslim subjectivity is something that many scholars (regardless of political affiliation) often find very problematic.

I maintain that, at least in Western Europe, and probably the North Atlantic as well as globally, there weren't any Muslims before 1989; certainly in Britain you can date it to that. That doesn't mean that there weren't physically people who went to mosques, ate halal food, and buried their dead facing Makkah. But as a political subjectivity, and as a public presence, Muslims were absent. So when *A Fundamental Fear* came out, there was already this process under way of the assertion of a Muslim identity. I remember a very senior academic who had written about Islam and its contemporary mobilization telling me, "In five years, it will all be over." (Alas, I have to add that, twenty years later, he is still saying the same sort of thing.)

The obituaries of Islamism keep being written. The contemporary Muslim mobilizations have been hitting the headlines for more than almost fifty years, and the end of Islamism has been predicted and anticipated repeatedly only to be deferred yet again. These prophecies of the demise of Islamism are not only a confusion between what scholars want to see and what they do see; they are perhaps a systemic failure: a failure that is not just simply predictive but philosophical, and a failure arising from a reluctance to accept that Islamism is not a fad or a superficial sociological trend but, rather, something profound.

Now, my hunch is that Islamism signals a transformation of world historical proportions: the assertion of Muslim identity has the same kind of significance as, say, the rise of nationalism in nineteenth-century Europe. This means that the ability of individual states to regulate, control, and domesticate this process is far more limited than they imagine. I think that this is specifically the hubris of Western plutocracies, because their political elites have a sense of themselves as being masters of the universe and believe that they are able to control, regulate, and domesticate this unruly planet. So, like the latter-day King Canutes, they try to roll back the tide of Islamism with colonial style occupations, drone assassinations, cruel and unusual punishments, and virtual mummification in the super-max prisons of the American gulag. The use of torture by the United States in its War on Terror has to be understood not in terms of whether torture is a useful tool for extracting information and defusing a ticking bomb somewhere but, rather, as a means of terrifying into a surly submission its Islamist enemies.

Now, if my hunch is correct, and Islamism is (for entirely contingent reasons) a world transforming tidal wave, then commanding the tide to halt by deradicalization, recolonization, social integration, or solitary incarceration is unlikely to be effective. Perhaps rather than trying to imitate Canute and replicate his failure, a more useful strategy may be to learn to surf this tide of history—although such prudent statecraft would require a different kind of skills.

The War on Terror is animated by desires to affix colonial solutions to postcolonial problems. I think one of the ways in which you can see the War on Terror is as an attempt to close the gap between Western values and universal values so that what cannot be done by persuasion has to be done by coercion. The War on Terror, then, has become the grammar of the world order in much the same way the Cold War was, and it is hollowing out many of the liberal democratic forms that many in Western plutocracies took for granted. So, while the Muslim question purports to be about "what to do with Muslims," the question behind this question is really about what the place of the West is in the world. There's a kind of subtext to that; it gets talked about on the surface of Muslim bodies, especially among some female bodies, but underlying the story is what the West means when it's no longer at the center of the world. This is why the Muslim question is so difficult to address: because it cannot be untangled from a Western question.

Earlier, you said you were quite influenced by Edward Said and
Orientalism. **How far do you think an Orientalist grammar remains**
hegemonic in narrations of the figure of the Muslim in the West?

I think that *Orientalism* remains dominant, and most political or governmental discourse is dominated by its categories. I think all the prescriptions that you see, from "we have to teach them English so they don't become a terrorist" to "we have to find the preachers of hate," are couched in Orientalist logics. In fact, the War on Terror has been used to attack the critique of *Orientalism*, and in a way, they'll carry on doing that because Orientalism isn't some sort of lifestyle choice. There's a reason why people support and invest in the Orientalist narrative: because it's ultimately about a sense of who they are. Unless they learn to tell different stories about themselves, they can't let go of Orientalism—unless it's taken away from them.

In your co-edited book *A Postcolonial People,* readers are
presented with a volume that concentrates exclusively on the
British South Asian experience. Could you talk about what
you think is significant about the relationship between British
South Asians and the postcolonial in the context of the UK?

I don't think there's any privileged significance attached to South Asian settlers in Britain and the postcolonial condition. What is interesting is that, in Britain, there is a confluence of different experiences of anti-colonial struggles: from the Caribbean, Africa, and South Asia. The juxtaposition of different racialized populations helped create conditions for the cross-fertilization of critical strategies and energies that could not be reduced to the particularities of the Caribbean, South Asia, or Africa. Urban Britain provided a platform where the legacy of the racial state that was the British Empire and the dominance of the Anglosphere came to be seen as being intimately linked in the perpetuation of what Du Bois described as the international color-line. It provided a common ground and common language to forge a common struggle in which anti-colonial, anti-racist, and anti-imperialist critiques could be more easily conjoined. This confluence of struggles and experiences is perhaps what gives the history of postcolonial settlement in Britain its specific flavor.

The book was novel in that it framed mass migration and settlement of South Asians in these islands through an explicit postcolonial prism. The postcolonial was not used as merely a descriptive replacement for, say, the postwar (like that found in the common refrain of "postwar immigration"), nor was the postcolonial reduced to just the end of empire; rather, it was used to undermine the conventions and framings by which much of the study of South Asian settlers was conducted. What I think *A Postcolonial People* did (as a collection) was to put in the forefront (of the analysis of the relationship between Britain and South Asian settlers) the problem of constructing a postcolonial sense of British identity. For example, you still have many anthropological and socio-logical accounts that remain locked into the belief of progressive assimilation, which makes each succeeding settler generation more "British" over time. You have narratives that tell us that the first generation directly affected by colonial-ism were somehow more quietist than the subsequent generations that became radical and disruptive because of their contact with Anglo-British society. These narratives of "corruptions of youth" circulate partly as a perennial anguish that the old feel for the young but also as a decontextualization of the differences in circumstances and structures that the pioneer settlers found themselves in. The pioneer settlers came as virtual guest workers; their commitment and invest-ment to specific locations was minimal. Confronted with racist attacks, flight was very often a viable option. Once these guest worker hostels turned into communities, the dynamics of the options available when confronted with rac-ism altered: fighting back become a viable, and even necessary, option.

A Postcolonial People wanted to recontextualize the settlement of South Asians in Britain away from narratives in which the movement of people from South Asia was presented as a form of time travel (immigrants arrive from the past into a future, represented by Britain). Away from narratives that sought axiomatically to assert that we need to study caste affiliations because they are South Asians, it was a rejection of the immigrant imaginary that governed the production of knowledge (popular as well as expert) on South Asian settlers. The chapters in *A Postcolonial People* were really trying to disrupt these essential-ist narratives by taking *Orientalism* seriously and interrupting the whole genre around the way in which we look at South Asians, which basically brought their experiences down to caste, religion, culture, and so on—in short, "sarees, samo-sas and steel bands." It's a collection that attempts to disrupt these narratives by telling an overall story about that complex and textured process.

Can you elaborate on your notion of the *immigrant imaginary* and the ways in which you think that such a concept has been mobilized to inform the practices of Europe or the West?

There is a particular way that South Asian settlers are talked about in Brit-ain, and specifically, the use of the term *immigrant* to describe people who have been born and bred here [in Britain] seems to me as little more than just inconvenient speech. The *immigrant imaginary* refers to a recurring group of analytical tropes and themes by which the relationship between European-esque societies and ethnically marked postcolonial populations are described and domesticated. It refers to the way in which the founding distinction of national democracies—that of citizen and foreigner—is interrupted by the appearance of postcolonial immigrants who are neither "proper foreigners" nor "proper citizens."

The immigrant imaginary has four main characteristics: First, it represents host societies and immigrants as being ontologically distinct. Second, it sets out the destiny of the ethnically marked as eventual dissolution and disappearance as the immigrant is consumed by the host. Third, the immigrant imaginary represents this progressive consumption in discrete and successive stages called *generations*. The concept of generation works to dehistoricize immigrants and remove them from the currents of history. The category of generation also polices the frontier between the West and the rest by continuing to keep racially marked immigrants as people without history. Fourth, the immigrant imaginary continually defers the moment of full consumption when the immigrant becomes one with the host. It is possible that countries based around migration and settlement outside the Afro-Eurasian ecumene may have a slightly different take on the immigrant imaginary, though I'm beginning to think that postcolonial migration is quite radically different, and as a consequence, the immigrant imaginary is becoming globalized—at least among nations buying into white privilege.

Your recent co-edited book, *Thinking through Islamophobia*, interrogates the very category of Islamophobia. Can you elaborate on how you specifically define Islamophobia and in what ways your approach differs from the term's conventional usage?

Abdoolkarim Vakil (who was co-editor of the volume) and I were dissatisfied by much of the debate on Islamophobia, which tended to get bogged down in whether there was a "phobia" of Muslims or Islam and whether it was justified or not. Rather than asserting the one true meaning of Islamophobia, we wanted to focus on the range of its deployment and look at the work the category of Islamophobia did intellectually, polemically, and in public policy terms.

Islamophobia is not something that can be simply analyzed etymologically, and it is not just about the irrational or rational fear of Muslims. Islamophobia problematizes and interrupts Muslim identifications. What this understanding allows us to do is examine the phenomenon in the way that it affects not just Muslims but also non-Muslims and see how it begins to structure the life opportunities of all people. Islamophobia is about the disciplining of Muslims by reference to a Westernizing horizon. Societies that represent themselves as Western or Westernizing articulate their Western character by the exclusion and regulation of Muslims. What is important about Islamophobia is that it has an uneasy relationship with other forms of exclusion, but it can't be read through antisemitism or simply racism. It is a racism for post-racial times.

What position do you think Muslims occupy in terms of questions around racism and the postcolonial?

I think the postcolonial explains a lot about the way in which Muslim subjectivity finds itself in the crossroads and crosshairs of so many different developments right now, partly because the postcolonial, by raising doubts and weakening the hierarchy between the West and the non-West, opens the possibility of a polycentric world. One of these polycenters is that which names itself Islam, and that in itself already carries out a certain kind of decolonial impulse. Currently, there are a series of ongoing struggles among Muslim populations that orbit around the sign of Islam. Now, because of the peculiarity of the global distribution of the Muslim population, there are no robust international structures that can facilitate the expression of Muslim agency; rather, the existing world order makes such expressions difficult.

The effect of all these developments is to produce a widening gap between the desire of an increasing number of Muslims to write their own history and the inability (or unwillingness) of the existing world order to accommodate these demands and desires. This is why the occupation of Palestine is emblematic of the postcolonial Muslim condition: because it reproduces the colonial and racial logics that preclude expressions of Muslim agency.

How far do you think black and postcolonial thought has been acknowledged in the social sciences, and to what extent do you think a decolonialization of the discipline is required?

I think decolonization is necessary because many of the social science categories and tools were made at a time when the demarcation between the Western and non-Western was very clear, and part of those key tools were about policing that frontier. Ideally, one would want people to be far better informed and have a greater historical awareness about these issues, and I would like to see such issues be more fully integrated in the discipline rather than almost ghettoized. I would also like to see race and ethnicity being treated in the analysis of nation formation. I think this would help unravel the complex story in which the category of "ethnic minority" only makes sense within a notion of a national majority.

Before the civil rights movement, I don't think there were any African-American studies departments in white elite universities in the United States, but now, you have a situation in which Ivy League universities compete to have the best African-American studies department. Alas, this is not the case in the UK, where the change to a multi-ethnic, multi-religious society is not reflected in a commitment to diversity in employment, curriculum, or teaching. Universities tend to be run by people who consider themselves to be nice and progressive—without a racist bone in their body—and will tell you that "it's terrible that there is institutional racism in HEI [Higher Education Institutions]." Alas, such candor rarely ever translates into sustained ameliorative policies.

It would be great if even one of the Russell Group universities took "diversity-as-democracy" seriously and translated its commitment to widening participation into widening the core curriculum of the university to make it fit for purpose as a crucible of contemporary multicultural citizenship. However, I don't think that is likely to happen anytime soon. The transformations that metropolitan local authorities experienced in the 1980s, which opened up the public sector to become reflective of the diversity of urban Britain, seems to have passed the university sector by. This is even true among those universities located in the thick of multicultural cities.

Postcolonial thought has to be included in the academy, not because of some affirmative action, but because it should not be excluded as a consequence of a systemic affirmative action that institutionalizes white privilege. Postcolonial thinking is not just for those who were colonized, since the European colonial enterprise affects more than non-Europeans; rather, the colonial enterprise helped constitute and consolidate a certain kind of Europeanness, a Europeanness that has become hegemonic. The emancipatory impulse of decolonization cannot come to a rest without decolonizing that Europeanness.

I suppose the university needs to take postcolonial thinking seriously because the world is changing, and universities can play a part in navigating these changes for society at large. The maps for such navigation can be grouped as being part of either Eurocentric social science or decolonial social science. In practice, trying to introduce even in homeopathic quantities changes to core modules that reflect the decolonial is very difficult. Postcolonial thinking is confined to the ghettoes of the discipline—the specialist elective modules, the obligatory "a week on racism"—while the suburbs of core components of degrees remain resolutely Eurocentric. Eurocentric thought points to the past, and the decolonial points to the future. The future of social sciences rests on their ability to be part of this post-Western world or risk going the way of alchemy.

Note

1.   For a critique of Rorty and nationalism, see Billig 1995.

Selected Key Works

Sayyid, S. (2003). *A Fundamental Fear: Eurocentrism and the Emergence of Islamism.* London: Zed Books.

———. (2013). "Empire, Islam, and the Postcolonial." In *The Oxford Handbook of Postcolonial Studies*, edited by G. Huggan, 127–41. Oxford: Oxford University Press.

———. (2014). *Recalling the Caliphate*. London: Hurst.

Sayyid, S., Ali, N., and Kalra, V., eds. (2006). *A Postcolonial People: South Asians in Britain*. London: Hurst.

Sayyid, S., Sian, K. P., and Law, I. (2013). *Racism, Governance and Public Policy: Beyond Human Rights*. London: Routledge.

Sayyid, S., and Vakil, A., eds. (2010). *Thinking through Islamophobia*. London: Hurst.

CHAPTER 11

Ronit Lentin

R onit Lentin is an associate professor in the Department of Sociology at Trinity College Dublin, Ireland.

Could you talk a little about your biography and what interested you in questions around race, ethnicity, and postcolonialism?

I was born in Palestine before the establishment of the state of Israel, so my childhood was informed by growing up in Israel. We were the first generation for redemption, and our parents had been saved from the Holocaust. We were Zionists through and through; we never questioned anything. That basically meant that one would go to the army, but I didn't go to the army because I had asthma. So I think that was an important point for me—not serving. At 18 years of age, I went to university instead (I messed up my first degree, but that's a different story). But I didn't do what everybody else did; I didn't have the "baptism of fire" of the army, and I'm very thankful to the state for that.

I didn't question much until 1967; my turning point was after the war. I was sitting with some friends in a bar, and they were shooting again in Syria, and I said to my friends, "Why are they still shooting when we won the war?" And one of them said, "Do you want me to explain it to you?" And using Marxist frameworks, he was able to show me how this war was actually not an attack on Israel but, rather, planned as part of the expansion. After that, for me, the penny dropped, and since then, there was no return, because once you know something, you can't *unknow* it. I was completely sold on the idea that Zionism was in fact a settler colonial movement. This was what really led my way.

Also, the experience of my own family, who came from Romania, influenced my thinking. They had to flee in 1940, and they were refugees for a whole year until they reached Palestine. They were very privileged because they had money. You needed a certificate that the British issued to people, and it was a thousand sterling per person. So my grandfather had four thousand sterling for the four members of his family, but it still took them a long time before they reached Palestine, and various things happened to them on the way. For example, I think of my grandmother being threatened at a railway station or that members of their family were taken to a camp in the north of Romania (it wasn't an extermination camp, but still it was a camp). All these things were very formative for me, although they [my family] didn't talk much about it. My PhD was later to be based around these particular issues.

Academically, my biography was unusual. I didn't finish my first degree, as I mentioned earlier. Time was messy after the war. Maybe the war is an excuse, but I didn't finish my first degree. I tried various other things, but they didn't work out, so then I worked in television for a while. I soon met my husband Louis, and we moved to Ireland. In all these years, I wasn't doing academic work, I was doing journalism. So I was living in Ireland, I had my children, and then, by chance, someone said to me, "Why don't you do a master's in women's studies?"—because feminism had always been very influential to me. It was 1990, which was late in my life. I was 46, but that master's was an eye-opener. It was great, and I thought academic work was brilliant. So I stayed and did my PhD in sociology, which was the work on Israel and the daughters of the Shoah. I've only been teaching twenty years in Trinity even though I'm 68, so in a way, I have a kind of bizarre academic trajectory in that respect.

The influences of both my Jewish and Palestinian experiences were very important to me, as I see all my scholarship as being linked to these particular moments, even though it may look a bit disparate at times. During my PhD work, I came across feminist methodologies, and this was a huge influence— Liz Stanley particularly. Audre Lorde's notion of "the Master's tools cannot destroy the Master's house" and the idea that we have to create new tools was also significant. But then I felt that many feminist academics recreated the same tools, so I found the language in some respects to be as obtuse as that of the men. I'm not sure that it led us to a real liberation from the chains. The notion of intersectionality in Nira Yuval-Davis's work was also important for me in the feminist literature. But a lot of the things I'm reading now around the decolonial are quite interesting. I'm currently reading Ramon Grosfoguel, who talks about the point of view of the Global South as opposed to the Global North.

I was also very lucky that Ireland became an immigration destination in the 1990s, because when I proposed together with a colleague a master's in ethnic and racial studies, it was at the right time. I'm still learning, and I feel I learn and develop all the time. Because I had a program to run as well as a course to teach about race and ethnicity, I had to find out about the theories around race and ethnicity—and I'm still finding out now.

How did you develop your sense of political consciousness?

The Zionist enterprise is really where I got my political consciousness as well as through the understanding of the enterprise as an oppressive system. Some people still talk about "no choice," or "everybody wants to kill Jews," "the world is against us," and so on, which is the discourse we grew up on. My parents were good people, middle class, and very good Zionists, but very interestingly, in my book *Co-Memory and Melancholia,* there is one chapter about my father, and just before he died, he started doubting the Zionist enterprise, but I don't know what his final thoughts on it were because he died before I was able to ask him.

The conversation in the bar after the war that I mentioned earlier was a big influence, as well as hanging around with a group called Matzpen, a Trotskyist fourth international group, who were saying what the young dissidents are saying now. They talked about getting out of the occupied territories already in 1967. They published an advertisement in the papers that said "we must get out," and they talked about a one-state solution. So these experiences of my lived reality enabled me to develop my theories. My early political consciousness therefore developed through Palestine and my anti-Zionist activism.

My activism was not really accepted in my family. I had arguments with my father, but my mother and I always agreed not to fight. My parents, later on, perhaps changed their Zionist position, because people who allow themselves to can see the other side. I have friends who sympathize with Zionism, but they are still very angry about what goes on in the West Bank checkpoints, for example; however, when I say there is no justification for a Jewish state, they part ways with me. That's the way it is; I can't undo it, and I can't undo who I am. There are many people who try to fight me, but it's not important; it's a price to pay, but it's a very small price.

When I was doing my PhD in Ireland, I remember reading the first article on racism in Ireland by Robbie McVeigh—who later became my co-writer on several books—and he wrote about the specificities of Irish racism and was very much positioned in the Stuart Hall tradition of theorization. His article, published in *Race and Class,* on the specificities of Irish racism really influenced me, and this is really what led me to start theorizing Irish racism. Some people say to me that Ireland is not the most racist place in the world, or that it's not as bad in Ireland, or that it's not as racist as other countries. But that's not the point for me, because the moment you read David Theo Goldberg, you understand that all modern nation-states are racial states. So it's not a question of who is more or less racist. This form of thinking really helped me develop my political consciousness intellectually, where we look to questions of the state as central to the production of racism.

Which thinkers have most influenced you and your work?

As soon as I started my PhD, I read Zigmunt Bauman's *Modernity and the Holocaust* and this really helped me in writing my thesis on the Holocaust through a sociological lens. Since then, I have met him and read many of his books. His understanding and critique of what he calls "liquid modernity" and his commitment to exposing what he calls "wasted lives" have remained an inspiration to my work and my thinking. I always return to reading him and teaching him, despite his focus on European modernity, and I am struggling to adapt my understanding of his work to non-European contexts. Similarly, my debt to Agamben has led me in new directions in recent years, and importantly, a recent book titled *Agamben and Colonialism* by Marcelo Svirsky and Simone Bignall has prompted me to adapt his theorization to colonial and anti-colonial conditions.

Early on, I was also very much influenced by feminist thinkers and feminist thinkers of color, in particular Patricia Hill Collins, bell hooks, and Nira-Yuval Davis. I've since parted company with Nira because she claims that my refusal to use the words of Palestinian women or to go out and interview them means my withdrawal into "identity politics," and I don't agree with her on this. But she did influence me in the beginning, particularly her work on intersectionality in *Gender and Nation*. She is actually responsible for my first collection, *Gender and Catastrophe*, because she asked me to write an entry for an encyclopedia of women's studies on gender and genocide, and this helped me develop my position and thinking for what later became *Gender and Catastrophe*.

I moved on to other thinkers in the field when I started teaching my master's program at Trinity College, so I was very influenced by Stuart Hall, particularly "Race the Floating Signifier." I was also influenced by Edward Said and his notion of not only *Orientalism* but also *The Question of Palestine,* which I translated into Hebrew. So I have a somewhat intimate knowledge of that book, and he's been hugely influential to me. David Goldberg and particularly his "racial state" notion have completely changed my thinking because, in the literature on race and ethnicity, there was, and still is, so much material that focuses on the psychological or the individual, which I always felt I was rejecting but didn't quite know how to articulate until David [Goldberg] published his book.

Now, I must say very openly that my daughter Alana Lentin has also influenced me a lot; people say the apple hasn't fallen very far from the tree, but I say the tree hasn't grown very far from the apple, because she did this work first.

Her clarity has helped me a lot, and co-editing *Race and State* with her was great. Alana did work mostly on anti-racism, but I felt racism was really an area that needed to be explored, particularly in Ireland, and that's when I decided to write my books *Racism and Anti-Racism* and *After Optimism: Ireland, Racism and Globalisation* with Robbie McVeigh, who was also great to work with and remains a big influence on my work.

In more recent years, I've been thinking more in terms of people who compare antisemitism with Islamophobia, so I think S. Sayyid's work has been particularly influential as well as some Muslim feminists that have been important to me: people such as Leila Ahmed, and also Nahla Abdo, who I have worked with. I am particularly interested in the way in which they explore the "othering" of Islam. So that's my trajectory that has led me to where I am today.

How do you understand the postcolonial, and what do you consider the main contributions of postcolonial thinking to be? Furthermore, do you think of yourself as postcolonial thinker, and would you situate your work within this genre?

Well, I never thought to situate my own work within the postcolonial genre; I would rather define myself as a race-critical theorist. Stuart Hall, Fanon, and Spivak, have been really influential to my thinking and continue to shape my understanding about the postcolonial, but we need to think more in terms of anti-colonial rather than postcolonial, because I have a huge problem with the "post." This comes from the post-Zionist argument; post-Zionists are considered to be critical, but some of them do not really reject Zionism, whereas I reject Zionism, and I reject colonialism. So yes, many postcolonial thinkers have influenced me, but to what extent have I really placed myself within this genre I'm not so sure.

Recently, like I said, I have been reading a lot around decoloniality, and I am understanding things a bit better about the subaltern and not only their right to speak but their need to speak. One thing I've learned from feminism is that you cannot speak from a point of privilege about the unprivileged. This is not a position people accept easily. I think postcolonial thinking has certainly contributed primarily to the notion that the Global South and the Global East need to speak for themselves, and this is very important. But then, what do we do as scholars in the Global North and the Global West? I think we have a real dilemma from our position as privileged scholars, and using the narratives of the subaltern is no longer acceptable in my own work.

Could you elaborate on your key findings in *Racism and Anti-Racism in Ireland*? And furthermore, to what extent do you think the economic crisis has affected racism, since part of your findings illustrate that economic prosperity brought racism to Ireland, which belies the conventional link made between poverty and the existence of racism?

For starters, our argument was contrary to what people were saying: racism was not brought about by migration; it existed a long time before "these people" came, and that's a really important point to remember. Also, migration is not such a new thing. One of the issues we argued was that migration in Ireland was a constant historical factor, so the Normans, the Celts, the Saxons, the Vikings, and so on, were all migrants, and this is what Irish identity is about—a mixture of all these people because they stayed and intermarried. So a "pure" Irish ethnicity, as people like to think of it, is actually a fiction. Second, racism has existed for several centuries; black people came to Ireland around the sixteenth century as slaves or as sailors and so on with the British. Then Jewish people came mostly in the 1880s, followed later by Chinese people, who came in the 1950s. Then the Italians and of course the Travelers, who are indigenous to Ireland though interestingly, people keep taking Travelers out of the equation when speaking about racism.

What we were suggesting in the book was that racism grew in times of prosperity as well as in times of poverty. When Ireland became prosperous, suddenly racism was talked about, particularly in 1997 in the European Year against Racism, where there was a committee set up by the government to talk about racism. And as McVeigh and I say in our second book *After Optimism,* there was a moment of optimism with that talk in that issues around racism could be addressed and understood. But in fact, that wasn't the case, and all those discussions have since gone.

The recession has affected the situation in that migrants were seen as coming in to plug in the labor shortages because Ireland needed labor. There was a prediction that we needed around fifty thousand migrants per year to keep prosperity, but now that prosperity has disappeared, migrants are represented as people who have come here to take "our" jobs. The recession has affected attitudes and the way in which people talk about migration. They talk more openly about migration today, so what they didn't say in 2008, they said in 2009 after the recession. The impetus to be politically correct during the boom has completely disappeared because the discourse after the recession was that we don't need to be politically correct anymore because "they" are just here to "take our jobs."

Whiteness is not challenged in Ireland today nor was it challenged before. Following Barnor Hesse and his work on white amnesia in Britain, I have written that there is a huge white amnesia in Ireland, where people do not recognize their privilege, and I think we need to acknowledge that—but it's becoming less and less popular as people increasingly deny the existence of racism. They claim we can't be racist because the government is supposedly anti-racist. For example, many people wouldn't agree that immigration policies are part of state racism because, after all, it's "common sense"; we can't have "too many migrants here," and so on. The discourse of neoliberalism continues to determine the terms of integration, immigration, and deportation policies, and to this day, we are still struggling with this. So the NGOs are saying deportation policies are OK because they are part of the immigration regime, provided they are done humanely and remain in agreement with human rights principles. But I'm saying, "Deportation is never OK," and critics say to me, "So do you want an open door policy?" And I say "Yes, sure, because you as an Irish white person want the right to go anywhere you want. So why shouldn't a Nigerian black person have the right to come here?" But people really don't want to hear that in Ireland.

So the main points about our book *Racism and Anti-Racism in Ireland* was to interrupt these discourses. It was the first book to actually say, yes, there is racism in Ireland; no, it's not new; yes, there is also racism against Travelers, who are the largest racialized group in Ireland; and no, it's not only about migrants. In that respect, it made a contribution.

What do you think is distinctive about the Irish postcolonial experience, and what do you consider the main consequences of the occupation of Ireland by the English to be?

That's a very big question, and there are many scholars who have theorized Ireland as a postcolonial entity, particularly Declan Kiberd and people of that nature. The most distinctive thing is actually that, in becoming independent, Ireland reinvented itself as an English country. It's very interesting, and Declan Kiberd's book *Inventing Ireland* really shows that the colonial model was reproduced—and we say that about Africa or India—but the exact same thing happened in Ireland. There are, however, some key differences from England; for example, there is a constitution and a different judicial system. Ireland was nonetheless modeled on England, and the differences were designed to mark Ireland as different. However, when we look at language, one can see quite clearly that the Irish language is not that prominent. Yes, you may have options on the ATMs to see the information in Irish Gaelic or English, but only 12 percent of the population speak Irish, so it's a minority language.

Having bought into the idea of the neoliberal state, Ireland has been hugely influenced by Britain—even though it wouldn't fully admit to it. If you look at its immigration policy, it is completely modeled on British immigration policies. For example, you have the 1905 Aliens Act in Britain, and you have 1935 Aliens Act in Ireland, which came into being shortly after the state was founded and not yet repealed. You also have the Common Travel Area, so Ireland has followed Britain closely in its policy, including the most negative one called "Direct Provision and Dispersal" for asylum seekers, which is horrible because asylum seekers are put in hostels as deportable subjects. The fear is that Ireland is the backdoor to Britain because, if somebody gets refugee status, then he or she will be able to go to Britain or the EU.

So, in that respect, Ireland is a postcolonial entity that has really reinvented itself in the shape of its colonial master. People in Ireland, for instance, are obsessed with the queen; they consume British television, British papers, and all that sort of thing—so it's been very influential. But beyond that, there are also some disavowals. While Ireland has never been a colonizing power, Irish people always served in the British Army and the British colonial administration. They have also served as missionaries in large numbers. So there has been a so-called cultural colonialism, and these things have not been fully addressed yet. It's very important to remember that Ireland was also part of the colonial enterprise, and having been both colonized as well as part of the enterprise makes this case all the more unique.

The implications for racism then become clear: Irish people have reinvented themselves as white; in the United States, for instance, there are important texts about this issue, including *How the Irish Became White* by Noel Ignatiev. David Roediger also wrote about it, and there are some interesting postcolonial thinkers here in Ireland, such as Luke Gibbons and Declan Kiberd, who I mentioned earlier, but their work is largely located in literary studies rather than in the social sciences—which in itself is also quite interesting. With all this, the point I would want to make is that it is very obvious that there is a desire by the Irish to Westernize and not to Easternize.

Your recent auto-ethnography, *Co-memory and Melancholia*, contributes to your extensive work around Israel and Palestine. Could you talk about the construction of collective memory in Israeli society and how this links with the memory claims of Palestinians?

The construction of memory in Israel is based on victimhood and very much on the Holocaust. The entitlement to the land of Israel, which actually is quite a recent invention (as argued by Shlomo Sand), is linked in recent times with the history of the Holocaust far too much. Therefore, when Palestine is constructed as a land without people for a people without land, it actually translates into daily entitlements in the territories, and we see this through the media and social networking sites and the way in which the settlers behave toward the Palestinians. We remember the Bible as if it happened yesterday, and we also remember all the years of victimhood in order to justify the entitlement we have on that land. Through this discourse, Palestinians are dehumanized.

The Palestinians themselves perhaps have a shorter memory span. They have been on the land for some hundreds of years, but it's not clear where they came from. Have they always been there, or have we always been there? And these things are played on all the time. There were many tribes in that space of land, so it's not clear who was what, and the idea of the Jewish nation or the Jewish people is an invention too, as it's not clear where Jews came from.

But in the memory of the history, there are clearly elements of remembering and constructing Jews in a particular way—that is, when they came to Palestine, they were represented as modernizing and modern, whereas Palestinians were represented as backward and unmodern—and these constructs continue to circulate to this day. So, for example, when the Israeli army destroyed the Bedouin village Al-Araqib for the sixty-sixth time in the last three years, the Bedouin people were constructed by the Israelis as an unmodern, primitive, and nomadic people without any technological advances or university degrees; they were basically seen as rubbish, not human. We can see then through their "modernization" the way in which the Israelis racialized "others" and disregarded what these people were. Israel does not want to believe that some people wish to live in their own way within this space, and the Israeli army, as a result, sees itself as completely allowed and entitled to demolish these villages despite the fact that the Bedouin people have been there for centuries.

So I think that the collective memory is constructed on these premises but, more specifically, in relation to the Nakba of 1948, which saw the evacuation and deportation of over three quarters of a million Palestinians from the land. The year 1948 is commemorated or remembered by the Israelis as their "war of independence," a war of "no choice," and this understanding for me ignores the element of violence that was involved in the creation of the Jewish State and its then occupied territory. As Ernest Renan would say, forgetting the violence involved in state formation is central to the formation of a nation. This forgetting also erases the fact that this was the intention from the very beginning— the whole land of Israel, the land of Israel from the river to the sea—and this is precisely what pro-Palestinian demonstrators say: "Palestine will be free from the river to the sea." This area has the entitlement of both these people; that's why I believe in a one-state solution; I don't believe in any other solution. Critics argue that the one-state solution would mean a Muslim state, and you see all the Islamophobic discourses about Muslim Jihads and so on, but I think the Jewish state of Israel is temporary.

Could you elaborate on your use of the "state of exception" (Agamben 2005) and the "racial state" (Goldberg 2001) in your rethinking of Israel-Palestine?

The state of exception according the Agamben is a state where the sovereign enacts a law that he takes himself out of; in other words, you enact a law for people who Agamben calls "bare life," whose lives are at the mercy of the sovereign. Yet the same law does not apply to the sovereigns "over there." Again, we do not have to go very far to see this on a daily basis. The army thinks it can destroy a village, and the law that gives it permission to do that does not apply to "these" people because if "they" try to enact a rebellion or an armed intifada in resistance to that, they would be "terrorists" or "jihadists."

What is important to remember about the state is that there is also a "state of emergency"; Israel is in a constant state of emergency, and the British-mandated emergency regulations enacted in 1945 continue to be re-enacted every year by the Israeli parliament. So we are actually ruled by a series of emergency regulations in a state of exception, which allows us, for instance, to call asylum seekers "infiltrators." But infiltrators are people who have no right to seek asylum; asylum seekers, however, do have the right to seek asylum, which is a human right according to all the conventions that Israel has signed. So Israel is a state of exception in that it both is part of the family of nations signing all these conventions and, at the same time, takes itself out of complying with them.

As for the racial state, again, it is interesting that early Zionist ideologue spoke about Jews as a race; many Zionist Jews argued that Jews were a race. Arthur Ruppin, for example, who lived in Germany before he came to Palestine, won an essay competition on eugenics in the 1930s.[1] Now, Jews are no more a race than the Germans were a race, but the Germans constructed Jews as a race on the way to the concentration camps. Today, Jews are constructing themselves as a race and constructing Arabs as a "subhuman" race in a similar way. The notion of transfer is also very clear—that is, transfer them to the seven Arab states—and you see this type of argument all the time: "What's the problem? Don't they have enough Arab states? Why do they have to live here?"

The whole notion of entitlement and the creation of homogeneity through schooling and through the army are inborn. I mean, you are subject to it from the time you are in preschool. I remember at school, soldiers would come in and give talks; we also went to a few military events so that we were prepared, and I even had pre-military training at school. Life is geared toward being in the army. Today, it is not working well, because many people are refusing to serve. But this is a country that was "there" first, and the nation was invented after; and it is a constant process, therefore it cannot *be* but racial.

Many people, however, continue to subscribe to the idea of Israel as an ethnocracy—the rule of one ethnic group—but you cannot call Jews an ethnic group because they are so ethnically diverse. If you believe in the concept of ethnicity—which I'm not sure I do—we have people from Yemen, Ethiopia, Germany, and so on, and they all look different and behave differently so they are actually ethnically very diverse. Ethnocracy relies on the fact that one ethnic group is superior to another, but I really think it is a question of race, again, a disavowed concept. Goldberg and Agamben therefore remain very important to my arguments in rethinking Israel and Palestine. More recently, I am trying to develop this further by adding two more frameworks: one is settler colonialism. I particularly like the work of Patrick Wolfe, who examines aboriginal people in Australia; I'd like to make the link there with Palestinians. The second is that I want to introduce the notion of decoloniality because it adds something to resistance that the frame of postcolonialism doesn't fully allow for me.

Your fascinating book *Israel and the Daughters of the Shoah* is a deeply personal account offering a unique feminist analysis to examine a number of complex and interrelated issues around Israeli society, Zionist discourses, gender, and the Holocaust. Could you elaborate on your main arguments and what you hoped to achieve with this piece of work?

As I said, this book is based on my PhD. The central notion was that, by creating itself as a new, active and masculine entity—through the creating of the so-called new Jew—meant that "he" would not be like "his" diaspora brethren; the diaspora and the Holocaust becomes feminized as a result. That is, the diaspora and the survivors of the Holocaust were portrayed in Israel as passive; they were called "human dust" when they came back. So particularly, Holocaust survivors had a really hard time on their return. This has changed a lot now, but at the time, Holocaust survivors were asked, why did you not resist? That was the main question asked. So the "new Jew" was constructed around the language of force and the idea that we will fight; thus the Holocaust is commemorated together with the few acts of resistance that happened.

We see then the notion of themselves as "new," "masculine," and "active" and diasporic Jews as "passive," "feminine," and "useless." But this is, in a way disingenuous, because we build so much on Jews having been victims, and therefore we need all this space—but then, at the same time, we also blame them for having been victims. What can you do? I always claimed that a mother holding a child's hand on the way to the gas chambers and saying, "It's OK. Don't worry. Mummy is here with you," is far more brave then somebody taking up arms. It's so hard, and that was not recognized then but is beginning to be recognized much more now, though. There is a lot of young scholarship and activism in Israel that is thinking about the Holocaust in a completely different way and taking up these very ideas.

I interviewed nine daughters of survivors, who were writers and filmmakers, and they basically told me their stories, and each of the stories they told had a particular trajectory that was very clear. Nobody spoke about it at home, and when they started talking about it, they spoke about it in gendered terms. They talked about how their families were not accepted, how they were ostracized, discriminated against, and seen as useless individuals. They also spoke of what it took for them as daughters of survivors to recreate, if you will, a post-Holocaust identity and to then write about having survive; many of them went on to be very successful writers.

Somebody asked me why there was such a small sample of interviewees. Now, if you look numerically, maybe there were thirty such women, so it's a third of the population, which was pretty good. But actually, this was qualitative work, and each story was so indicative, so I really felt the stories vindicated my analysis. One particular story that kept being published is "My Sister on the Beach." This is the story of a group of pre-state militia men bringing to safety on a beach in Palestine a survivor girl who had been in the concentration camp from one of the boats that illegal immigrants came on to Israel. On her back is supposedly tattooed "for officers only." The militia men assumed that she was tainted, that she was used and sexually abused. However, they said to her, "You are our sister, and for you, we will do everything." The subtext is that "we are the strong men," "we are many—you are one," and "you are tainted—and we are pure," so there was a very clear masculine element there.

Masculinity was so inborn in the way we grew up, including sexual harassment, that it was an everyday occurrence. Many Israeli women experience sexual harassment; it's part of Israeli men's entitlement—"we are entitled because we serve in the army, so you open your legs." It was very blatant; it's a very blatant society.

How do you understand the Jewish diasporic experience in the context of the postcolonial condition, and what challenges face the Jewish diaspora today?

I don't think the Jewish diasporic experience can be understood simply through the postcolonial framework because Jews have supposedly been living in the diaspora for two thousand years. Jews have always had a parallel existence, and they still do today; it's rooted in the notion of survival. The diasporic experience is, in a way, an emblematic Jewish experience. They say you can take Jews out of the diaspora, but you can't take the diaspora out of Jews, and it's so true. There is a ghetto mentality, and what they're doing in Israel is creating a ghetto, surrounded by all these walls: on the border with Egypt so that "infiltrators" will not come in, around the Palestinian villages, and around gated communities—it's a very self-protective and self-preserving mentality, which is a very diasporic feature.

Now, in terms of the challenges facing the Jewish diaspora today, it's very interesting that the Jewish diaspora is beginning to increasingly be disenchanted with Israel. For example, more and more American Jewish youth are saying no to the occupation. Israel and the Holocaust are the two building blocks in the construction of Jewish identity in the diaspora. The Holocaust has very much become an edict: "You must remember so *it* will never happen again." But what is *it*? I always ask, does *it* include what has happened to the Palestinians? And it doesn't for most people, but those for whom it does and who are against the occupation are taking this position precisely because they love Israel and they want to remain Jewish, not because they want to see the end or the destruction of Israel. So they want Israel to be a better place where people can live in harmony while remaining Jewish, but there is a tension there between Jews who oppose the occupation and Jews who support it, and this is one of the main challenges today.

The other challenge is that of intermarriage. The increase of intermarriage means that the children will not necessarily be Jewish because, according to Orthodox Judaism, if you don't have a Jewish mother, you're not Jewish. So there is a slow moving away. Jewish people have left Ireland—which is typical of many small Jewish communities—to go to America, Britain, or Israel because there weren't enough Jews to have a Jewish life. Yet they go, and very often what happens to them is that they get away from Jewish life—so it's full of contradictions. There is a real concern how to remain a Jewish people. Maybe there are the same sorts of challenges for Sikhs. For example, Sikhs who wear the turban are clearly Sikh, like those Jews who wear the garb are also very obvious. But those who don't are not; they are just like everybody else. The main question, then, is, will there be a Jewish people in three generations?

Do you see any parallels in terms of representation, racialization, and institutionalization between the antisemitic discourse of the nineteenth century and the current Islamophobic discourse in the wake of the War on Terror?

We definitely see the same discourses from the 1930s about Jews being reproduced to construct the figure of the Muslim now. The constructs included things like Jews are a fixed culture; there are too many of them; we can't see them; they have dual loyalties; and so on. The same thing is being said about Muslims today. Now, although Jews were not constructed as terrorists—they were constructed as financial dangers, as seen with *The Protocols of the Elders of Zion* and the idea that they were colluding to dismantle the world order as it was known; the same sort of thing is being said about Muslims that they are colluding to create Islamic regimes everywhere with Sharia law and so on, but many Jews fail to recognize this similarity because they too are part of the Islamophobic discourse.

There is a lot of fear, I think: both of Jews previously, as "financial actors," and of Muslims now, as supposedly "armed actors." Jews were definitely constructed as a danger, and Hitler created this very well. They were seen as both Bolsheviks and capitalists and, therefore, a danger to the German nation. There are very close parallels, and that's why, when I teach antisemitism, I always teach it in conjunction with Islamophobia—precisely because the two are so interrelated. And I think S. Sayyid's work around this is brilliant.

In both cases, there is also a very gendered element in terms of the constructs. In relation to Islamophobia, we have the very typical image of the veiled Muslim woman who needs "rescuing" by white women and white men; it is their mission to "liberate" and "free" these women from the Muslim man. This notion is also prevalent in contemporary gay discourse; for example, Adi Kuntsman and her colleagues show how white gays want to "liberate" Muslim gays from supposedly homophobic Muslim regimes.

So there is a gendered element here, and in relation to antisemitic constructs, there was the figure of the Jewish "usurer" who was always masculine. The shylocks and so on, and then the "wandering Jew," were also always portrayed as male. There is not one picture of a Jewish woman in all these antisemitic caricatures. Jewish men then were largely constructed as predatory, while Jewish women, on the other hand, were constructed as sexually attractive—the "belle Juive." But we see the same tropes circulating in relation to the construct of black men and black women too, so I think this clearly demonstrates the way in which processes of gendered racialization continue to take place in the construction of all marked groups.

Your important book *Gender and Catastrophe* examines the gendered impact of violence against females in extreme conditions (e.g., war, genocide, ethnic cleansing, and the Holocaust). Could you elaborate on your analysis and the way in which women in such situations become markers of the nation?

Like I said earlier, Nira Yuval-Davis was influential in the birth of this particular work. Her argument was that women are "ethnic subjects" in relation to various things, and their role in particular is to reproduce the next generation; therefore, by controlling women, we control the ethnicity of the next generation. But women also become symbols of the nation. It is interesting that, in all nations, you have a symbol that is always a figure of woman—for example, *La France*, *Mother Ireland*, *Germania*, and *Britannia*—so it's very clear that there is an investment in controlling women, because there is an investment in controlling what comes out of the womb. Freud spoke of penis envy, but I think womb envy is more appropriate because women can produce human beings in their bodies and men can't, leading to male envy and anger.

Women, then, are to be both protected and attacked. I have written about the notion of "femina sacra" in recent years, gendering Agamben's notion of "homo sacer," the bare life that can be killed by the sovereign with impunity yet cannot be sacrificed because he's impure. With femina sacra, we see the idea that the figure of the woman can be both raped and killed with impunity, like in the Serbian situation where Serbian soldiers carried out mass rapes of Bosnian women, and rape, in this instance, was used as a tool to alter the structure of the enemy's ethnicity.

Interestingly, in relation to Israel and Palestine, comparatively, there were not that many rapes of Arab women by Israeli soldiers, and the reason here is racism; the women are constructed as "too dirty to touch." Although there were certainly cases of rape during the 1948 war, by and large, rape is not as prevalent a practice in this case compared to, say, in the Congo, Bosnia, or Rwanda because Arab women are considered to be "subhuman." What I found most interesting in all the chapters of the book was the way in which the women in each of the cases were positioned as vessels of the nation, and this idea is definitely something that has continued to develop in my work today.

Could you talk a little about the relationship between race and the state and how this shapes racism across Europe, particularly against the backdrop of the "post-racial"?

First of all, I think that there is a huge rise in racism, and not just state racism. There is also a huge rise in extreme right-wing movements and skinheads, particularly in eastern Europe. But I think that, increasingly, immigration policies and deportation policies are the main phenomena of the link between race and state—yet the post-racial EU and post-racial United States claim that this is not racism but rather about the rational control of "our" population. The nation-state seems to still want to assert its authority even though it is in many ways in decline—at least economic decline. For example, Ireland sold its soul completely when it gave the banks a guarantee of four hundred billion Euro and gave control over to the World Bank and the International Monetary Fund. While it lost its sovereignty in economic terms, it still has a very strict immigration policy, so nation-states remain the precinct police who control the comings and goings of immigrants. But very few people see immigration and deportation policies in terms of racism, and there is a failure to recognize this in relation to the increase of racism today.

But what is more interesting is to look at non-Western societies where whole populations are being racialized by the West. Through the decolonial approach, we are able to see that the coloniality of power remains, and even though the colonial era is over, by and large, the West still controls the non-West through economic and military terms. The fact that Obama can send drones to Yemen with impunity shows the strength of the state and the racialization and the dehumanization of whole societies. How can the United States bomb Yemen? What is going on? Obama has failed in terms of foreign policy. He has retained the United States as a global colonial power, and for me, this actually fortifies the notion of the racial state. The concept of the racial state is applicable today more than ever, but at some point, this controlling of "immigrant" populations will collapse. Take climate change for example; it's a doomsday scenario, but the time may come when there will be no food, people will be desperate, and there will be waves of people fleeing. At some point, our privilege will cease to matter.

To what extent do you think postcolonial/black thinking has been acknowledged in the social sciences, and what do you hope to see emerging from the new generation of scholars engaging with questions around race, ethnicity, and postcolonialism?

I think it depends on which social sciences you are speaking about. In Ireland, race-critical thinking has not been acknowledged properly. In Britain, race-critical scholarship is more developed because there are some major thinkers there like (the late) Stuart Hall and Paul Gilroy. We don't have anybody of that stature in Ireland, because the issue of Irish exceptionalism is still very powerful today. France has not particularly accepted this concept either, as with Germany, where they don't even speak of racism. It's the elephant in the room across many European societies, so Britain is an exception in that respect, contributing to the debates around these issues.

The post-racial notion is so strong, and anti-racism has been completely diluted. For example, in Ireland, race equality units are being amalgamated into the human rights commission. So the everyday experiences of people of color are written out of the equation. What is also scary is that scholars are also failing to talk about these issues. Somebody said to me, "Oh, Ronit. You're becoming irrelevant. You've said this so often, it's not important anymore." Yet I'm always being asked to contribute to this area because not many people are talking about it—there is a real tension there. The language of racism is clearly changing. It's framed in terms of integration, which means the topic of research is also changing as a result, and this is worrisome. Therefore, postcolonial and black thinking in this country have not had much of an influence, and when I look at young scholars, I wonder how many of them are doing the work or are allowed to do the work.

The work on migration being done now in Ireland is about migrants who are professionals, high tech, Polish and white—"lifestyle migrants." So the discourse has completely changed. We are not talking about migration anymore but, rather, about mobility. It's tough in Ireland to maintain this type of race-critical postcolonial scholarship, but it's important to remind people that these issues have not gone away. There is clearly a gap, and I hope young scholars are able to fill it with critical work around precisely these issues. I also hope that their voices will be heard and that their ideas will be taken up in the future.

Note

1. Arthur Ruppin (1876–1943) was a Zionist thinker. His works include *The Jews in the Modern World* (1934).

Selected Key Works

Lentin, R. (1997). *Gender and Catastrophe*. London: Zed Books.
———. (2000). *Israel and the Daughters of the Shoah: Reoccupying the Territories of Silence*. Oxford: Berghahn Books.
———. (2010). *Co-memory and Melancholia: Israelis Memorialising the Palestinian Nakba*. Manchester: Manchester University Press.
Lentin, A., and Lentin, R., eds. (2006). *Race and State*. Newcastle: Cambridge Scholars Press.
Lentin, R., and McVeigh, R., eds. (2002). *Racism and Anti-Racism in Ireland*. Belfast: Beyond the Pale.

CHAPTER 12

Paul Gilroy

Paul Gilroy is a professor of American and English literature at King's College London.

Could you talk a little about your biography and how you first got into the field of race, ethnicity, cultural studies, and postcolonialism?

I am of a certain generation. I grew up in London, and London is the place where the world is available if you want to find it. My parents had been politically active in different ways, so I was influenced a lot by them. I grew up as a kid going on demonstrations in my pushchair, from anti-apartheid to "ban the bomb." My mum was very involved, and my dad had been in the Communist Party. I suppose I came of age on the end of Black Power, and when I was doing my A levels, Black Power was in the air. I read Black Power literature and thought about all those sorts of issues.

Obviously, 1968 was significant. Enoch Powell made his speech, and I was 12 years old then, so I was beginning to go out and the skinheads were around. At times, you had to run for your life or they would attack you in the street. I think I was about 11 when I was attacked in the street by these kids. They didn't really hurt me, but I remember they were eating fish and chips, and as I walked toward them, they started throwing their fish and chips at me. I remember being hit in the face by this very vinegary chip and being very frightened. I didn't know what was going to happen, and I could taste the vinegar in my mouth. So I began to really wonder about what was going on.

It sounds silly to talk about the racism of those years, but it was constant in some respects. Today, people don't talk about black people eating Kit-e-Kat.[1] In those days, you weren't only supposed to go back to where you came from (which was always a challenge for me, as I was born in Bethnal Green) but there was also the daily racism one had to put up with, from Kit-e-Kat, to "coons," to "Jungle bunnies,"[2] and so on, and these kinds of things were just constant features of London life. For me, they were educative, I suppose. So when you ask how I first got into the field of race, ethnicity, cultural studies, and post-colonialism, I would say I was born into it, and in order to understand your own experience, you need to find the tools to interpret it and to understand its historical setting. I went to Black Power and, from there, into other things looking for those resources.

How did you develop your sense of political consciousness?

I developed it from family but also when I was still at school; we thought the revolution was coming. We did actually think that the revolution was coming, and there was a very strong counterculture around. It was there in the music; it was there in what you read; and it was there in poetry. I suppose, in a small way, I led an activist life; I was involved in politics in school.

I remember David Frost used to have a discussion show on television. In 1972 or 1973, it was all about different forms of protest in England, from the miners, to the trade unionists, to Black Power people. One day, everybody was summoned into the studio of ITV, and I went with a couple of my friends who had been involved in the struggle of school children in London to keep our cheap fares on the buses and trains. In those days, we used to pay a half fare on the bus, and that was to be taken away from us, so we were revolting about that. So I guess I sort of had an activist sense, although I wasn't in a political party or anything like that (that came later), but my sense of political consciousness came from my parents and from the turbulence that was going on in the world at the time.

I was very involved with making music, being a musician, and in the culture that the music created, particularly around those ideas of revolution that were very pronounced, very visible, and very palpable. The mood of the moment was that the world was changing. In 1969, I remember going to the Isle of Wight festival to see Bob Dylan play there and encountering the White Panthers, Mick Farren, and people like that, and I was actually a bit perplexed by that encounter.

I'd read about some of those issues in *Rolling Stone* magazine (we all used to read *Rolling Stone* in those days). *Rolling Stone* was not what it's become now. It's very glossy today; back then, it was almost an underground publication. For example, it had covered the Chicago trials in the previous year in great detail, so we derived a lot of our political knowledge from reading that and from looking at the alternative films being made at that time, films like *Zabriskie Point* and *Punishment Park* by Peter Watkins the English filmmaker. So there was a coherent counterculture if you wanted to inhabit that. I don't know about other cities because, at that time, I'd barely been out of London, but London was overflowing with revolutionaries; it was overflowing with revolution; it was overflowing with not just the hippies but also those at the political edge of "hippydom"—squatting, festivals, and so on.

The *Oz* trial of 1970 was also very important to me.[3] I remember we sat in our school classroom wondering about whether to join in when we saw the advert in *Oz* magazine for what would become the infamous SkoolKids issue. I think we were just too lazy, too stoned, and too out of it to go do that. But when the trial came on, I remember I went to the court in the Old Bailey and sat there for several days and watched the trail. It was a very interesting and politicizing experience for me because I'd never been in a court before and I'd never heard a judge before. I certainly had never heard a judge like Michael Argyle. The prejudices of Michael Argyle and his odious and hateful behavior in that court, the way he spoke to John Mortimer, and the way he spoke to the defendants in the *Oz* trial—all this had a very big effect on me politically.

What thinkers have most influenced you and your work?

In terms of people I know, Stuart Hall has influenced me a lot, and my partner Vron Ware has influenced me a lot because, when I met her, I was 22, and I had just read her pamphlet, *Women and the National Front*. She'd written it when she was working at *Searchlight* with Maurice Ludmer, and since that time, I have been constantly influenced by her—her perspectives, her morality, and above all, her clarity. I'd pick those two out of people I know. I did know C. L. R. James a very little bit. After *The Empire Strikes Back* came out, he wrote me a very nice letter, so I went to go see him and then went on to have a couple more meetings with him. So he really influenced me a lot. Fanon, too, very much influenced me, and Du Bois and Richard Wright. And then June Jordan, the African-American essayist and poet, influenced me a lot, and again, she was someone whom I had contact with and have some nice letters from. bell hooks was a big influence on me too, but more in a sibling sort of way.

George Orwell I think about a lot. I've always been very affected by his example. People don't like him because of his politics or because of his occasional lapses, but I always really admired him. I admired his writing first of all, and then his example. After he left the colonial police service, the first thing he did was to get his hands tattooed. So when he went back to English polite society, all the posh bastards wouldn't be able to get past the fact that his hands were tattooed, and that's always been kind of interesting for me.

The people who taught me have also influenced me; I've mentioned Stuart already. He was my teacher, but there were other teachers who really affected me: Cora Kaplan, who is a literary scholar; Gillian Rose, who was a sociologist and philosopher (she died a few years ago); and Donald Wood, another Caribbean historian who taught me when I was at Sussex as an undergraduate in my first year there. He was the one who told me to read Fanon and C. L. R. James. So my teachers, in their writing and in their example of what scholarship was, really influenced me and the way in which my work developed.

I was also influenced by the Panthers and figures like Huey Newton. The Panthers were socialists of some sort. They were leftists, and I found it easier to connect with them compared to, say, Malcolm X, because I was never really comfortable with what I took to be the nationalist side of Malcolm. Now I know more about Malcolm, and I understand more about the history of how his ideas developed. Of course, Muhammad Ali and the example of him refusing to fight in Vietnam were also important, but at the time, I didn't really like the nationalism of it. I felt that it was too obviously—or seemed so to me as a young teenager—an inversion of the forms of oppression found in the United States, and I didn't really like that. I didn't think that rewiring the polarity of that system was enough of an answer. Even then, I felt it was something that had to be disposed of.

In terms of musical influences, it's a miracle, really, to have lived through those years. I don't know where to start with that side of my story; I mentioned Dylan already. He was a huge influence on me, and Hendrix, who was living in London, was a very big influence on me, but I didn't always understand his politics. I knew there was a politics there, and I didn't really work it out in print until my last book *Darker than Blue*, where I tried to explore that. He had been a soldier, so one of the things about him was that he never really seemed to have had any other jobs apart from being a musician and a soldier. He was important to me because of his utopianism.

James Brown was also really, really important to me, and he came to the Rainbow in Finsbury Park in 1972. I've still got the ticket from that night. Brown alerted me to the significance of wordless screams. His performances pointed to the deep structures of the slave sublime. Bob Marley was around, and I remember going to see him playing in a pub in Fulham. It was late 1972 or early 1973, and we were all rushing down the stairs after he'd finished his set to go and speak to him, and he began to be very important to me because hearing *Catch a Fire* changed my life quite a bit.

There were other people too, like Sly and the Family Stone, Miles Davis, and the Voices of East Harlem. But I would have to pick out Hendrix, James Brown, Sly, and Bob Marley. With Bob Marley, I didn't really like the way his music changed as a result of his apparent relationship with Chris Blackwell. I felt he'd sold out, but initially the promise and the creative explosion that *Catch a Fire* represented impacted me and my view of the world. Obviously, Rastafari and Ethiopianism were in that explosion too, and forty years later, they're still there.

My mum had an old copy of the University of the West Indies report on the Rastafari movement in Kingston, Jamaica (1960), which is a very important social science document. It's a very important piece of the political anthropology of Caribbean societies. I read that document, and it really provided a sort of poetic frame for my connection with what I took to be as a Caribbean idiom of Black Power.

How do you understand the postcolonial, and what do you consider the main contributions of postcolonial thinking to be? Furthermore, do you think of yourself as postcolonial thinker, and would you situate your work within this genre?

I suppose I do think of myself as a postcolonial thinker, and I would situate my work within that genre to some degree. I don't think that postcolonialism should just refer to literary scholarship done by posh people of Indian heritage in American universities, so yes, I would consider myself to be part of that conversation. C. L. R. James wrote an essay called "Black Studies and the Contemporary Student" in which he attacked the idea of black studies as therapy in universities or colleges and schools. I feel about postcolonial thinking the way he felt about black studies, which is that it offers an opportunity to tell an alternative history of the world. Postcolonial thinkers should seize that chance to tell an alternative history of the world.

Could you talk about your early involvement in the Centre for Contemporary Cultural Studies at the University of Birmingham? Do you think there is a connection between the objectives of cultural studies and postcolonial studies?

I went to Birmingham, and I didn't know that I wanted to be an academic. It didn't occur to me that that would happen in my life. I thought I might be a primary school teacher or a musician or a planner—something like that. But when I finished my undergraduate degree at Sussex, I felt like I hadn't finished my thinking, and I wanted to go on a bit more. I applied to do a master's, and Birmingham was the only place I applied. Some people tried to warn me about going there and said, "Go do sociology of literature at Essex instead." I nearly did, as I really liked what they were doing. So those were the two options I had to think about. But why did I decide to go to Birmingham? I knew it. That was a big factor because I had been involved with a woman who lived in Birmingham, so I had some sort of idea of Handsworth, and that was interesting to me.

Handsworth also appealed to me because I knew some of the roadies for the band Steel Pulse, and one of them, Andy Bowen, was involved with producing and managing. He arranged for me to get together with David Hinds, who was the leader of Steel Pulse. David and I were the same age, and we were sort of struggling with some of the same things. I remember going to talk to him in his apartment up there, spending the afternoon with him playing the guitar, and thinking, "Well, OK. Birmingham's all right. I can do this for a bit." So that helped me choose to go there.

I really respected Stuart Hall. This was just before *Policing the Crisis* came out, so I didn't go there because of *Policing the Crisis*. Although I knew that there was that sort of work in the background, I didn't really know that much about it, but I had seen *Resistance through Rituals* in the bookshop. It's a book about working-class culture that they collectively produced in Birmingham. I looked at it and thought to myself, "If one can do this kind of thing at a university, then that's the university I want to go to." So that's what I did. When I got there, there weren't a lot of black people, I was very good friends at the time with a guy named Bob Williams-Findlay, who was a poet and would later become an influential activist for people who were disabled. Bob had a big impact on me. We shared a great love of Kafka. Bob was a Trotskyist, and he had a great rhetorical flourish. He was a great orator, and he and I started the race and politics group. The third person in the mix at that time was Valerie Amos, who had written her master's thesis on the history of racialization in the nursing profession.

So we started this group, and we began to recruit other people and drew others in. Hazel Carby came in quite early on, but it was Valerie, Bob, and I who started it. It was very energizing and very exciting because it was a collective project, and it was something that was beyond our individual research yet was judged to be necessary in that moment of pedagogy. I learned a great deal from the other people in that group: from Andy Green, who is at the Institute of Education now; from Robin Wilson; from Valerie, in a funny way; and from Hazel. Our conversation continues to this day, so we are still teaching each other's work.

There were a number of other people in Birmingham who were very supportive and helpful to me: John Clarke, who writes about social policy; Paul Willis, who was very kind, respectful, and thoughtful; and Hazel Downing, who had wrote her PhD on new technologies. She was the first woman to finish her PhD in the cultural studies center. So there were a lot of interesting people around there. The year that I went, in my class, there was Michael Denning, who is now a professor at Yale; David Batchelor, who is a very famous artist; and Michael O'Shaughnessy, who is now a singer in the Spooky Men's Chorale; as well as Adam Seligman, Ioanna Nicolaidou, and Guillermo Sunkel. We were a crop of amazing people—refugees from Chile and Greece, insiders, outsiders. Although we were being lectured to and were learning from our teachers, we also kind of taught each other, and for some reason, that suited me.

In terms of the connection between cultural studies and postcolonial studies, I'm not really comfortable with the formalization of these fields. Basically, I'm with the eleventh thesis of Feuerbach. The point is not simply to interpret the world but to change it. So, when these areas of work become "fields," there are questions one has to ask oneself about the value of them. I've been influenced by Georg Lukacs, and he argues about the reification of bourgeois forms of knowledge, so in my own practice, as a writer, thinker, and intellectual—although not always as an academic—I don't really respect the boundaries placed between fields because it seems to me that those divisions are just symptoms of the reification of knowledge. I don't think that knowledge gains from being reified.

There are connections between every so-called field, and that's why we are drawn to multidisciplinary work. Cultural studies is a multidisciplinary project, and at its best, I guess I'd say postcolonial studies was also a multidisciplinary enterprise. So we are drawn to multidisciplinary work because we reject that reification. This probably sounds like a transmission from the valley of the dinosaurs, but that's what I think. If you take a bit more time to understand, to breathe, to be curious, and to pursue your curiosity in a range of different directions, then I think you will do more interesting work.

The Black Atlantic has been incredibly influential to the field. Could you elaborate on your rethinking of diaspora and how it feeds into your powerful critique of Afrocentrism and Eurocentrism as means of reformulating ideas around culture and cultural nationalism in the wake of modernity?

Well, I suppose what I was trying to do with the notion of diaspora was to say that diaspora wasn't just migration. A lot of people want diaspora to be migration, but it's not; it's something more than that. It's a certain kind of migration that's really prompted by violence, conflict, and the idea of flight. I was trying to fight for diaspora to mean more than just migration.

When I went off to live in the States, I wasn't in a new diaspora. I was electively choosing to migrate, which is a very lucky and privileged thing to be able to do. So the first thing is that I didn't just want diaspora to mean migration alone. The issue is this: How do people become present to one another politically? How is that mediated through technology, print, sound, or by the movement of real bodies? And how does that becoming present together fit with the limits of a methodological nationalism that privileges the contours of national states as the focus of interpretation or focus of research?

Obviously, my mum had been a migrant, so I understood what migration had done to sociality, culture, history, literature, and so on—in her life and in my life. I wanted to try to find a different angle on those notions of connectedness. I'd read Robert Farris Thompson; he's who coined the term _black Atlantic_, and he was my colleague at Yale. He's an art historian and anthropologist, and he's done some very interesting work. For him, it was about the idea that there were African survivors that found their way into the New World. Then they were reanimated, brought back to life; they were intact. So there they were in Africa, and then they reappeared in the New World in the Western Hemisphere. It seemed to me that that was too simple a view of culture because it suggested that things weren't altered in their displacement, in the flow from one place to another. I wanted to accentuate the transformations that happened. I wanted to show that, when you put something into a ship, that isn't the end of it; it could be the beginning of something else. So those were the kind of ideas that I was working with.

In relation to the critique of overly centered and nationalist thinking, Afrocentrism and Eurocentrism are not the same kinds of phenomenon, but they are centered in that they work within the fundamental code of a methodological nationalism that I reject. They see the national state as a founding unit, an essential principle of political thought, of political theory. Eurocentrism is bigger than that, in the sense that it also implies a kind of making of the world in a pattern that is centered on Europe, and it seemed to me that Afrocentrism hadn't done that, really.

It's the same thing that I described earlier, when I said that rewiring the contours of a system of thought that privileged one set of experiences of one place or one space over others and making it into a space you liked and identified with didn't solve that problem, it just repeated the problem. So I wanted to offer some alternative ways of managing that pressure, and I found them in the poetics of what I suppose I'd want to call pelagics—thinking about long-distance travel over water, thinking about ships and shipboard life. I'd been very influenced by not only Robert Farris Thompson (although I rejected his theory) but also Peter Linebaugh and later Marcus Rediker and the work that they were doing toward the book that would eventually be published as *The Many-Headed Hydra*.

In your groundbreaking book *There Ain't No Black in the Union Jack*, you challenge both intellectual and political discourses and practitioners around race, particularly their failure to engage with race issues adequately. To what extent do you think the politics of race have changed from 1987 to now, especially with the increasing emphasis on the so-called post-racial?

That's a big one, isn't it? It's very difficult to answer that question. The politics of race have changed significantly. They have been changed above all by the entrenchment of the neoliberal revolution, but there are also great similarities too. What I was trying to do in *There Ain't No Black in the Union Jack* was to say that people talk about class, people talk about gender, but they don't talk about race, and race interpretively has to have the same sort of epistemological valency that these other systems of interpretation and critique have, and I do believe that. But I don't like the language of intersectionality, although there is something about the language of intersectionality that points beyond that formula; it asks how these things become entangled and offers a new theoretical problem or object when we ask the question of how these systems of domination, subordination, inequality, expropriation, and exploitation can be articulated together. I wanted to ask that question in a serious way.

Another thing about this particular book was that, for me, I had begun—by the time that I'd written *The Black Atlantic*—to see that racisms produced races, not the other way round. That's a hard one for people. I think many people think that race is nature, that it's in the body and the world, and if we look round the room, we see the different classifications we can put people into. They think that racism just comes along after nature made those basic differences and then pollutes them in the world by distorting them into a hierarchy. Instead of saying everything's beautiful, everything's equally wonderful, racism makes it into a hierarchy and places black people on the bottom, white people on the top, and we'll quarrel about who's in the middle. I don't really buy that way of thinking.

It seems to me that racisms as systems for making meaning, as systems for exploitation, as systems of power, control, domination, government, law, science and aesthetics produce races; they generate and assemble—I prefer orchestrate—them. That's not the same thing as saying that they are natural phenomena that get misrecognized. If you want to be an anti-racist in the latter model, you say we will keep race as natural difference but get rid of all the racism that comes along secondarily and messes it up. A lot of Americans take this position: the idea that racism intrudes on the beauty of racial diversity. They think they can have racial diversity without the prejudice, the inequality, the penal system, or Jim Crow; they want to retain the natural difference rather than to denature race.

What I'm saying is that there is no nature "there" underpinning sociality. All those racial actors are generated by the systems that are committed to a racial order, or a racial hierarchy, and once we get rid of those systems, we don't know whether the things that we now call "races" would even survive. Maybe they would, maybe they wouldn't, and maybe there would be even worse ways of doing bad things to each other. That's perfectly possible too, but I think that we might be better off without that particular way of doing bad things to each other.

I see race as a political ontology, as something that follows from the deployment of racial orders, the life of racial orders, and systems in the world. I don't see race as an innocent variety of natural difference that underpins society and history. When I think of races as socially constructed, it's not that there is natural difference and then social construction gets added on top. What I mean by social construction is that racism usually enters the world through war, violence,

exploitation, conquest, and things of this kind, and from its historical opera-
tions, local races emerge as part of the resulting racial orders. However, the idea
of race as natural difference is still dominant. There are lots of ways in which it is
cemented and reproduced, and I don't just mean by sport. There are lots of ways
in which we see it entrenched, for example, through the politics of diversity and
corporate multiculturalism that thrive on the idea of "natural" racial difference.

**When you wrote *There Ain't No Black in the Union Jack*, it was
perhaps the last years before the unified black subject fragmented
into constituent African-Caribbean and Asian parts. Since then, there
has been the emergence of a Muslim political subject. Consequently,
how do you see the relationship between Islamophobia and racism?**

I think that these mythic Muslims are racial creatures; I think they are, and
when we talk about Islamophobia, we need to ask what Islamophobia is. I
suppose I prefer to call it *misoxeny* (like misogyny), which means the hatred
of the Xenos, the hatred of the stranger. I think the figure of the Muslim is
assembled from things like the politics of immigration law as well as from a
kind of populist racism, so you couldn't really have—certainly not in Britain
and in Europe—the patterns of Muslim hatred that we have now without the
anterior history of a racial politics. Those things are intimately connected to one
another. Obviously, I'm not comfortable with any over-integrated or finished
political subject, so the Muslim political subject is an orientalist fantasy. You'll
meet a lot of Muslims before you meet the Muslim political subject, and that's
just in the nature of the way the analysis is offered.

We have a clash of civilizations supposedly going on around us, but I don't
know, or I've never met, the Christian subject presented in that discourse. Even
Anders Breivik, the Norwegian man who slaughtered all those young people
in such a vile way a couple of years ago, said he was a cultural Christian; I
thought that was very interesting. In other words, I'm a Christian, but I don't
believe in God, and actually, my Christianity has nothing to do with heaven,
salvation, or sin. There's therefore a certain cultural disposition that is extracted
from "fantasy Christianity," and I think those kinds of pressures yield a cultural
Christianity; they yield a clash of civilizations and the Muslim political subject.

The level of analysis that's being articulated in those anxious, fearful encounters with Muslims is something that derives from an older political conflict of
doubt about the leaky borders of racial groups—in particular, around the ways
that incoming settlers from postcolonial places are judged to be people who are
intruding into, corrupting, corroding, or polluting the life of a nation that is
supposedly clean, free of pollution, stable, and free of disruption before they
arrive. I don't buy that account of the history of the UK.

After Empire examines the relationship between the end of imperial rule and its impact on Britain around issues of multiculturalism and racism. Could you elaborate on these arguments in light of Britain's support of imperial adventures of the American Empire?

In the 1950s, people really wanted American stuff in the UK. Richard Hoggart's book *The Uses of Literacy* considered the impact of American culture on life in this country. Hoggart is in Leeds or somewhere, and he's looking at some people going into the new Milk Bar, and in the Milk Bar, there's a jukebox, and on the jukebox there's rock and roll. Part of the concern of cultural studies in their original formative moment has been defined by the cultural impact of American life and American modernity in Europe.

In the things I've written on African-American culture in European countries, there's a sense in which I talk about black culture being part of the clearing up after the war. In the 1970s, Tony Benn, E. P. Thompson, and a lot of people on the British Left—even though they might have been very friendly and had personal relationships with Americans and American culture—were concerned about American imperialism as something that was kind of engulfing British life and interests. Tony Benn, at one point in the late 1970s and early 1980s, was talking about Britain as a country that had been colonized by America, so I think there is a kind of a secret history of the relationship between England and America that's being played out in the second half of the twentieth century, and much of the concerns with culture and politics that come into play derive from that.

So what we are faced with today is living out the twilight of that relationship, and it's odd because those forces and those flows of information, of personnel and of ideas, have created the neoliberal experiment around us that is often felt as a kind of Americanization, and that Americanization of everyday life is very ambivalently held. There are some people who like the idea of being entirely responsible for themselves and their own fate; I think generationally a lot of young people find it liberating. For example, not every one of my young colleagues is in the trade union. They don't see the value of that necessarily. Perhaps they feel that there's a form of freedom involved in taking possession of your own selfhood and your own fate, of imagining that you can be responsible for your own fate; that's a powerful fantasy, so I think all that is being worked out in the support of the American Empire.

Perhaps Tony Blair and Gordon Brown were the last ones to be simply and unambiguously obsessed with America. The results of Blair's relationship with Bush are some of the things we are still struggling with today. As the Conservative Party dies as an organization, and as our British politics become a different kind of affair than they were when people were members of mass-based political parties, the relationship with America will change. On some level, people hate

"Merikins," but at the same time, they are captivated and fascinated by a version of American modernity that they find exciting. It's the romance of Americana, even in its dystopian forms, that people are invigorated by.

I don't know where that's going to end. We see it in the language; we see it in the way in which the technology works, and the politics of race are a part of that too. What does the March on Washington really have to do with the UK? Beyoncé isn't just a radiant exemplar of American modernity; there's also a kind of uber-femininity there that people are certainly taking note of. It becomes part of the way that they understand themselves as women or girls, and there are other examples of that. The Obamas might be another example that we could draw out in the same way. So, in terms of British politics of race, it turns into an argument about where our black celebrities are. Why don't we have Beyoncé? Or when are we going to have an Obama? Is it going to be Chuka Umunna, or is it going to be Adam Afriyie? And that's about the sort of boundary of it. *After Empire* was trying to say that there's a bit more going on than that!

Many of the neocon supporters of the War on Terror have cast this conflict as war between liberalism and Islamofascism. Given your opposition to both the Iraq War and black fascism, could you perhaps suggest how one could navigate between these contending claims?

Ha! I have problems with the idea of Islamofascism, but that doesn't mean that Islamofascists don't exist. I mean, there are [Islamofascists] because fascism, as the great revolution of the twentieth century, touches everything that we know in our world. And there are black versions of that; there are white Aryan versions of it; there are Jewish versions of it; and there are Christian fundamentalist, white power, white supremacist versions of it, and so there's no surprise if there's also a Muslim version of it too. These expressions are the routine currency of our modernity or our postmodernity—however you want to see that. The problem is in recognizing the provenance of the new fascisms when we encounter them and understanding where they came from, being able to identify them correctly. I think there's a challenge involved in doing all that, and our teaching around race is something that has to rise to that challenge.

I got a lot of stick for raising the issue of black fascism, but we—modern folks—are kin to all that, unfortunately, as well as understanding where it arises in the enlightenment project of Europe and where, in particular, it touches the understanding of what national states might be and nations might become. If we are going to build nations and make states of our own, we have to be careful about the tools, the intellectual equipment and resources, as well as the analytical habits that we bring to bear on those processes. The history of Liberia, the history of Haiti, the history of Ethiopia—the three independent states of the black world in the twentieth century—each of them has things to offer to us in our understanding of the history of fascism.

Again, people didn't really see why I was going on and on about fascism in *Between Camps*, but perhaps we need to know more, not less, about fascism and how it works at the level of everyday life, how it arises in terms of its history, how it links with questions of political solidarity, how it works with political symbols, how it manages the relationship between political power and information, and how it relates to advertising and things like that. I don't think we've really explored that as deeply as perhaps we need to—even now.

One can single out the place of the body in fascist politics as being particularly resonant. Let's stick with the Beyoncé example for a moment. What are the attributes of that as an ideal body? I'm not talking about Beyoncé—I don't know what Beyoncé actually looks like, because I see an endlessly photoshopped, edited, and entirely virtual Beyoncé that is represented and projected in the world as a kind of ideal female body. It's the relationship between the ideal and the lived reality that's the issue. I guess you could make similar arguments about the porn bodies that are so much a part of people's lives now as well as the saturation of Internet culture and computer use with pornography. We need to think a little about the politics of the body in that light as something that might connect with the figuration and production of the ideal body in the world of pornography, or similarly, to think about that in relation also to the fascist world, at the 1936 Olympics. That's a massive subject, but I just want to point to those links. It's not a way of saying, "Aha! What you thought you were doing when you were watching Jessica Ennis was actually secretly fascist!" I'm not saying that, but I am saying that there are historical connections, and I was thinking a lot about that when the Olympics were in London—about the relationship between 1936 and the recent national spectacle, the ideal body, the heroic story, and the scripting of our national moment of becoming at ease with ourselves. I think that there are more connections there than there are differences, and it's worth having that conversation out in the open.

Against Race examines the extent to which the progress of the civil rights movement, decolonial mobilizations, and anti-racism projects have been dismantled and calls for the rejection of race in favor of a new political language. Do you see this language in operation today, or is it a language "to come"?

I don't see the language in operation today, and is it a language to come? I hope so; I don't think there's any reason to suppose that the programmatic part of it can't be reached. It boils down, on the one hand, to the idea of planetary humanism and, on the other, to the idea of racisms producing races, rather than the other way around. I don't think I've begun to win any of those arguments yet. But when the electricity starts going off, when the water starts to rise, when the river Thames is lapping up past us, who knows what things people are going to judge to be important? I don't necessarily think, for example, that the national state as a piece of political technology is going to be able to survive the impact of climate change; I'm not so sure that's going to happen at all. You might find, for example, that all the people that live around a body of water are going to have to find some way of acting together in order to survive, and that just won't send them away from the water toward their national states somewhere else on higher ground, but it might send them into some sort of kin relationship with each other that they haven't had before.

The methodological argument that came out of *The Black Atlantic* was about taking bodies of water as negative continents and then seeing how the edge of the water—the places on the rim, as it were, of the water—corresponded or connected at the time, and what the trade was, and what the various things were that were circulating there. The sea becomes a place that hosts these mixtures, and I think that kind of approach can be extended. It is likely to be part of the way in which we see things begin to alter as climate change becomes more apparent to people.

The humanistic part of it, planetary humanism, is still a useful way of naming a problem. If you are thinking about representative democracy, you're probably wondering how many people there are in India. How many people are there in China? We're talking about billions and billions of people, so emergent planetarity has to engage their understandings of themselves, their lives, their morality, their ethics, their hopes, their fears, and their anxieties about the future, so if it is to be truly worldly, we don't know what that's going to look like. I am not going to say that it's impossible for that to happen or that it is such a tainted, utopian idea that it's not even worth discussing. I'm not going to do that, because we don't know what's going to happen.

You have been a pioneer in cultural studies and a lead thinker in race, ethnicity, and postcolonial thinking. What do you see as the main thread that stitches your diverse range of works together?

My hatred of nationalism I suppose is the thing that stitches everything together—my hatred of nationalism. I am a sort of dinosaur humanist in that sense; I have been influenced by people like Stuart Hall and C. L. R. James, and there's a strand in Marxism that follows that line. Gramsci might be part of it; Lukacs might also be part of it. It's the side of Marx that goes back to the 1844 manuscripts, to the sense of Marxism as a philosophical anthropology of a certain kind. So that's one of the things that also helps stitch things together.

And the other thing, I suppose, is this sense of a critique of productivism—that is, Marxism is attractive for its philosophical anthropology but, to me, repellent for its productivism and its view of labor as the center of everything, so I am trying, as many people have also tried, to put the account of work ethics alongside an account of play ethics. It derives from the history of the black Atlantic, the history of the people who were enslaved, and who therefore didn't look to work as a means to freedom but looked instead at creativity, play, art, and culture as offering them freedoms that the world of work didn't afford them. Those are the fundamental ideas to be found within my work.

In the contemporary academy, to what extent do you think postcolonial/black thinking has been acknowledged in the social sciences, and what do you hope to see emerging from the new generation of scholars engaging with race, ethnicity, and postcolonialism?

Has postcolonial/black thinking been acknowledged in the social sciences? No, not really. The struggles I have had really demonstrate that. To give you a small example, to make someone like Du Bois part of the history of sociology, you'd think people would be keen to do that, but they're not. And there are interests involved in the parochialization of social scientific knowledge, not its cosmopolitanization. Of course, there are people who want that, and there's a conflict between the two sides, but I don't necessarily think we could say that the cosmopolitans are winning that struggle. I think we'd have to say it's too soon to see what the outcome would be.

What would I like to see emerging from the generation? I'm glad there *is* a new generation; that's the first thing. And I'd like to see a successor analysis to the one that was offered in *There Ain't No Black in the Union Jack*. I would like to see someone write an *Ain't No Black in the Union Jack*–type book that spoke to the situation that we are in now, and I don't really see why that couldn't be done. In a way, I'm a bit surprised that [it hasn't,] following the London riots a few years ago (maybe I'm just ignorant and that work's going on somewhere), but I haven't seen much of that work seriously rising to the challenge. I do wonder what makes people hesitant, because there are lots of young people who could do that if they thought it was in their interest as scholars, academics, sociologists, or anthropologists. I wonder if they are intimidated out of doing it because it's not thought to be "real" scholarly work.

When I wrote that book, I didn't have a job—and I didn't think I'd ever get one—so probably I was a bit freer to try to not follow the rules or to not follow the scripts. But I wonder, with the way that career paths operate today, if people are a bit fearful; I wonder about those pressures. Perhaps it's also a bit about a loss of a certain perspective, and maybe that's one of the things that made the riots different this time, because a lot more people were saying, "They're scum," "They're just after trainers," or "They're going shopping without money," and they weren't really prepared to say, well, actually, maybe we need a different sort of explanation rather than the one that says that they are just out for themselves and therefore it doesn't need to go any further than that.

If we lived in a world in which racism "is finally and permanently discredited and abandoned" (Bob Marley 1976), what do you imagine would be the biggest differences that we would see? In other words, what would a world without racism look like?

Well, I don't know the answer to that. I do think that a world without racism wouldn't mean a world without stupidity or cruelty or selfishness, and the ingenuity of people in doing awful, hurtful, evil, and wrong things to each other knows no boundary. Its relationship with racial orders, racial categories, and racial histories is a very contingent one, so I wouldn't want to think that, by getting rid of it, we would get rid of every problem we've ever had—but I still think we'd be better off without it.

You can look at what's happened in South Africa as a very interesting empirical case to pursue the partial dismantling of apartheid. You can't undo in 10, 15, or 20 years what's been in place for 200; that's not going to happen. But there is a sort of uneven development of that going on in the South African case, an uneven development of the undoing of race that is very important. So that's one thing.

The other thing I suppose I'd say is that we have to adjust our understanding of these questions—"a world without race" to a non-teleological way of thinking—so it's not just about thinking about the future. It might also mean looking at the past in a different way, thinking about worlds that existed without racial categories, and then looking at those historical precedents. There are places in the world where people managed to get by and work through their differences and dwell together, despite differences of faith, caste, language, religion, or law. So it isn't just a matter of speculatively thinking about the future; it's about looking at human history, thinking more carefully about those instances where that has been possible in the past, and trying to work out what it was about those societies that made that possible.

That's why I got interested in this notion of conviviality: because it speaks to the experience of the Iberian Peninsula and the time before the Jews and the Muslims were expelled from what became Spain and Portugal. Maybe even all those great cities of the so-called Middle East—the Cairos, the Baghdads, the Jerusalems—the places where that ability to dwell together and be together (which was destroyed by nationalism later on) are worth revisiting. Perhaps there are aspects about the ways in which the histories of those places operated that we might need to take another look at.

Do you think in the contemporary landscape that the postcolonial retains any of its critical and political energy? Or has it become part of the neoliberal branding of lifestyle options?

I hope it hasn't just become part of neoliberal branding. Well, there's obviously a conflict here, isn't there? And the uneven take on of the idea of the postcolonial across the disciplines is very much a symptom of that. So, for example, postcolonial literature: you can go and do a course in that, but could you go do postcolonial anthropology or postcolonial sociology? I don't know the answer to this because it seems to me that the answer has not yet been worked out. I suppose the issue will turn on whether people will export sociology or take their sociology degrees to China, India, or other places, and whether those issues will be made part of the curriculum of these forms of knowledge by the people who will take up the disciplines and work with them in other places outside of Europe.

It seems to me that that's going to be the test, really, because those people might have a different reason for thinking about Du Bois; the history of conquest; the building of colonial states; or the development of anthropological or sociological theories of pluralism. That's a question that is going to be settled in the future and by the way the disciplines develop outside of Europe. And if they do, it may be that these forms of knowledge will just die, and everyone will just be doing their MBA and nothing else will matter—but I don't think that will be the case.

Notes

1. Kit-e-Kat refers to a brand of cat food sold in the UK.
2. "Jungle bunny" is a racist, pejorative term to describe people of African descent.
3. *Oz* magazine was published between 1963 and 1969 in Sydney, Australia. Editor Richard Neville moved the magazine to London in 1967. Regarded largely as an underground publication, the magazine was subject to two famous obscenity trials, the first in Australia in 1964, and the second in the UK in 1971. In both trials, the magazine's editors were acquitted on appeal after being found guilty and punished with harsh jail sentences.

Selected Key Works

Gilroy, P. (1982). *The Empire Strikes Back: Race and Racism in '70s Britain*. London: Hutchinson/Centre for Contemporary Cultural Studies.

———. (1987). *There Ain't No Black in the Union Jack: The Cultural Politics of Race and Nation*. London: Hutchinson.

———. (1993). *The Black Atlantic: Modernity and Double-Consciousness.* London: Verso.

———. (2000). *Against Race: Imagining Political Culture beyond the Color Line.* Cambridge, MA: Harvard University Press.

———. (2004). *After Empire: Multiculture or Postcolonial Melancholia.* London: Routledge.

———. (2011). *Darker than Blue: On the Moral Economies of Black Atlantic Culture.* Cambridge, MA: Harvard University Press.

———. (2013). *Between Camps: Nations, Cultures and the Allure of Race.* London: Allen Lane.

CONCLUSION

Postcolonial Crossroads
Between the Devil and the Deep Blue Sea . . .

> We always knew that the dismantling of the colonial paradigm would release strange demons from the deep, and that these monsters might come trailing all sorts of subterranean material. Still, the awkward twists and turns, leaps and reversals in the ways the argument is being conducted should alert us to the sleep of reason that is beyond or after Reason, the way desire plays across power and knowledge in the dangerous enterprise at thinking at or beyond the limit.
>
> —Hall 1996, 259

The opening quote by Stuart Hall illustrates the complexities, potential risks, and rewards around the task of enervating the colonial discourse. Irrespective of the grisly ghouls and frightening fiends that the undoing of the colonial paradigm might throw out, for Hall, this is clearly a venture well worth pursuing, and one that can perhaps be achieved through a serious engagement with a postcolonial language. The postcolonial is a practice, not just a theory. In other words, postcolonial thought has a performative dimension that exceeds its expression in academic fora. Thus a collection of conversations about the postcolonial is not only a series of reflections but also a complicit part of the production and extension of the postcolonial project.

The postcoloniality of this book has two main dimensions: First is the content provided by the 12 interviewees. Although some of the thinkers in this text may not identify themselves as "strictly" postcolonial thinkers, their thinking is undoubtedly shaped by the postcolonial in that they each challenge, critically interrogate, and unsettle the hegemonic discourse of the West. This is the very heart of postcolonial thinking—that is, a conceptual and ontological understanding rather than an empirical concern.

The second dimension is provided by the structure of this volume. An attempt has not been made to provide a comprehensive and complete biography of each of the thinkers and their works but, rather, to use the medium of conservations to elicit improvisational and provisional engagements with postcolonial motifs to populate, develop, and enrich the sense of the postcolonial. The conversational modalities allow for the intersectional and interdisciplinary interweaving between life and work, between experience and reflection, and between postures and positions. These thinkers tell stories about how they engaged with the postcolonial or how the postcolonial engaged or recruited them. Their journeys uncovered that, whether they prefer to describe themselves as critical race thinkers, feminists, historians, or geographers, the question of racism—and thus the postcolonial—is central to their work.

The relationship between racism and postcolonialism is therefore significant and cannot be untangled, as one cannot understand the birth of racism outside Western colonial projects. In other words, out of Western colonialism arises racism—from explicit color-based hierarchies, segregation, and racial classifications to implicit workplace discrimination, assimilation policies, and the all too familiar "I'm not a racist, but . . ." Western colonialism marks, oppresses, and silences the "other," furnishing the binary between the West and the rest (Hall 1992), and although some may argue that formal frameworks of colonialism have been dismantled, one cannot help but see that its vestiges continue to haunt us through structures of racism that remain embedded across contemporary Western plutocracies.

The emergence of modern society is supposedly the foundational concern of the social sciences; however, given that the formation of modernity, coloniality, and racism were imbricated with each other, it is ironic to note how the sociological imagination is reluctant to consider racism as something intrinsic to modernity—and thus the formation of modern social relations—in the way it does class.[1] Racism and its analysis remains a minority concern both as a study of those deemed to be minorities, and professionally, that those who study it are often located at the margins of the profession.

The postcolonial focus on modernity and coloniality opens the path to a reconsideration of topics (that conventional social sciences and humanities have tended to marginalize) and, in doing so, provides us with a more fruitful account of not only how the world we live in came to be but also how it can be. As Walter Mignolo writes, "The strength of postcolonial theorizing resides in its capacity for epistemological as well as for social and cultural transformation. It is helping, furthermore, to redefine and relocate the task of the humanities and the cultures of scholarship in a transnational world—that is, to take the humanities and cultures of scholarship beyond the realm of modernity and their complicity with national and imperial states" (Mignolo 2000a, 126).

This collection has not attempted to uncover the "authentic" postcolonial thinker; rather, it has aimed to show a variety of postcolonial journeys that can help broaden the debates around how we are to (re)configure the postcolonial in current times. The (auto)ethnographic conversations with the 12 thinkers have told the story of awakening and the possibility of transformation. Not only has the collection discussed the main arguments of the thinkers and their contribution to the development of postcolonial studies, but it also has attempted to open up the space in understandings around the way in which the postcolonial condition impacts biographies and life stories as a means to trace their intellectual trajectories.

This book has attempted to offer a different path to the naturalized route that many of us may only know. The postcolonial represents the fork in the road and perhaps entails more twists and turns, but the promise of the decolonial makes every step along this journey more meaningful, more purposeful, and more transforming. Daring to follow the signs that point to the postcolonial when you are confronted with the crossroads is a terrifying choice, because you have dared to take a different path, to see a different world, and to make new rules. This book has aimed to signal readers to the postcolonial as a means to disrupt the colonial through the opening of a series of routes that each, in their own right, offer different stories but ultimately lead to the same objective—that is, to tell a different history of the world.

From this collection, what are we to understand by the postcolonial? There is a boundary between those who are ambivalent about the postcolonial and those who are more strident about its formations and formulations. Going through the various accounts offered, we do not uncover an "essence" that determines the postcolonial, but rather, we are given a series of overlapping but non-congruent commonalities that provide a repertoire for a range of its uses within contemporary academic conversations and interventions. All the thinkers in this collection emphasize different takes on the postcolonial, but not at the expense of other viewpoints; there is a remarkable coherence in the shape of the postcolonial as it emerges through these pages.

In Chapter 1, Sara Ahmed points to the textured nuances of European colonialism and its relationship to racism. Ahmed explores how our contemporary times (through culture, politics, education, etc.) have been shaped and framed by imperial enterprises. For Ahmed, the postcolonial relates to not only specific times and spaces but also a theoretical vocabulary to unsettle and disturb Western narratives as they appears in the everyday—that is, in the very object of our disciplines. Engaging closely with questions of race and embodiment, Ahmed sees the postcolonial as a critical site for conceptual and practical work.

In Chapter 2, David Theo Goldberg's epistemic potentialities of the postcolonial take a central place in his account as he sets out a series of commitments that he elucidates as being constitutive of the postcolonial project. For Goldberg, postcolonial thought depends on a deep anti-essentialism for the opening up of new objects of analysis. He points to the necessity of examining historical conditions, both structural and analytical, in order to understand contemporary relations of power between the Global North and the Global South. Goldberg's reading of the postcolonial emphasizes its deployment as an instrument of critique directed primarily at the hegemonic assumptions that underlie the epistemological and ontological grounding of the current assemblage of power/knowledge bequeathed to us by the European colonial enterprise.

Catherine Hall, in Chapter 3, is perhaps the most explicit in pointing to the centrality of the permutations of the postcolonial. Her understanding of the postcolonial as the continuation of the governed difference between colonizer and colonized raises important questions around power, inequality, and self-determination. Hall's conceptualization of the postcolonial moment as constitutive of the moment of recognition of race being *inside* the society, rather than outside, draws our attention to the impact of political and cultural transformations in Britain.

Boaventura de Sousa Santos's Chapter 4 formulates his take on the postcolonial in relation to the framing of a Global North and a Global South, and he does so self-consciously by bringing up debates around decolonization and anti-hegemonic praxis. For Santos, the postcolonial unsettles the key narratives of Western modernity, and central to his analysis is the critique of what he defines as the *abyssal line*, the line that separates the metropolitan societies from the colonized societies. Santos is also concerned with understanding the diversity of imperial systems as a means to add texture and complexity to postcolonial thought.

In Chapter 5, Vron Ware's interest in the postcolonial and post-imperial is linked to wider questions on empire, global wars, and geopolitical challenges. She is concerned with not only how the postcolonial relates to the idea of historical memory but also the way in which the world is very much defined by European colonialism and the United States. Ware's specific interrogation of whiteness opens the question of how imbricated whiteness is in the process of nation building and belonging. Her take on the postcolonial draws on the proximity between the postcolonial and the ex-imperial in the construction of masculinities and femininities as embodiments of nations and nationals.

Ash Amin examines in Chapter 6 the way in which the postcolonial permeates debates around space, globalization, culture, and political economies. For Amin, postcolonial thought signals the intricate and complex crossings of the hegemonic and subaltern, and he is drawn to the anti-hegemonic reconfiguration that the postcolonial promises. Amin, in his biopolitical analysis of urban spaces and their enmeshment in the networks of global flows (financial, cultural, industrial, etc.), points to the way in which the postcolonial impacts the geopolitical and the geo-cultural. His emphasis on the interplay between the local and the global, the spatialization of the postcolonial, and its appearance in urban morphologies help concretize our understanding of the postcolonial condition.

By focusing on how the postcolonial affects every day lives through the construction of cities and the transformations arising out of their connectivity to the global, Amin reminds us of Gramsci's insistence on the materiality of hegemony: the postcolonial cannot be confined to English literature curriculums but has to be acknowledged as a living force structuring lives. What emerges from Amin's account is a vision of the postcolonial as a political economy of the urban.

Avtar Brah, in Chapter 7, foregrounds the postcolonial as a product of the imperial reach of current neoliberal logics that continue to govern the world as a global entity. She sees the postcolonial as a means to critically examine the contemporary global system and challenge structures of authority and dominance that continue to regulate unequal relations of power between countries and between regional blocks. Brah exercises postcolonial thought as a way to interrogate how such structures impact and effect questions of identity formation across multiple axes.

Howard Winant's Chapter 8 draws our attention to the continuation of empire in the modern world, in fomenting and expanding the postcolonial by deferring the moment of decolonization through new forms of colonialism and imperialism found all over the globe. As the Global South remains subject to the neoliberal capitalist enterprises of the Global North, he questions the degree to which societies are able to make valid claims for their postcoloniality. Winant emphasizes the necessity for the postcolonial to be understood and practiced as a pedagogy rather than as an abstracted decontextualized philosophy. He believes that it is this pedagogic function of the postcolonial that can help leverage justice and combat the neo-colonial dispensation.

For Heidi Mirza in Chapter 9, the postcolonial denotes an interrupting of universal time and the concomitant mixing and stirring of various temporalities. That is, she sees the postcolonial as the historical linking of the past with the present to understand the challenges and possibilities in the contemporary space. The postcolonial, in this sense, allows for the critical examination of complex connections between past, present, and future. As such, Mirza alerts us to the point that, although discourses shift and change over time, racism and colonialism remain very much intact as they continue to impact racialized and gendered bodies.

S. Sayyid's analytics in Chapter 10 point to the complex ways in which anti-universalism interacts with anti-essentialism. He is critical of the use of the anti-essential to displace the critique of universalism. The postcolonial rescues from Eurocentric post-metaphysical thought the necessity of anti-universalism. Conceptualizing the postcolonial as the weakening of the violent hierarchy between the West and the non-West, Sayyid draws attention to the post-Western aspect of the postcolonial. The postcolonial then appears to mark a transition in the relations of power that expose the contingency of the contemporary ordering of the world and, in doing so, opens a decolonial horizon. For Sayyid, the production of power/knowledge can no longer be organized around what he describes as a second axial age in which the difference between the West and the rest became the axis of the world. It is this second axial age against which the postcolonial critiques (including within them anti-positivist and post-Orientalist energies) are directed.

In Chapter 11, Ronit Lentin is concerned about the postcolonial and its contamination with ideas associated with post-Zionism. As such, we see her problematizing of the "post" in her account and the preference for the decolonial. Questioning the privileges of the Global North and the concomitant inequalities of the Global South, Lentin critically engages with the racial state and its persistence in postcolonial times. For her, the racial state continues to define and limit the opportunities of those found on the wrong side of the color-line.

Paul Gilroy, in Chapter 12, emphasizes the complex methodological issues arising from a serious and sustained engagement with the postcolonial. This is a recognition of not only the multidisciplinary character of postcolonial studies but also a normative claim on behalf of the postcolonial as a form of scholarship rather than neoliberal scholasticism. Gilroy's admonishment that the postcolonial should not be reduced to simply the outputs of privileged literary writers in elite institutions designates the postcolonial as not simply a discipline or a genre but as more of a possible alternative vision of the world. This sense of an alternative vision is something that runs through all the interviewees' accounts, often biographically in terms of their engagements, interests, and appreciation for the contingency of the present as well as in terms of an analytical horizon, which sees the possibility of alternative worlds, a hope for a better future, as well as a method for weakening the incessant and insidious demands of the current hegemonic order.

My journey, in a way, reflects this quest for alternative undertakings, not fully cognizant often of this sensibility but still guided by a sneaky feeling that the hegemonic accounts didn't quite fit, at least for me. This, in a way, marks the transitional nature of the "post" knowing that the colonial order can no longer hold, and not knowing what will take its place as something to hold on to. It is this moment of detachment and dissatisfaction with the colonial—without the solace of a new dispensation—that helps some of the writers in this volume embrace the decolonial—that is, to see the postcolonial as something to be radicalized and deepened as a move toward an all-encompassing liberation.

The postcolonial sensibility, once disavowed and at the same time proclaimed in the very fabric of contemporary societies—cuisine, fashion, music, aesthetics—has become the background against which people enact their lives in many parts of the world. It's not just the takeaways or the rhythms and blues but, more prosaically, the jostling and erosion of an uncontested and uncontaminated white privilege; the refusal to take seriously the narratives of Eurocentric self-aggrandizement; and the reluctance to be mobilized for colonial wars. These all point to the myriad ways in which the postcolonial cannot be confined to metropolitan drawing rooms and elite common rooms. It seems that we are all postcolonial now. Given this postcolonial sensibility, how does one explain the persistence of coloniality? What kind of triangulation brings us colonial-style occupations and gunboat diplomacy?

There is a sense in which the thinkers in this book are at a loss to understand the depth of depoliticization that has occurred before their very eyes, in which the ethnic is celebrated superficially, European empires are denigrated and at the same time rebranded as ecumenical entities, and the epistemic energies of the postcolonial have been translated into the chronological so that the postcolonial signals the end of the chapter in colonialism, imperialism, and white supremacy. However, the postcolonial cannot be rebranded so easily, as the very heart of the postcolonial is the transformation of the balance of power; the hierarchy that held up the world between the West over the non-West cannot function as it once did. Without that violent hierarchy, the colonial order cannot be sustained, white supremacy cannot be maintained, and the South cannot be contained. This is life in the interregnum; colonialism is dying, and a new world is waiting to be born, "Whatever their theoretical take on the multiple hypotheses that inform constructions and conflations of the philosophical, the phenomenological, and the sociological other, postcolonial scholars of the future will have to remain, at least in part, students of other knowledges" (Slemon 2013, 700). As postcolonial scholars of the future, and as students of other knowledges, we see that, as the sun gradually sets on the contemporary West, a decolonial horizon is in our reach, and with that, the possibility of another story of the world to be told. In the words of Malcolm X, "It is only after the deepest darkness that the greatest light can come" (2007, 498). And that, perhaps, is what all the thinkers in this book have been saying in my quest to find the postcolonial.

ਨਿਰਭਉ

Nirbhau

Without Fear

Note

1. Reed 2006, 112–17, offers a detailed account discussing the neglect and exclusion of race and gender in social theory.

Further Reading

The following provides a list of texts referred to in the interviews throughout the collection.

Agamben, G. (2005). *State of Exception*. Chicago: University of Chicago Press.

Assad, J. (2007). *Desiring Arabs*. Chicago: University of Chicago Press.

Bauman, Z. (1991). *Modernity and the Holocaust*. London: Polity Press.

Bhabha, H. (1994). *The Location of Culture*. London: Routledge.

Bloch, E. (1986). *The Principle of Hope*. Cambridge, MA: MIT Press.

Borges, J. (1998). *Fictions*. London: Penguin.

Carby, H. (2000). "White Woman Listen! Black Feminism and the Boundaries of Sisterhood." In *Theories of Race and Racism: A Reader*, edited by L. Back and J. Solomos, 389–403. Oxon: Routledge.

Chatterjee, P. (1993). *The Nation and Its Fragments: Colonial and Postcolonial Histories*. Princeton, NJ: Princeton University Press.

———. (2012). *The Black Hole of Empire: History of a Global Practice of Power*. Princeton, NJ: Princeton University Press.

Cock, J. (1980). *Maids and Madams: A Study in the Politics of Exploitation*. Johannesburg: Raven Press.

Collins, P. (2008). *Black Feminist Thought: Knowledge, Consciousness, and the Politics of Empowerment*. New York: Routledge.

Crenshaw, K. (1996). *Critical Race Theory: The Key Writings That Formed the Movement*. New York: New Press.

Davis, A. (2011). *Women, Race, and Class*. New York: Random House.

Davis, N. (2011). *The Politics of Belonging: Intersectional Contestations*. London: Sage.

Derrida, J. (1978). *Writing and Difference*. Chicago: University of Chicago Press.

Du Bois, W. E. B. (1996). *The Souls of Black Folk*. London: Penguin.

Dyer, R. (1997). *White: Essays on Race and Culture*. London: Routledge.

Evans, S. (1980). *Personal Politics: The Roots of Women's Liberation in the Civil Rights Movement and the New Left*. London: Vintage.

Fanon, F. (1986). *Black Skin, White Masks*. London: Pluto Press.

———. (1994). *A Dying Colonialism*. London: Avalon Travel Publishing.

———. (2001). *Wretched of the Earth*. London: Penguin Modern Classics.

Ferguson, R. (2003). *Aberrations in Black: Towards a Queer of Color Critique*. Minneapolis: University of Minnesota Press.

Fish, S. (1989). *Doing What Comes Naturally: Change, Rhetoric and the Practice of Theory in Literary and Legal Studies*. Oxford: Clarendon.

Frankenberg, R., and Mani, L. (1993). "Crosscurrents, Crosstalk: Race, 'Post-coloniality' and the Politics of Location." *Cultural Studies* 7, no. 2: 292–310.

Freire, P. (1996). *Pedagogy of the Oppressed*. 2nd ed. London: Penguin Education.

Fukuyama, F. (1992). *The End of History and the Last Man*. New York: Free Press.

Gibbons, L. (1996). *Transformations in Irish Culture*. Cork: Cork University Press.

Goldberg, D. (2001). *The Racial State*. Malden, MA: Blackwell Publishers.

Gopinath, G. (2005). *Impossible Desires: Queer Diasporas and South Asian Public Cultures*. Durham, NC: Duke University Press.

Griffin, J. (2010). *Black Like Me*. New York: Signet.

Grosfoguel, R. (2007). "The Epistemic Decolonial Turn." *Cultural Studies* 21, no. 2: 211–23.

Hale, G. (1999). *Making Whiteness: The Culture of Segregation in the South, 1890–1940*. London: Vintage.

Hall, S., Critcher, C., Jefferson, T., Clarke, J., and Roberts, B. (1978). *Policing the Crisis: Mugging, the State and Law and Order*. London: Palgrave Macmillan.

Hall, S., and Jefferson, T. (2006). *Resistance through Rituals: Youth Subcultures in Post-War Britain*. 2nd ed. London: Routledge.

Hartigan, J., Jr. (1999). *Racial Situations: Class Predicaments of Whiteness in Detroit*. Princeton, NJ: Princeton University Press.

Harvey, D. (2006). *Spaces of Global Capitalism: Towards a Theory of Uneven Geographical Development*. London: Verso.

Hesse, B. (1997). "White Governmentality: Urbanism, Nationalism, Racism." In *Imagining Cities: Scripts, Signs, Memories*, edited by S. Westwood and J. Williams, 85–100. London: Routledge.

Hoggart, R., Hoggart, S., and Hanley, L. (2009). *The Uses of Literacy: Aspects of Working-Class Life*. London: Penguin Modern Classics.

hooks, bell. (1999). *Ain't I a Woman: Black Women and Feminism*. Boston: South End Press.

Ignatiev, N. (1995). *How the Irish Became White*. London: Routledge.

James, C. L. R. (1969). *Black Studies and the Contemporary Student*. Detroit: Friends of Facing Reality.

Jones, S. (2006). *Antonio Gramsci*. London: Routledge.

Kiberd, D. (1996). *Inventing Ireland: The Literature of the Modern Nation*. London: Vintage. First published in 1995.

Kristol, I. (1972). "The Negro Today Is Like the Immigrant Yesterday." In *Nation of Nations: The Ethnic Experience and the Racial Crisis*, edited by P. Rose, 197–210. New York: Random House.

Kuntsman, A., and Miyake, E., eds. (2008). *Out of Place: Interrogating Silences in Queerness/Raciality*. York: Raw Nerve Books.

Latour, B. (1996). *Aramis, or, the Love of Technology*. Cambridge, MA: Harvard University Press.

Linebaugh, P., and Rediker, M. (2012). *The Many-Headed Hydra: The Hidden History of the Revolutionary Atlantic*. London: Verso.

Lorde, A. (1984). *Sister Outsider: Essays and Speeches*. New York: Crossing Press.

Massey, D. B. (2005). *For Space*. London: Sage.

McClintock, A. (1995). *Imperial Leather: Race, Gender, and Sexuality in the Colonial Contest*. New York: Routledge.

Mignolo, W. (2011). *The Darker Side of Western Modernity*. Durham, NC: Duke University Press.

Mohanty, C. (1984). "Under Western Eyes: Feminist Scholarship and Colonial Discourses." *Boundary 2* 12, no. 3–13, no. 1: 333–358

Nkrumah, K. (1975). *Neo-Colonialism the Last Stage of Imperialism*. Bedford: Panaf.

Painter, N. (2011). *The History of White People*. New York: W. W. Norton.

Puar, J. (2007). *Terrorist Assemblages: Homonationalism in Queer Times*. Durham, NC: Duke University Press.

Rich, A. (1995). *On Lies, Secrets and Silence*. New York: W. W. Norton.

Roediger, D. (1994). *Towards the Abolition of Whiteness: Essays on Race, Class and Politics*. New York: Verso.

———. (2005). *Working Toward Whiteness: How America's Immigrants Became White: The Strange Journey from Ellis Island to the Suburbs*. New York: Basic Books.

———. (2007). *The Wages of Whiteness: Race and the Making of the American Working Class*. London: Verso.

Rorty, R. (1989). *Contingency, Irony, and Solidarity*. Cambridge: Cambridge University Press.

Roy, O. (1996). *The Failure of Political Islam*. Cambridge, MA: Harvard University Press.

Said, E. (1978). *Orientalism*. London: Penguin.

———. (1994). *Culture and Imperialism*. London: Vintage.

———. (2003). *The Question of Palestine*. London: Vintage.

Sayyid, S., and Vakil, A., eds. (2010). *Thinking through Islamophobia*. London: Hurst.

Simone, A. (2004). *For the City Yet to Come: Urban Life in Four African Cities*. Durham, NC: Duke University Press.

Smith, M. G., Augier, R., and Nettleford, R. (1960). *The Rastafari Movement in Kingston, Jamaica*. West Indies: University College of the West Indies, Institute of Social and Economic Research.

Spivak, G. (1998). "Can the Subaltern Speak?" In *Marxism and the Interpretation of Culture*, edited by C. Nelson and L. Grossberg, 271–313. Urbana: University of Illinois Press.

———. (1999). *A Critique of Postcolonial Reason: Toward a History of the Vanishing Present*. Cambridge, MA: Harvard University Press.

Stoler, A. (2002). *Carnal Knowledge and Imperial Power: Race and the Intimate in Colonial Rule*. Berkeley, CA: University of California Press.

Subrahmanyam, S. (2006). "A Tale of Three Empires: Mughals, Ottomans, and Habsburgs in a Comparative Context." *Common Knowledge* 12, no. 1: 66–92.

Svirsky, M., and Bignall, S. (2012). *Agamben and Colonialism*. Edinburgh: Edinburgh University Press.

Thompson, E. (1991). *The Making of the English Working Class*. London: Penguin History.

Thompson, R. (1984). *Flash of the Spirit: African and Afro-American Art and Philosophy*. New York: Random House.

Thrift, N. (2007). *Non-representational Theory: Space, Politics, Affect*. London: Routledge.

Wallerstein, I. (2004). *World-Systems Analysis: An Introduction*. Durham, NC: Duke University Press.

Wittgenstein, L. (1958). *Philosophical Investigations*. Oxford: Basil Blackwell.

Bibliography

Agamben, G. (2005). *State of Exception*. Chicago: University of Chicago Press.

Alessandrini, A. (2000). "Humanism in Question: Fanon and Said." In *A Companion to Postcolonial Studies*, edited by H. Schwarz and S. Ray, 431–50. Oxford: Blackwell.

Anwar, M. (1998). *Between Cultures: Continuity and Change in the Lives of Young Asians*. London: Routledge.

Arendt, H. (1968). *Antisemitism: Part One of the Origins of Totalitarianism*. New York: Harcourt Brace.

Ballard, R., and Ballard, C. (1977). "The Sikhs: The Development of South Asian Settlements in Britain." In *Between Two Cultures: Migrants and Minorities in Britain*, edited by J. Watson, 21–56. Oxford: Blackwell.

Bauman, Z. (1991). *Modernity and the Holocaust*. London: Polity Press.

Behdad, A. (2000). "Global Disjunctures, Diasporic Differences, and the New World (Dis-) Order." In *A Companion to Postcolonial Studies*, edited by H. Schwarz and S. Ray, 396–409. Oxford: Blackwell.

Billig, M. (1995). *Banal Nationalism*. London: Sage.

Brah, A. (2003). "Diaspora, Border and Transnational Identities." In *Feminist Postcolonial Theory: A Reader*, edited by R. Lewis and S. Mills, 613–34. Edinburgh: Edinburgh University Press.

Butalia, U. (2000). *The Other Side of Silence*. London: Hurst.

Butler, J. (1997). *Excitable Speech: A Politics of the Performative*. New York: Routledge.

Dreyfus, L., and Rabinow, P. (1983). *Michel Foucault: Beyond Structuralism and Hermeneutics*. Chicago: University of Chicago Press.

Du Bois, W. E. B. (1996). *The Souls of Black Folk*. London: Penguin.

Fanon, F. (2008). *Black Skin, White Masks*. London: Pluto Press.

Foucault, M. (1995). *Discipline and Punish: The Birth of the Prison*. London: Vintage.

———. (1998). *The History of Sexuality Vol. 1: The Will to Knowledge*. Harmondsworth: Penguin.

Gabriel, D. (2013). "Race equality in academia: time to establish black studies in the UK?" *The Guardian*. http://www.theguardian.com/higher-education-network/blog/2013/jul/25/race-equality-academia-curriculum.

Gilroy, P. (1993). *The Black Atlantic: Modernity and Double-Consciousness*. London: Verso.

Goldberg, D. (2001). *The Racial State*. Maiden, MA: Blackwell Publishers.

———. (2008). *The Threat of Race: Reflections on Racial Neoliberalism.* Oxford: Wiley-Blackwell.

Hall, S. (1992). "The West and the Rest: Discourse and Power." In *Formations of Modernity,* edited by S. Hall and B. Gieben, 275–320. London: Polity Press.

———. (1996). "When Was 'the Post-Colonial'? Thinking at the Limit." In *The Postcolonial Question: Common Skies, Divided Horizons,* edited by I. Chambers and L. Curti, 242–60. London: Routledge.

Heidegger, M. (1962). *Being and Time.* Translated by J. Macquarrie and E. Robinson. New York: Harper and Row.

Larsen, N. (2000). "Imperialism, Colonialism, Postcolonialism." In *A Companion to Postcolonial Studies,* edited by H. Schwarz and S. Ray, 23–53. Oxford: Blackwell.

Law, I. (2009). *Racism and Ethnicity: Global Debates, Dilemmas, Directions.* London: Routledge.

Levy, D., Sznaider, N., and Oksilloff, A. (2006). *Holocaust and Memory in the Global Age.* Philadelphia: Temple University Press.

Lorde, A. (2007). *Sister Outsider: Essays and Speeches.* New York: Crossing Press.

Mail Online. (2006). "Muslim Veil Is a Symbol of Women's Oppression, Says Jowell." *Daily Mail.* http://www.dailymail.co.uk/news/article-410622/Muslim-veil-symbol -womens-oppression-says-Jowell.html.

Marley, B., and the Wailers. (1976). *War.* London: Island Records.

Mignolo, W. (2000a). *Coloniality, Subaltern Knowledges, and Border Thinking: Local Histories/Global Designs.* Princeton, NJ: Princeton University Press.

———. (2000b). "Human Understanding and (Latin) American Interests: The Politics and Sensibilities of Geohistorical Locations." In *A Companion to Postcolonial Studies,* edited by H. Schwarz and S. Ray, 180–203. Oxford: Blackwell.

Modood, T. (1994). "Political Blackness and British Asians." *Sociology* 2, no. 4: 859–76.

Mouffe, C. (2005). *On the Political.* Abingdon: Routledge.

Rajan, R., and Park, Y. (2000). "Postcolonial Feminism/Postcolonialism and Feminism." In *A Companion to Postcolonial Studies,* edited by H. Schwarz and S. Ray, 53–71. Oxford: Blackwell.

Ray, S. (2000). "Postscript: Popular Perceptions of Postcolonial Studies after 9/11." In *A Companion to Postcolonial Studies,* edited by H. Schwarz and S. Ray, 574–84. Oxford: Blackwell.

Reed, K. (2006). *New Directions in Social Theory: Race, Gender and the Canon.* London: Sage.

Riley, N. (2012). "The Most Persuasive Case for Eliminating Black Studies? Just Read the Dissertations." *The Chronicle of Higher Education,* April 30, 2012. http://chronicle .com/blogs/brainstorm/the-most-persuasive-case-for-eliminating-black-studies-just -read-the-dissertations/46346.

Roberts, B. (2001). *Biographical Research (Understanding Social Research).* London: Open University Press.

Rosenthal, G. (1993). "Reconstruction of Life Stories: Principles of Selection in Generating Stories for Narrative Biographical Interviews." *The Narrative Study of Lives* 1, no. 1: 59–91.

Said, E. (1978). *Orientalism*. London: Penguin.

———. (1994). *Culture and Imperialism*. London: Vintage.

Sayyid, S. (2003). *A Fundamental Fear: Eurocentrism and the Emergence of Islamism*. London: Zed Books.

———. (2006). "BrAsians: Postcolonial People, Ironic Citizens." In *A Postcolonial People: South Asians in Britain*, edited by N. Ali, V. Kalra, and S. Sayyid, 1–10. London: Hurst.

———. (2010). "Out of the Devil's Dictionary." In *Thinking through Islamophobia*, edited by S. Sayyid and A. Vakil, 5–18. London: Hurst.

Sayyid, S., and Hesse, B. (2006). "Narrating the Postcolonial Political and the Immigrant Imaginary." In *A Postcolonial People: South Asians in Britain*, edited by N. Ali, V. Kalra, and S. Sayyid, 13–31. London: Hurst.

Sayyid, S., and Zac, L. (1998). "Political Analysis in a World without Foundations." In *Research Strategies in the Social Sciences: A Guide to New Approaches*, edited by E. Scarbrough, and E. Tanenbaum, 249–67. Oxford: Oxford University Press.

Sian, K. P. (2013). *Unsettling Sikh and Muslim Conflict: Mistaken Identities, Forced Conversions and Postcolonial Formations*. Lanham: Lexington.

Sian, K. P., Law, L., and Sayyid, S. (2013). *Racism, Governance and Public Policy: Beyond Human Rights*. London: Routledge.

Slemon, S. (2013). "Afterword." In *The Oxford Handbook of Postcolonial Studies*, edited by G. Huggan, 697–702. Oxford: Oxford University Press.

Spivak, G. (1998). "Can the Subaltern Speak?" In *Marxism and the Interpretation of Culture*, edited by C. Nelson and L. Grossberg, 271–313. Urbana: University of Illinois Press.

———. (2000). "Foreword: Upon Reading the *Companion to Postcolonial Studies*." In *A Companion to Postcolonial Studies*, edited by H. Schwarz and S. Ray, xvi–xxiii. Oxford: Blackwell.

Travis, A. (2011). "Young Black Men Make up Four in 10 of Youth Jail Population." *The Guardian*, October 25, 2011. http://www.theguardian.com/society/2011/oct/26/young-black-men-youth-jails.

University College London (UCL). "Legacies of British Slave-Ownership." http://www.ucl.ac.uk/lbs.

X, Malcolm. (2007). *The Autobiography of Malcolm X (with the Assistance of Alex Haley)*. London: Penguin Books.

Yancy, G. (1998). *African-American Philosophers: 17 Conversations*. New York: Routledge.

———. (2002). *The Philosophical I: Personal Reflections on Life in Philosophy*. Lanham: Rowman and Littlefield.

Žižek, S. (2011). *Living in the End Times*. London: Verso. First published in 2010.

Index

Printed and bound in Great Britain by
CPI Group (UK) Ltd, Croydon, CR0 4YY